CM01163709

The Hauraki Gulf
AN ICONIC KIWI PLAYGROUND

The Hauraki Gulf
AN ICONIC KIWI PLAYGROUND

JANE KING

Bateman

Text © Jane King, 2017

Published in 2017 by David Bateman Ltd
30 Tarndale Grove, Albany, Auckland, New Zealand

www.batemanpublishing.co.nz

A catalogue record for this book is available from
the National Library of New Zealand.

ISBN 978-1-86953-950-4

This book is copyright. Except for the purpose of fair review, no part may be stored or transmitted in any form or by any means, electronic or mechanical, including recording or storage in any information retrieval systems, without permission in writing from the publisher. No reproduction may be made, whether by photocopying or by any other means, unless a licence has been obtained from the publisher or its agent.

Publisher: Bill Honeybone
Book design: Cheryl Smith, Macarn Design
All photographs as listed on page 231
Printed in China through Colorcraft Ltd, Hong Kong

This page: Pa Beach, Great Barrier Island.
Opposite: Sunset over Little Barrier Island.

Contents

Introduction 7

Great Barrier Island 11
Sarah Harrison – Potter 25
David Watson – Creator and curator 35

Little Barrier Island 39
Steve Clarke – Pilot 46

Tiritiri Matangi Island 53
Ray and Barbara Walter – Enlightened guardians 62

Rangitoto Island 71
John Walsh – Bach owner 84

Motutapu Island 93

Rakino Island and The Noises 103
Andy Light – Skipper 106

Browns Island 113
Ingrid Visser – Scientist 118

Motuihe Island 129

Waiheke Island 135
Penny Whiting – Sailor 146

Rotoroa and Pakatoa islands 153
Alan Good – Boatie 162

Ponui Island 171

Kawau Island 175
Sir George Grey – Controversial leader 192
Helen and Dave Jeffery – Lodge owners 204

Motuora Island 211

Moturekareka Island 215
Karen Elliott and Dan McGowan – Coastguards 218

Bibliography 227

Image credits 231

Acknowledgements 231

Auckland CBD from Rangitoto Island.

Introduction

Whilst researching this book I met many wonderful people, all enamoured by the Hauraki Gulf in one way or another. I spent time with people who live, work, sail, fish, fly, research, adventure, conserve and love spending time in the gulf; they each shared unique stories and experiences of the place they hold dear.

I was captivated by the spirit and appreciation with which people spoke about the gulf and was struck by the common threads that ran through their stories. The majority of people I talked to expressed how incredibly lucky they feel to have such a unique, beautiful marine environment and natural playground on Auckland's doorstep. They shared their excitement at the prospect of discovering new places, 'hidden gems' that are abundant among the islands. And they waxed lyrical about the limitless opportunities for fun and adventure, and the chance to escape the frantic pace of their busy lives to relax.

The Hauraki Gulf islands are so rich with unique geographical landscapes, natural beauty and resources, and a favourable climate, that many settlers before us fought battles in order to be able to spend time there. Where ancestors fought, we can now play, and what a magnificent playground we have available to us.

The Hauraki Gulf held a special place in the hearts of two of the greatest New Zealanders we have ever known. Sir Edmund Hillary and Sir Peter Blake both spent happy childhoods exploring the gulf and both, during their lifetimes, expressed great appreciation and gratitude for the experiences, life lessons and pleasure the gulf afforded them.

Sir Peter Blake, one of the world's most celebrated yachtsmen, adventurer, environmentalist and leader, grew up in Bayswater on the North Shore and spent many hours messing around in boats in the waters of Auckland's Waitemata Harbour and the Hauraki Gulf. 'I had as good a time then as sailing around the world years later,' he said in his book, *Adventurer*. Sir Peter's achievements continue to inspire many young sailors who have come to understand that the gulf is the perfect training ground for the best sailors in the world.

Sir Edmund Hillary, the legendary mountaineer, adventurer, philanthropist and Kiwi hero, grew up in Auckland and had a deep love for the Hauraki Gulf. In his book *View from the Summit* he expressed his wish that, when he died, his ashes 'be spread on the beautiful waters of Auckland's Hauraki Gulf to be washed gently ashore' on the land of his birthplace. 'Then the circle of my life will be complete,' he wrote. It was fitting that his ashes were

Rangitoto Island from Tiritiri Matangi Island.

scattered in the gulf by his family from aboard the *Spirit of New Zealand* in February 2008.

The gulf is a special place for many past, present and future generations – the devoted conservation efforts of a number of organisations, trusts and volunteers over the last few decades have regenerated the health of many of the gulf island environments. Endangered species of birds, wildlife and plants have renewed hope for their future safety with the protection and sanctuary that the carefully tended gulf islands provide.

I have loved exploring the gulf islands and learning more about sailing, cruising, marine life, water sports, fishing, conservation, and the variety of outdoor and water-borne adventures that are the recreational lifeblood of the region. Each gulf island has its own personality; a cocktail of characteristics, varied landscapes, scenic beauty, rich history, and people with a deep connection and love of the land and sea.

This book is not intended to be a guide book or a comprehensive history but a celebration of the beautiful natural land and seascape, the diverse array of opportunities that the Hauraki Gulf islands provide for fun and recreation, and the stories of the people who live, work and love spending time in this one-of-a-kind aquatic playground.

Whangapoua Beach from Windy Canyon, Great Barrier Island.

Pa Beach, Great Barrier Island.

Great Barrier Island

WILD OPEN SPACES, BREATHTAKING NATURAL BEAUTY

Great Barrier is probably my favourite island in the whole world. Not just because it helps make the Hauraki Gulf such a wonderful marine playground by sheltering it from the ocean swell, but also because of the many special places there.

– Sir Peter Blake

Tranquil, rugged and unspoilt, Great Barrier Island feels more far-flung and remote than it actually is. The Hauraki Gulf's largest island (and New Zealand's sixth largest island) lies at the eastern edge of the Hauraki Gulf Marine Park – 90 kilometres north-east of Auckland and 16 kilometres north-west of the Coromandel Peninsula. Often described as an 'untouched wilderness', the island's landscapes are diverse. Blessed with many sweeping expanses of white sand, lush native bush, forest-clad ranges and pinnacles, bluffs and ridgelines, pretty coves, tidal creeks and natural harbours with crystal clear waters – the natural beauty of the island is astounding. Port Fitzroy, on the west coast, has been described as one of the finest natural harbours in the world. At Christmas and New Year, the harbour fills with boaties all geared up for some of the most outstanding party celebrations in the world.

The lowdown on Barrier

Great Barrier, or 'Barrier' as it is known by locals, is 40 kliometres long and about 20 kilometres wide (at its widest) with a chain of 23 smaller islands and clusters of rocks scattered around the coastline: the Broken Islands, Kaikoura (Selwyn) and Motuhaku islands, amongst others, lie off the west coast. Rakitu Island (also known as Arid Island and a remnant of a volcano around nine million years old) lies off the north-east coast.

The maze of islands, bays, coves, inlets and natural harbours make Great Barrier a boating wonderland. The fiord-like ports of

Fitzroy and Abercrombie are the ultimate picturesque playground in which to cruise, sail, relax and enjoy the natural aquatic heaven.

The expanse of the island is relatively large (274 square kilometres) and the number of residents small – around 800 people live on Barrier permanently. The islanders are an independent, self-sufficient crowd; many locals relish the open spaces and small population. They appreciate living in a wild and beautiful place, and for many of them it would be disastrous if ever that changed.

The main settlements on the island are Tryphena, Claris, Whangaparapara and Port Fitzroy. All but Port Fitzroy are in the south of the island where the majority of Barrier Islanders live. (The north of the island is mostly Department of Conservation land.) The different styles of abode on the island reflect the different lifestyles of the people who live there. There are wooden baches, cabins, old hippy shacks from the 1970s, inhabited old fishing boats propped up on land, self-built alternative lifestyler properties, larger solidly-built timber homesteads (many of the first European settlers' homes still exist), farmhouses, more modern properties, and some new and sleek architecturally designed properties – many perched high on hillsides with 180-degree ocean views. There's something for everyone wherever they are on the lifestyle spectrum. Accommodation options for visitors are also varied – from backpackers and basic camp sites to luxury cliff-top lodgings.

Ferries from Auckland to Great Barrier arrive and depart from Tryphena – the sailing time can vary, particularly when weather conditions are rough. On a good day the journey should take four-and-a-half hours. Flying is a smoother, faster option taking between 20 and 30 minutes depending on the aircraft. There are several operators offering daily transfers, with the choice of either aeroplane or helicopter. Barrier Air fly a number of routes to Great Barrier Island. The flights are scheduled according to seasonal demand and available on request from Auckland Airport, North Shore Airport, Hamilton, Kaitaia and Whangarei. It is also possible to fly from Whitianga, on the Coromandel Peninsula, to Great Barrier Island with Sunair.

Supplies to the island are variable and the boats come in to Tryphena and Port Fitzroy weekly (weather permitting). With only a handful of small grocery stores on the island, stocks of certain items can quickly run out. Café menus and staff have to be very flexible as a result.

The island has no mains power or public water supply; many residents harness their own power using solar or wind energy, or have their own generators. Rain water is collected in tanks, and visitors staying on the island are asked to be mindful of the limited infrastructure and conserve energy and water. Anyone reliant on hairdryers – this is not the place for you. Hairdryers are considered the power-sapping enemy and can't be used in most of the island's lodgings.

The island has a relaxed pace of life, likely perpetuated by the sense of being off the grid. Music on the island is provided by award-winning solar-powered radio station Aotea FM, based in Claris. The station operates during daylight hours and is so popular it's streamed around the world – comments on their Facebook page prove it.

Living without mains power doesn't come without challenges. When medical emergencies occur, being off the grid suddenly becomes troublesome. There are no hospitals or emergency services, so airlifting very sick or injured people to the mainland is the only option.

Jim Bergman, who founded Great Barrier Air in 1983, explained that back in the 1980s he would volunteer to fly to Great Barrier to pick up injured or sick locals to take them to the mainland. There were no helicopters in those days and he didn't want any of the other Barrier Air pilots flying at night as it was 'dangerous as hell.' At night, with no electricity, the island was pitch black and it was difficult to locate the airfield with no lights to guide him. The airfield was just a paddock in those days, and often boggy if it had been raining. The emergencies often happened at night. 'People had a lot of accidents. Saturday nights over there were dynamite ... the island was dry and the only alcohol they had over there was what you took yourself,' he said. 'But when they opened the Tryphena club, which was allowed a licence because it was a club, there was only one narrow road and people would get on their bikes with no lights, and in their cars with no brakes or lights – there were accidents everywhere,' according to Jim.

In later years, one policeman was installed on the island. 'He was just as bad as the locals,' Jim laughed. When emergency flights were needed, Jim would call the policeman and ask him to contact some of the locals to get them to turn on their generators – some of the residents would be sober enough to switch on a few lights to help him see the island. The policeman would then go to the pub, round up the locals and get them to drive their cars to the airfield

Towards Port Abercrombie from Glenfern Sanctuary.

Port Fitzroy Harbour.

where they would attempt to park their cars in two straight lines, opposite each other, to create a runway of sorts – lit by headlights The result was often pandemonium; it was a dicey old business for the pilots getting in and out of there. Some of the cars didn't have working headlights and after an evening's drinking the locals would park their cars in strange formations. 'You never knew where the cars would be parked,' Jim shook his head as he recalled.

These days the airport has a runway and its own generator. The roads on the island are much improved, although remain narrow and winding, and mostly gravel – except for the main road (now tarsealed), which the locals, amusingly, refer to as State Highway 1. Whilst passing each other on the narrow roads, the locals have a friendly and understated custom – they acknowledge passing cars, almost without fail, by a casual lift of one finger from the steering wheel and sometimes a slight nod of the head.

To get around and see the island it is necessary to drive, as there is no regular public transport, but to be able to assimilate the natural beauty of the surroundings, enjoying the sights at a slower pace is so much more rewarding.

If exploring the island on two wheels is more your thing, there are mountain bike tracks and quiet coastal roads on which to ride around Great Barrier. Mountain bike hire and guided cycle tours are available through Paradise Cycles in Whangaparapara.

Kiwis and tourists alike visit Great Barrier, particularly during the summer months, to relax and enjoy extended holiday trips on boats, explore wild spaces, pristine white sandy beaches, walking tracks, mountain biking trails and to sea kayak, dive and snorkel. The opportunities to unwind or embark on an adventure are endless.

WHITE CLOUDS, LONG OR OTHERWISE

The Maori name for Great Barrier Island is Aotea, meaning white cloud. In local tradition, the island also has an association with the ancestral waka (canoe) Aotea, which was said to have visited during the great migration in the thirteenth century. The definitive meaning behind the name of the island is unknown. If the Aotea canoe discovered the island because of a white cloud hanging over the land, it would have been quite a coincidence! It therefore seems more likely that the island was named after the canoe – but no one can be certain.

The same uncertainty also applies to the naming of Aotearoa, New Zealand. Aotearoa – aotea (white cloud), roa (long). In Te Ara, the Encyclopedia of New Zealand, the possibilities open up even further: 'Aotearoa is made up of either two or three words, *aotea* and *roa* or *ao*, *tea* and *roa*. *Aotea* could be the name of one of the canoes of the great migration, the great Magellan cloud near the bright star Canopus in summer, a bird or even food; *ao* is a cloud, dawn, daytime, or world; *tea* white or clear, perhaps bright, while *roa* means long or tall.'

The question is intriguing and locals on Great Barrier have a favourite story: they like the version that suggests that the people aboard the ancestral canoe saw the Aotea cloud, sailed around it, and discovered another (much larger) Aotea cloud – Aotea-roa!

Palmers Beach.

Work on display at Shoal Bay Pottery.

Creativity thrives

The thriving arts scene on the island manifests in a number of galleries and studios showcasing local artists' work. The Great Barrier Island Heritage and Arts Village, situated in Claris, holds regular exhibitions and sells works from local artists and craftspeople. Much of the art and crafts are inspired by the island. There are works of sculpture, wood and stone carving, pottery, sculptural and homeware pieces, woven flax baskets and bags, and paintings and photography – all inspired by island scenes and Maori legends.

The buildings that make up the arts centre are old European settler homesteads. The Grays' family home, one of the early pioneering families, is currently being renovated to become a new museum. Beyond Claris, the Tryphena Art Trail includes nine characterful galleries and studios to explore. The studios include works of pottery, jewellery, quilting, painting, woven designs, mosaics and wood carving.

Many residents on the island are involved in the tourism industry, and although they love their sparsely populated island, some do say they would benefit from an extended tourist season. Many of the locals rely on income generated from New Zealand's summer break, from Christmas through to February. Although visitor numbers during summertime can peak at around 3000, a longer, more sustained period of visitation rather than a huge peak would help them greatly.

Aquatic antics

Nature designed the coastline of Great Barrier perfectly for water-based activities. Whether sailing, cruising, sea kayaking or fishing, the clear water and deserted coastline are a unique waterscape offering truly special experiences. The marine life around the islands' shores is abundant: bottlenose dolphins, orca, Bryde's whales, seals, turtles and little penguins are all regularly sighted.

In a recent study, Massey University marine biologist Sarah Dwyer discovered a significant population of bottlenose dolphins off Great Barrier. She also discovered that these dolphins can be found close to the Barrier shores all year round. The bottlenose dolphins are nationally endangered and prior to Sarah's study were only known to have permanent populations in Fiordland, the Marlborough Sounds, off Westport, and in the Bay of Islands. As the bottlenose dolphins are coastal dwellers, they are particularly susceptible to the impacts of humans and boats.

Visiting vessels to the island will find sheltered access via the west coast where there are three natural harbours, wharves and sheltered anchorages. Fiord-like terrain creates landlocked natural harbours around Port Fitzroy and Port Abercrombie. Tryphena and Whangaparapara are also stunning natural harbours. There are wharves at Okupu, Whangaparapara, Port Fitzroy, Tryphena (the ferry wharf), Schooner Bay and Blind Bay. The east side of the island is exposed to the Pacific Ocean swell so there are no wharves there – but it is possible to launch into the Whangapoua estuary at high tide.

Fishing on Great Barrier is a way of life for many of the locals and a keenly anticipated activity for many visitors. There are a number fishing charter operators on Great Barrier with experienced fishermen offering half- and full-day trips. The Barrier is known for great snapper and kingfish – hapuka, trevally and blue cod can also be found depending on seasons and weather. Diving for crayfish and spearfishing are both very popular activities – Barrier is well-known for its favourable crayfish habitats.

One activity the Hauraki Gulf islands are not known for is surfing, and there is good reason for that as most of the islands are too sheltered. Great Barrier is the exception – the combination of expansive east coast beaches and ever-shifting sandbanks make for spectacular surfing conditions. The largest of the famous four surf beaches on Barrier is Kaitoke Beach. Two kilometres of white sand arcs gently from Sugarloaf Hill to a cluster of rocks beyond which the beach extends further to Palmers Beach. The best sand bars can usually be found at Palmers Beach and at the Kaitoke Creek mouth.

Medlands Beach.

Medlands Beach, named after one of the earliest European settler families, is just south of Kaitoke Beach and provides good surfing in all conditions. The beach has consistent sandbanks that extend the length of the beach, either side of Memory Rock, which stands in the middle of the beach. It is one of the most popular beaches on Barrier as it is easily accessed from Claris.

Awana Beach is a breathtaking landscape featuring a huge and dramatic, steep-sided rock at the north end, which looks as if it has surged up out of the beach at a 45-degree angle. A Maori pa site exists on the rock – it easy to see why such a naturally fortified position would have been chosen. The surf break at Awana is one of the best on Great Barrier; the sign at the entrance to the beach describes the barrel waves on offer as 'punchy, powerful and hollow … suitable for intermediate and expert surfers.' The steep profile of the beach contributes to the more difficult surf conditions here. Rips are common and swimming can be dangerous.

Further north, a short walk from Okiwi airfield, is the Whangapoua estuary, described as 'one of the most dramatic, fertile and beautiful river estuaries in the entire country.' The walk out across the river flats takes a while but is worth it. Whangapoua is known for excellent right-hand surf breaks at the mouth of the estuary.

Exploring the underwater world of Great Barrier, and its surrounding islands, by snorkelling or scuba diving is a must-do for underwater enthusiasts. It would take a very long time to exhaust the number of stunning dive locations – the options are many and varied as the East Auckland current provides temperate conditions which support rich eco-systems. The chain of islands that span the 40-kilometre length of the island offer a huge number of diversely different locations to dive. The Broken Islands, Rabbit Island, Rakitu Island and The Pigeons – a group of rocks west of Whangaparapara with a large drop-off – are popular diving locations.

Shipwrecks aren't short on numbers either – 24 vessels have seen the wrong side of the ocean surface in the last century. The *Wairarapa* (see page 28), sunk in one of New Zealand's worst maritime disasters, is one of the most popular wrecks to dive on the north-west side of the island near Miners Head. There is also the *Wiltshire*, off Rosalie Bay on the south-west coast (see page 30). The clear water provides excellent visibility and the underwater terrain has volcanic rock formations, seaweed forests and abundant marine life to explore.

Barrier's beauty – best discovered on foot

From the wonderful views and the unique bush at the top of Mt Hobson, to the kauri dams, the bush streams, the wetlands and the hot springs, there are many good tracks where you can experience the New Zealand wilderness the way it should be experienced.

– Sir Peter Blake

There's an endless supply of beaches, coastal walks and a network of over 100 kilometres of well-formed tracks to get your stride on. Some tracks navigate dense and sheltered forest, and native bush; others are more exposed with ascents leading to rocky ridgelines, rewarding walkers with magnificent panoramic views of the deserted north coast beaches and out to the Pacific Ocean. Depending on the hiker's appetite, the walking track menu caters to all kinds of timeframes, scenic splendour, and exertion levels. Planning a walk that passes or ends at the Kaitoke hot springs, with hot pools to soak the muscles, and waterfalls and swimming holes to cool off in, comes highly recommended by locals and visitors.

The hillier walks like Windy Canyon and hiking to the summit of Mt Hobson (621 metres) take on steep climbs and steps up to scenic ridgelines and bluffs. At the island's highest point, Hirakimata (Mt Hobson), the panoramic vista and inevitable photos will definitely instil envy among friends. Mt Hobson is the remains of an ancient eroded volcano which was formed around 9 million years ago and last erupted around 4–5 million years ago.

The spectacular pinnacles and bluffs in the highlands of the island are all deeply eroded volcanic rock. The type of rock is uncommon – obsidian breccia, which is made up of rock and volcanic glass (obsidian) pieces. This is formed in unusual circumstances where lava is suddenly chilled and fractured. As rain and streams have flowed over the rocks they have become eroded and exposed.

From the top of Mt Hobson, on a clear day, you can see the entire island, then on to Rangitoto and Auckland, the Mercury Islands and Cape Colville to the south. Black petrels nest around the sheer rock faces, where steps and boardwalks have been constructed to protect them.

If a multi-day walk appeals, the Aotea Track – a 25-kilometre loop of the mountainous area of the island – is a beautiful mix of terrain and can be completed easily in three days. There are huts to bunk down in at Mt Heale and Kaiaraara – the views from Mt Heale include Little Barrier Island and across the Hauraki Gulf. Large storms damaged parts of the Aotea Track in winter 2014 and sections had to be closed, but repairs have been completed and all tracks are now open. Sadly, during the storms, the Kaiaraara dam, one of the most impressive historic structures from the island's timber industry, was washed away.

Some of the many steps leading up Windy Canyon.

Variety prevails on the Aotea Track as a diverse array of flora and fauna reveals itself through every twist and turn. The path includes stretches of easy flat sections, steep inclines, streams, swing bridges, and mature and regenerating forests of rimu, kauri and kahikatea. The tranquil wetlands, streams, ridges, bluffs and mountains do not fail to challenge and delight walkers.

If running is more your thing then in October each year the Wharf to Wharf Marathon takes place from Port Fitzroy to Tryphena. The course is hilly and rewards participants with continuously beautiful scenery and spectacular views atop hills to splutter and catch your breath to. The event caters to serious runners as well as those seeking more fun than competition. There are options to run, mountain bike, or walk the marathon or half-marathon distances. There is also a duathlon (bike and run) event. The event is organised by local volunteers who are welcoming and take pride in their enthusiastic cheering-on of runners, walkers and bikers – the event has been described as 'New Zealand's friendliest marathon'.

A substantial safe haven

Two-thirds of the island, most of the central and northern region, is conservation estate which is managed by the Department of Conservation. Since the 1970s kauri forest regeneration, species-recovery and pest eradication (particularly rats and feral cats) projects have improved and replenished much of the island environment.

The Department of Conservation manage a large expanse of land on Barrier (around 12,000 hectares). Their work involves maintaining the Aotea Track and its two huts, the mountain bike tracks, and six campsites on the island. The benefits of the conservation work are flourishing – the island and surrounding water boast healthy kauri and mangrove forests, 500 species of plants, abundant birdlife, and 70 different species of fish.

Many of the island's birds, reptiles and amphibians are rare or extinct on the mainland and so rely on the protection of safe island havens. High above the forest canopies the North Island kaka, a large and loud brown parrot, can often be heard and sometimes seen. What the kaka lacks in numbers it makes up for in volume with a repertoire of harsh, guttural sounds and whistles. The tomtit, North Island robin, brown teal, and black petrel can also be found nesting on the higher ground and slopes of Mt Hobson. (The black petrels are often detected by the nostrils before they are seen.) The morepork, grey warbler, kingfisher, bellbird and silvereye can also be seen and heard around the island.

One of New Zealand's most endangered lizards, the chevron skink, is so rare it can only be found on Great Barrier and Little Barrier islands. The Maori name is 'niho taniwha' meaning 'teeth of the taniwha'. The name sounds fierce but the teeth refer to the distinctive V-shaped markings on its back and not its gnashers. Chevron skinks may not have the taniwha's roar but they can grunt or squeak if disturbed. They are susceptible to dehydration so live near streams, creeks and damp places. The skinks have survived as none of the usual rodent suspects made it to the island.

A unique conservation success story on Great Barrier has been planned and delivered by Glenfern Sanctuary. The picturesque estate, including Fitzroy House, overlooking the blue water of Port Fitzroy harbour, is a carefully managed pest-free environment for endangered species of plants, birds and wildlife. The sanctuary roots were planted by world champion sailor Tony Bouzaid, who sadly passed away in 2011. He loved the island and wanted to restore native trees, plants and birdsong to Great Barrier. He planted over 15,000 trees and erected a two-kilometre rodent-proof fence around his property as part of his endeavour to create a safe paradise. His vision has been achieved with an immense amount of cooperation from nearby landowners, the Department of Conservation, and graft by Glenfern staff and volunteers over 20 years.

Glenfern Sanctuary, with the assistance of the Kotuku Peninsula Charitable Trust, has recently extended its footprint and manages not only the Glenfern estate but also the Kotuku Peninsula, which spans 260 hectares. Visiting Glenfern Sanctuary and walking the Glenfern Trail through regenerating and ancient native forest is captivating. The two kilometres of trail are bustling with birds. Fantails follow walkers and flitter across the path as tui fill the air with their repertoire of exquisite sounds – of all the birdsong, the tui beatboxing never gets old.

Ascending through the forest, there is still evidence of the storm damage from the winter of 2014. Wind and torrents of rain caused flash-floods through the hillside gullies of sanctuary land and many trees were brought down by the storms. Climbing higher still, a swing bridge leads to a 600-year-old kauri tree, a majestic king of the forest – its size is mesmerising. The track continues past a black petrel burrow and out of the trees to a clearing at Sunset Rock. Here are some of the best views on Great Barrier so it is well worth spending some time at this natural lookout; the panoramic views across the harbours of Port Fitzroy, Port Abercrombie, Kaikoura Island and the Broken Islands are awe-inspiring. The forest-clad and hilly peninsulas stretch out towards the open ocean and their coastlines meander, forming intricate coves and inlets flanked by deep blue water – reminiscent of the Marlborough Sounds and equally beautiful. A memorial to Tony Bouzaid is mounted upon Sunset Rock – his remarkable legacy appreciated by all who visit.

Brown teal, North Island robins, black petrel, giant weta, and chevron skinks are some of the endangered species that can be found at Glenfern. Guided tours are available and should be booked in advance.

Tangata whenua on Aotea

The Maori history of Great Barrier began peacefully but became fractious with conflict and battles. After the Aotea canoe visited the island, Tainui and Te Arawa people settled and lived peacefully on the island for over 300 years. During the late 1600s the Ngati Manaia (Ngatiwai) people from Northland and Marutuahu tribes moved to Aotea and began settling. The death of a Ngati Manaia woman (killed by Ngati Tai) caused all-out war, as chief Rehua (who had married a Ngati Manaia woman), his son, and Ngatiwai tribes descended on the island to fight bloody battles and take over the northern half of the island.

Peace was temporarily achieved as marriages between the tribes forged improved relationships, until Rehua was murdered, burnt to death at his home on Rakitu Island as revenge for the battles and killings he had instigated.

Battles commenced throughout settlements on the island as Rehua's son avenged his father's murder and killed many Ngatiwai. The Ngatiwai managed to retain the south of the island and built relationships with Coromandel Ngati Maru. The island remained peaceful and the tribes intermarried and established a solidarity that was to last. In the 1820s Ngapuhi people from Northland invaded and raided Aotea causing large-scale destruction and death.

Rehua's people remained relatively unscathed as they had close links with Ngapuhi and things settled down until 1838 when a visiting Hawke's Bay tribe, Ngati Kahungunu, caused offence to some of the local women and were said to have stolen food. The women sent word of their humiliation back to the Coromandel Ngati Maru and, with Rehua's encouragement, fierce fighting began again. A large battle was fought at Whangapoua with huge loss of life on both sides. What was left of the Hawke's Bay iwi left the island and the Marutuahu were resentful at the losses they had endured by helping Ngati Rehua. In a final act of vengeance, a Marutuahu chief sold the island to his son-in-law William Webster and his timber-trading business partners, William Abercrombie and Jeremiah Nagle. The result of this transaction is still unresolved to this day – Ngatiwai lost all of their land.

The following years saw Ngati Rehua ignore the land sale and resettle on the island. The Crown bought land on Aotea and allowed Webster and his partners a small portion of what they believed they had purchased. The Crown and European settlers arrived and bought large areas of land to farm. Ngatiwai had lost everything and petitioned the Crown for many years for land on which to live. In the 1850s the Crown afforded them land at Motairehe (Katherine Bay). Today, their descendants still own and inhabit a tiny portion of the land their forebears once populated.

Later in the eighteenth century, Europeans and Ngatiwai built relationships as European whaling boat sailors traded resources. The Europeans landed in larger numbers in the nineteenth century searching for natural resources.

The naming of things

In 1769 Captain James Cook, on his first voyage on the *Endeavour*, was searching for the 'great southern continent,' believed to be an enormous undiscovered landmass at the bottom of the world, when he discovered New Zealand. He had been aware that Dutch explorer Abel Tasman sighted the land 100 years previously, but that he had not charted the land or come ashore. Whilst sailing along the North Island's east coast Cook sighted and named the island now known as Great Barrier Island. In *Captain Cook's Journal*, he recounts his voyage around and into the Hauraki Gulf. Sailing from Colville Bay down to the Firth of Thames, Cook named the bay after the swampy mangroves that reminded him of the River Thames in London. The Thames in 1769 would have needed to be considerably cleaner than it is now for Cook to have likened it to a body of water in which plants could grow. Or perhaps he had been partaking in a tipple or two of rum that evening whilst writing his journal. (The alcohol supplies on *Endeavour* were generous – the ship's supplies list included 250 barrels of beer, 44 barrels of brandy and 17 barrels of rum.)

As Cook sailed north he identified many natural 'good harbours' – Auckland is now one of them. Within the Hauraki Gulf, he observed 'a chain of large and small islands which I have named Barrier Isles ...' Cook recognised the protection these 'barrier isles' afforded the gulf from the mighty Pacific Ocean, and named them, recognising their function and usefulness.

The 'Great Barrier' could have provided an even greater barrier had it remained part of the Coromandel Ranges. The land was once a long volcanic chain of rock. During the last ice age the land was carved out and eroded by glaciation. When the glacial ice melted, the land flooded and the elevated mass at the end of the peninsula was disconnected, becoming Great Barrier Island.

James Cook observed the Maori people in the gulf and in his journal he described them: 'They are a strong, well made, active people as any we have seen yet, and all of them paint their bodies with red ochre and oil from head to foot, a thing that we have not seen before. Their canoes are large, well built and ornamented with carved work in general as well as most we have seen.'

Incidentally, Captain James Cook, during this first voyage on the *Endeavour*, was a lieutenant, not a captain. His journal of the voyage *Captain Cook's Journal – The First Voyage* probably took an age to write. Perhaps he was a captain by the time the journal was published, which would have worked out conveniently – Lieutenant Cook doesn't have quite the same ring to it. (James Cook was captain of his second voyage in July 1772 where he and his crew sailed further south than any other crew had sailed before, crossing the Antarctic circle and disproving the theory of there being a great southern continent.)

Boom and bust on Barrier

Not long after Captain Cook's charting of New Zealand, many more European ships were to arrive. In 1791, the very first whale hunters began their nasty business in New Zealand waters. Whaling had begun in the South Pacific as a result of the British needing cargo to fill their empty ships, having offloaded convicts in Australia.

In the early 1800s the growth of the whaling business was frighteningly fast. Numbers of British ships dropped off for a while, but American and French vessels were quick to take up the slack.

The American and European vessels were staffed with international crew including Pacific Islanders and Maori. Although the Maori crew numbers were few, they were attracted to whaling as an opportunity to travel.

The Napoleonic wars saw an influx of British ships into New Zealand waters again as they fled from attacks by the French off South America. New Zealand waters were at their busiest with whaling ships in 1839, when it was estimated that 150 ships from the United States and 50 from other nations were operating.

Whaling hubs were established in New Zealand on the North Island – in the Bay of Islands initially. As the whaling business increased, a whaling station was established on Great Barrier in 1856 at Whangaparapara. It is hard to believe, given New Zealand's current stance on the practice, but whaling led New Zealand's economy during the nineteenth century. The slaughtering of whales continued throughout the nineteenth century until some whale species reduced to such an extent that they became too scarce to find.

It wasn't until 1986 that New Zealand finally banned whaling. Evidence of the frenetic whaling days still exists at the bottom of the harbour at Whangaparapara where whale bones still lie. It was a boom-and-bust business that decimated whole whale populations in the process.

Another boom-and-bust enterprise was the kauri timber industry. The boom in the mid-nineteenth century saw periods of intense logging destroying enormous forests in record time. The timber industry didn't slow down until the mid-twentieth century, when the kauri trees had almost all been felled and only tiny areas of the original forest survived.

Until recently, one of the island's most impressive historic landmarks, a remnant of the kauri logging days, was the Kaiaraara dam. It was built in 1926 for the Kauri Timber Company and stood 40 metres tall on the Kaiaraara Stream below Mt Hobson. It was one of the largest timber dams ever built in New Zealand, an impressive feat of engineering, but was destroyed by storms in the winter of 2014.

The kauri driving dams were extremely robust. The sturdiness required to hold back the force and weight of large numbers of kauri logs floating in tonnes of water was immense. Large numbers of kauri logs would be fed into the dam waters, the dam would then be tripped and the gate would open, driving the logs downstream. The sight and sound of a mass of kauri logs flying down the hillside must have been something to behold.

The Kauri Timber Company had a lot of work in the early twentieth century. Not only did the sawmill at Whangaparapara process the logs from Great Barrier Island, it also managed timber rafted in by sea from the Coromandel and from as far away as Northland. The old sawmill ruins remain today at Whangaparapara, a reminder of the short-lived industries on Great Barrier.

The European settlers relied heavily on the timber industry for jobs and income so there was little thought given to the fact that the trees had taken thousands of years to grow. By the 1950s many thought the kauri tree species would be wiped out entirely. The logging stopped just in time, and on Great Barrier, the kauri that survived only did so by being too difficult to reach. The industry died out when the forests did in the mid-twentieth century. Some of the old tramlines that were used by the logging industry live on and are now walking tracks on the island.

SARAH HARRISON – POTTER

Sarah Harrison is a potter based in Shoal Bay, a short walk from Tryphena wharf. Her Shoal Bay Pottery shop sits tucked under a nectarine tree in a peaceful spot with views of Shoal Bay from the front window, exuding character and charm even before you set foot inside. Stocked with beautifully crafted works of pottery, art and sculpture, the colourful array of work inside is a treasure trove of practical and decorative pieces including work by other local artists. Summer is the busiest time for Sarah when visitors flock to the island and stop by her shop.

Useful pieces of homeware – pots, bowls, plates, mugs and vases together with decorative tiles – all with unique designs and inlays, are designed and produced by Sarah, who also creates wall hangings and sculptural pieces. Her work is inspired by, and reflects, the natural beauty of Great Barrier and the gulf, depicting shells, seahorses, fish, whales, bright stars and the natural landscape.

Sarah is a born and bred Barrier Islander. Her father moved to the island in the 1960s and Sarah grew up there. She studied ceramics at art school in Auckland before returning home to pursue her passion as a potter. Over the last 20 years, Sarah has grown and evolved her craft and her studio – she has an impressive set-up which she has worked hard to establish. It includes her shop, extensive studio space and three kilns.

Studio space behind the shop extends out the back to include two gas kilns where her work is fired at temperatures up to 1300 degrees Celsius for up to 10 hours. I was in awe of the unflinching

Work for sale at Shoal Bay Pottery.

trust a potter must have to place their work into an oven capable of incinerating just about anything, but Sarah says that with her experience, she's not fazed by it at all.

More recently, Sarah extended her kiln firepower when a community of 20 people, including a visiting Scotsman who designed the kiln, collaborated over the course of a month to build a wood-fired kiln. It is an impressive structure, a work of art in itself, even more so when you consider the thought, design, hard graft, time, care, and people-power that it took to create. Sarah proudly showed me her new 'beastie' and explained that she is still 'learning how to drive it,' while finding new inspiration and ideas with different techniques. She is excited about the different effects that can be created with the wood-fired kiln. By firing work and adding rock salt in the latter stages of the process, the salt creates a surface sheen which is unique and the finish is different to a glaze. The creative possibilities are endless and Sarah sometimes fires work in the wood-fired kiln and then again in the gas-fired kiln to achieve different effects.

Sarah's work continues to be inspired by the Barrier and she is constantly learning and evolving as she exercises her creativity in new ways whilst trying out new designs and techniques.

Her pottery studio is an artist's dream – a large space dedicated to creating and housing her work, full of shapes and vibrant colours. There are sketches, drawings, clay and pottery pieces in various different stages of production – some domestic homeware pieces and some sculpture. Both Sarah and her studio exude a calm, orderly creativity.

A founding member of the Community Arts Centre at Claris, Sarah was part of the Arts Trust that managed the centre for many years. She recalls a number of keen artists who used to meet in the old school hall years ago, dreaming about how great it would be to have an arts facility, a gallery and a museum. They didn't just dream about it, they worked together to make it happen, and in doing so they also saved and restored some historic family-owned buildings in the process. The Arts Centre showcases and sells works from local artists, puts on exhibitions, and organises and hosts weekend workshops. Locals and visitors to the island take part in art, craft and pottery workshops over winter weekends.

Great Barrier Island is a beautiful place and Sarah's latest project is taking steps towards keeping it that way by encouraging people to think differently about waste management. Recently, a few friends helped Sarah rebuild a shed on her property – her vision was to give the shed a new lease of life as a space where people could come and leave unwanted items which could then be rehomed rather than becoming landfill. She describes her new venture as a 'repurposing hub, a dump shop, resource centre,' or alternatively, as she likes to call it, 'the rat shed.'

Whatever people decide to call it, it's a great concept and will no doubt be valued by those who obtain new treasures as well as those who appreciate the effort to reuse or reinvent items rather than waste them. Hopefully it will also help change the mindset of those who aren't quite as good at recycling and managing their waste. Apparently the same issues that are evident on the mainland also occur on Barrier. Despite being surrounded by jaw-droppingly beautiful landscapes wherever you go, there are still people who remain oblivious of the environmental connection between putting their recyclable materials in the appropriate recycle bins as opposed to putting them in landfill bins. I found this surprising considering Barrier Islanders' pride in their independent lifestyles and self-sufficiency, but as Sarah pointed out, 'being self-sufficient doesn't necessarily mean they're any good at dealing with all their shit.' She's absolutely right and her new project is a small but creative way of changing the culture for the better.

Sarah Harrison's Shoal Bay Pottery shop.

Two of Great Barrier's shipwrecks

The SS *Wairarapa*

On the stormy night of 29 October 1894, the SS *Wairarapa*, a 285-foot, 2000-tonne steamship, with approximately 235 passengers and crew on board, was sailing from Sydney to Auckland when the ship lost course in fog. The visibility was minimal and yet the ship was flying at great speed despite the treacherous conditions. Passengers and crew alike had been frightened by the speed of the ship and had asked Captain McIntosh to slow down. He didn't.

Shortly after midnight, the ship crashed into rocks at the bottom of the high cliffs at Miners Head on the north-west coast of Great Barrier Island. High seas and heavy winds blasted the ship and it listed sharply to one side, submerging many lifeboats and making them impossible to launch.

Many passengers were in bed when the ship struck the rocks and it was said, in *The Colonist* newspaper, that the passengers did not panic (which is hard to imagine) as they tried to find safe positions on the bridge, at the forefront and in the rigging of the ship. Twenty minutes after the ship's collision, the lights went out and the chaos was intensified by complete darkness. High winds and giant waves continued to batter the ship throughout the night.

Huge waves crashed across the decks sweeping people, cargo, and even horses and sheep into the raging, stormy sea. Survivors reported that 16 horses that were being transported were untied from their stabling and were swept off the ship into the water. It is believed that many people in the water were injured, crushed and killed by the flailing horses. The scenes must have been diabolical.

Some survivor accounts say that Captain McIntosh remained on the bridge for many hours until he and others who had gathered there were washed away by an enormous wave. Some accounts say the captain jumped into the sea, accusing him of cowardice and suggesting he had committed suicide.

The ship lurched and listed throughout the night but somehow the masts of the *Wairarapa* remained intact. Many of the survivors who had managed to cling to the mast and rigging were rescued the next day. A couple of lifeboats had been successfully launched and saved many who had slid or been washed away from the ship. Lifejackets had also played a large part in saving passengers who had been flung from the ship in darkness. A small number of survivors had been strong swimmers and had strenuously battled the surging swells to make it ashore.

The wreckage was a scene of devastation that the European and Maori settlers on the island were unaware of until the next day. When daylight came, two of the ship's crew volunteered to attempt to swim to shore with a rope line that they hoped could assist people

Captain John McIntosh, who was at the helm of the SS Wairarapa *when it sank.*

28 THE HAURAKI GULF

from the shipwreck to the rocks. Their courageous attempt was prevented by the raging waves that smashed against the rocks, battering and bruising them badly. They were forced to let go of the line and only just managed to save themselves.

When the sea calmed down a few hours later, steward Burgess Kendall bravely swam the line to shore, although not without difficulty. He had spent the previous 12 hours clinging to the rigging with only his pyjamas for warmth. Suffering from exhaustion, cold and cramps, his heroic act secured a lifeline that saved 50 lives. Kendall was later acknowledged as New Zealander of the Year.

The exact number of crew and passengers travelling on the *Wairarapa*'s last voyage is unknown. It was believed that many of the children on board had not been registered as passengers. It was estimated that around 235 people were on board and that approximately 121 died, while 114 were saved.

Local Maori who assisted with the rescue, shelter and transportation of the survivors were also generous in gifting land at Whangapoua beach as a burial site. This kind gesture provided a peaceful place of rest for many who sadly perished so far from home.

In the aftermath of the disaster there were allegations that Captain McIntosh of the *Wairarapa* had been racing, intent on a fast voyage in a competition for the fastest voyage time. In previous weeks the *Wairarapa* had apparently set a record time for crossing the Tasman on the same route. It was said that competitions between ships' captains for the fastest crossing were commonplace. Speed supposedly equalled superior seamanship. Not in this case. Far from it.

The wreck of the SS Wairarapa, *Miners Head, Great Barrier Island.*

Other stories from survivors claim that Captain McIntosh had been acting very strangely throughout the voyage and could have been sick, drunk or both. There was speculation that Captain McIntosh was suffering from influenza and had been self-medicating with whisky. Other stories said he was in a mad rush to get the 16 racehorses he was transporting to port in time for an important race. The speculation continued as an inquiry into the disaster began.

The outcome of the inquiry found Captain McIntosh to be at fault. It was not proven that he had been racing or intoxicated, but he had been found culpable of taking the ship on the wrong course and not making allowances for the dangerous conditions.

The SS *Wiltshire*

Another shipping disaster off Great Barrier Island, which luckily had a much less tragic outcome, was that of the SS *Wiltshire*. In 1922 the *Wiltshire*, a 596-foot, 12,000-tonne freighter, was in stormy weather en route from Liverpool to Auckland when it collided with rocks at Rosalie Bay.

The ship broke into two pieces and everyone feared the worst. Once news of the disaster was received in Auckland the wireless station put out a call to all shipping in the area to assist with a rescue effort. Many vessels responded to the call and heroic efforts were made in a long and drawn-out rescue hampered by unrelenting storms.

Some of the British seamen clung to the wreckage for up to 40 hours. The *New Zealand Herald* described how the crew must have felt as they waited to be rescued and endured '... the gnawing bitterness of idleness. There was little or nothing they could do to help themselves. Numbed in mind and body, famished by hunger and thirst till physical exhaustion overtook them, they could

The wreck of the SS Wiltshire.

only cling to what remained of their ship and commit their lives to providence.'

Thanks to many rescue vessels and the locals onshore who worked tenaciously through days and nights to ensure the safety of all those stricken on the *Wiltshire*, the rescue operation had succeeded. Everyone had been brought to safety. Even the ship's cat was saved and lived to meow another day.

After the long, drawn-out agony came heartfelt thanks from the crew. The ship's captain heartily and repeatedly thanked all of Auckland for their kindness, friendliness and heroic efforts; 103 lives had been saved. A lone snake was also found alive in the wreckage of the ship. The newspapers reported that the snake was 'killed and photographed.' Not necessarily in that order. More good news washed up on shore in the following days with the ship's cargo, one the largest cargoes brought to New Zealand for a long time (4000 tonnes), delivered itself in waves to islanders.

Reportedly the gift that kept on giving, the *Wiltshire* supplied locals with cigarettes and tobacco (there are stories of great anguish expressed by smokers when finding huge volumes of soggy cigarettes), 30,000 yards of calico, cotton, bedding, paper, varnish, hundreds of golf balls and English china crockery. There were also barrels of whisky, soggy mailbags and even furniture, bathtubs and carpets – some of which, allegedly, still exist in older properties today. Not the whisky of course. That would have been dealt to with a fair degree of immediacy.

Top: Seaman Kehoe and the SS Wiltshire *cat, who was saved from the wreck.*
Bottom: Survivors being winched from the wreck of the SS Wiltshire.

GREAT BARRIER ISLAND 31

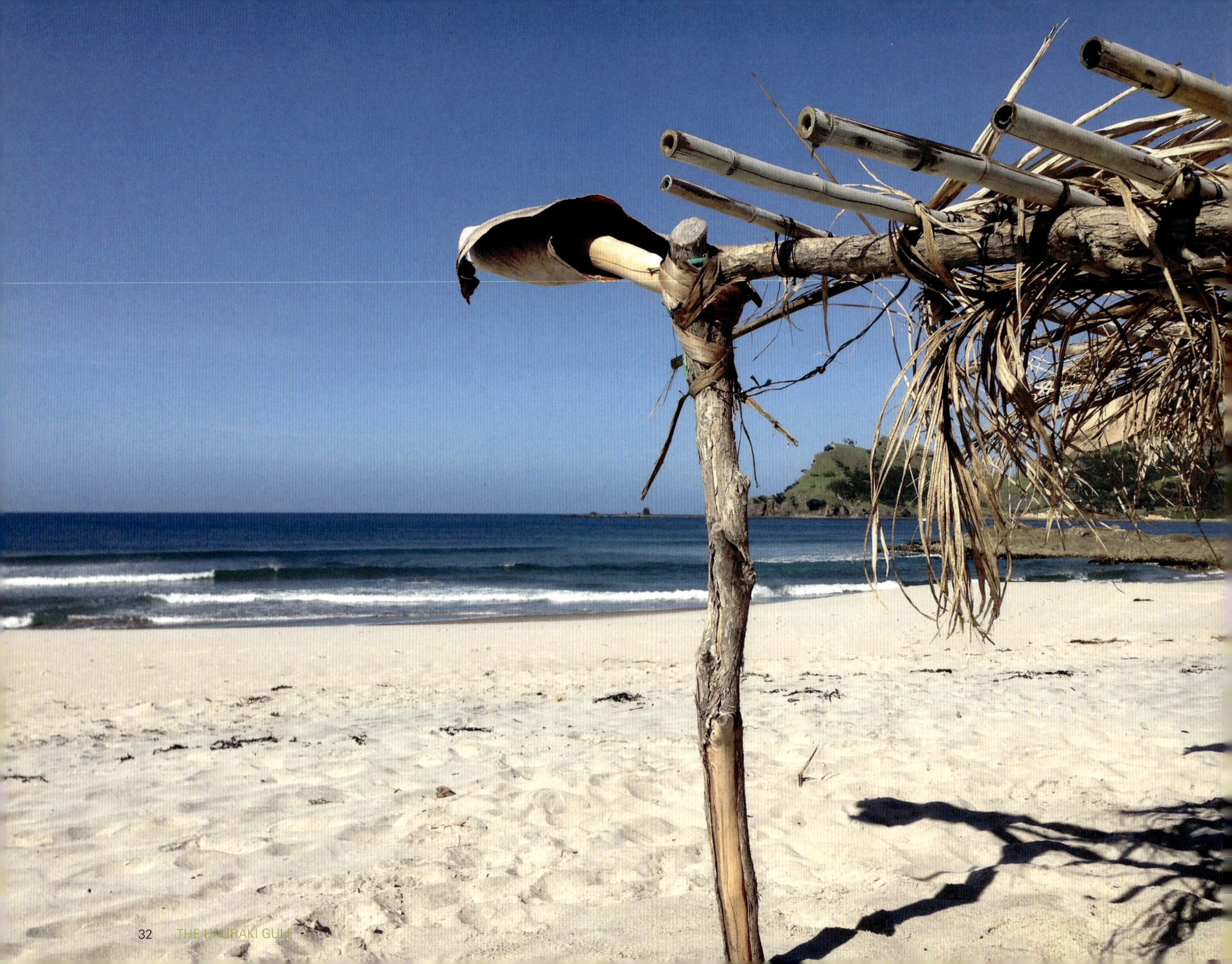

PIGEON POST

The *Wairarapa* disaster highlighted Great Barrier's isolation and the lack of timely communications with the mainland as a concern. In 1897, a Mr Fricker of Okupu came up with a clever business idea and launched a solution to the problem – pigeon post. A message that used to take days could now be sent and received in a few hours.

In 1896, Great Barrier Island was the first place in New Zealand to use pigeons to carry messages (called 'flimsies') over the sea to the mainland. The messages were written on tissue paper and wrapped around the pigeon's leg. When the pigeon arrived the message was retrieved, stamped and delivered. The first pigeon post service was in such demand that a rival pigeon post company was set up in competition with Mr Fricker's within a couple of months. The pigeon was not only used for emergency communications; the pigeon-grams conveyed breaking news, shopping lists, orders from the mainland to the Kauri Timber Company, requests for doctors and general letters.

In 1898, it was suggested that an adhesive stamp could be an easier way to attach the message to the pigeon's leg rather than tying it with string. This idea was put into practice and the world's first airmail stamp was airborne!

Pigeons could carry multiple messages at a time and delivery times were recorded. The first pigeon message delivered from Great Barrier to Auckland took an hour and three-quarters. The fastest recorded pigeon, Velocity, at peak fitness, had a personal best of 50 minutes (125km/h)! Pigeon-gramming was the social media of the day; you could stick your message to a pigeon's leg, and boom – a couple of hours later, via the cloud (usually a long white cloud) your data would be transferred and delivered to the recipient's inbox (pigeon loft). Pigeon post was used until 1908 when an underwater telegraph cable was put in place between Tryphena and the mainland – spoiling the fun for lots of the feathered friends who were made redundant.

DISASTERS SOLD NEWSPAPERS THEN AS THEY DO NOW

A few days after the *Wairarapa* disaster, on 5 November 1894, the *New Zealand Herald* printed a rather insensitive article which began: 'The story of the wreck of the *Wairarapa* furnishes one of the most thrilling tales of the era that has ever come to light, and, as a consequence, the demand for papers has been almost unprecedented. On Thursday, Friday, and Saturday last, many thousands of extra copies of the *Herald* were printed.' You can almost see the dollar signs in the eyes of the *Herald*'s circulation manager that day. Not much has changed since then.

'WHEN I'M CLEANIN' WINDOWS'

It wasn't only bad weather conditions and the erratic behaviour of the *Wairarapa*'s captain that led to loss of life. Earlier in 1894, eight months before the *Wairarapa* was shipwrecked, a seaman lost his life during a voyage to Melbourne. On 23 February 1894, The *Thames Star* reported that as the *Wairarapa* sailed through the night 'a seaman named Wellsteal fell over-board while engaged in cleaning the ship's side, and was never seen again.'

Awana Beach with pa site on the steep-sided peninsula.

DAVID WATSON – CREATOR AND CURATOR

Whilst having a nose around the Milk, Honey and Grain Museum, you quickly get a real sense of the social and industrial history of Great Barrier Island – the pioneering families who settled there, and the journeys and adventures they embraced to make a living and enjoy a unique lifestyle on the island. You also, almost on entry to the museum, get a sense for the enthusiasm, passion and sense of humour of the museum's curator. There are facts, figures and fun things to interact with in these three cosy cabins crammed full of historical artefacts, photographs, stories and contraptions. David Watson is a natural storyteller. He loves to piece together fragments of information with objects that he buys, borrows, finds or goes searching for, in order to create a picture of their context in the past. He has built up a unique and quirky collection of stories that you won't find in any book (except his!) or on the internet.

Don't be fooled by the name of the museum. The history and tales of milk, honey and grain production on Great Barrier are evident but there is so much more – pieces that cover just about everything else that has happened on the island over the years. There are items that were salvaged from some of the Great Barrier shipwrecks; contraptions that will likely give you a fright and a giggle; equipment and tools from the gumdigging, agriculture, timber, mining, whaling, and boat-building industries; and beekeeping and honey-making equipment – and that's just for starters. The museum also has two other separate sheds to explore, an old creamery and a replica honey shed, which contains an original wooden honey press.

David Watson at his Milk, Honey and Grain Museum in Claris.

David Watson is a longtime Barrier Island resident. He first visited Great Barrier as a schoolboy in 1965 and fell in love with the place. He felt that visiting the island was like stepping back in time and he enjoyed the smaller population. He liked the old cars and gravel roads – the quieter lifestyle appealed to him even as a boy, and after a subsequent visit in later years, he moved to Great Barrier and bought land at Medlands Beach in 1972 (with a deposit of $100!).

David worked as a primary school teacher and beekeeper and enjoyed producing honey far more than school lesson plans. In 1993, wanting a change, he sold his land in Medlands and moved to Claris where he decided to pursue his passion and start a museum. Having always been interested in people and how things used to be, David enjoyed talking to the older folk on the island, particularly those who had known some of the island's gumdiggers. He is especially glad to have gathered the information and stories about gumdigging 'as all of the folks who knew about it have since passed away.'

David often used to find out about the gumdigging characters and then head off tramping in the bush looking for their old gumdigging sites to find out more about them as well as getting an idea of how they lived and worked, and maybe finding a few items for his collection. David often sketches, very skilfully, what he finds to bring it to life for the museum.

David's museum collection expanded considerably when historic pieces of machinery from Les Todd's Tryphena estate came up for sale after his death. The Todd family were one of the first European families to settle on Great Barrier. Les Todd had been quite a hoarder, and David obtained items from the *Wiltshire* shipwreck as well as farming machinery for his rapidly growing collection.

Some of the items David has from the *Wiltshire* shipwreck he found himself. He explained that even nowadays when storms hit the island and the wind gets up, there are still small bits and pieces from the *Wiltshire* wreck buried in the Kaitoke Beach sand dunes. As the wind whips up the sand, new pieces of timber or fragments of the ship are often uncovered.

Back in 1922 when the *Wiltshire* lay broken in two pieces and beached on rocks off Rosalie Bay, the rough seas washed the loose cargo up onto Kaitoke Beach. Local people found all sorts of goods which they hastily stashed away. A huge trove of tobacco, entirely ruined by the water, washed up – to the disdain of the island's smokers who lamented such a fine stash coming to such a soggy end. Stories of locals scurrying off with kegs of whisky and immediately burying them for safekeeping are common. Sadly, stories of those same people not being able to find their stashes are also told.

David explained that nothing of the *Wiltshire* was wasted, in fact 'everything that could be unscrewed was unscrewed' and timber from the ship was hauled ashore and used for building on the island. Some families, notably the Gray family (one of the original Great Barrier families), salvaged enough timber to build the majority of their substantial house. Incidentally, the Gray family house still exists and has been restored and relocated to the Claris Community Arts Centre site where there are plans for it to become a new museum. David hopes people will still visit his museum when the new one opens – undoubtedly they will; it has too much character to miss.

David's curation philosophy is based on having a bit of fun: 'You've got to amuse people ... inform and entertain them.' He definitely does that and as a result often hears loud shrieks and laughter coming from the museum as visitors discover the tricky little bits of humour that David has carefully installed. Unfortunately, I can't disclose any details – no spoilers allowed. The Milk, Honey and Grain Museum is open most days during daylight hours whether David is there or not. It's well worth a visit – it is a wacky little place housing historical gems and information that can't be found anywhere else. David has also written a book about the history of the island including some great insights into the lives of the European pioneering families and their antics – *Ye Olde Barrier Scrapbook*, which can be purchased at the museum.

Kaitoke Beach and Medlands Beach from the air.

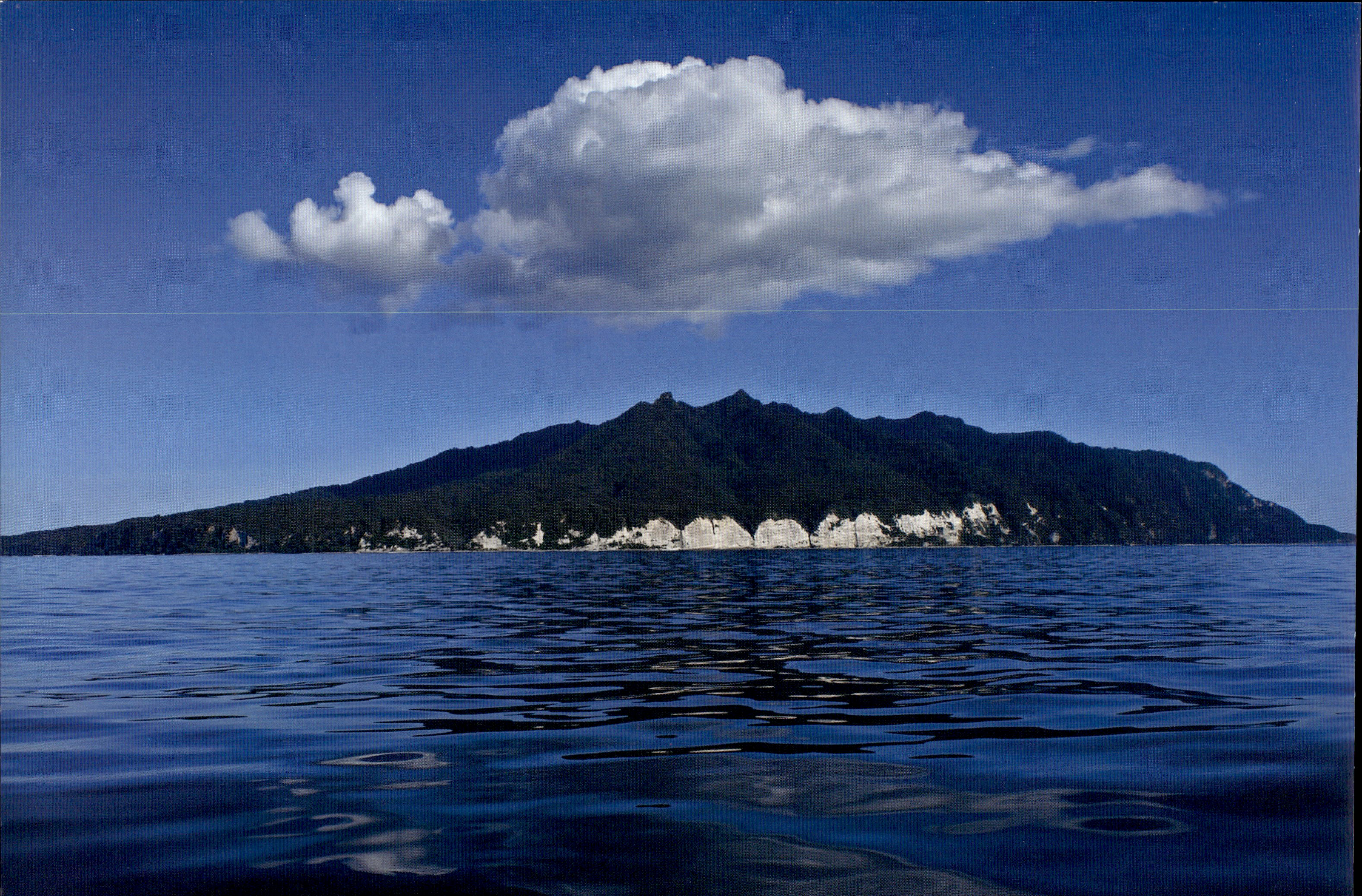

Little Barrier Island

THE BOTANICAL JEWEL IN NEW ZEALAND'S CROWN

Little Barrier Island – or Hauturu as it's known in Maori – is a beautiful, unspoilt, botanical jewel, which is critically important for the conservation of many of New Zealand's endangered plant and wildlife species. Described as 'the most intact ecosystem in New Zealand' and 'one of the most important reserves of its kind in the world,' as well as 'an invaluable refuge for rare and endangered plants, birds and animals whose mainland habitats have been destroyed', you get a sense of the magnitude of this place – it is an extremely precious nature reserve.

The lay of the Little Barrier land

Little Barrier Island is an extinct and eroded volcanic cone, which is thought to be around three million years old. The most recent volcanic activity occurred over a million years ago and the volcano is now extinct. The island (3083 hectares) is almost circular in shape and about 5 kilometres in diameter. Little Barrier can be seen from Auckland and even from 80 kilometres away it's easy to see that it has steep-sided cliffs and, as such, is almost impossible to access. There is one level corner of land on the island, Te Maraeroa Flat, which is made up of alluvial soil and surrounded with large rugged boulders that continue out to rocky beach and into the ocean. Te Maraeroa is the only place with relatively safe access via Te Tikoki Point.

A range of mountainous peaks runs through the centre of the island – the highest point is Mt Hauturu, which is 722 metres, above sea level. The steep terrain extends throughout the island, and deep valleys and streams radiate out from the central point, Mt Hauturu, slicing through the volcano, almost dissecting it in places. The high and low areas of land offer different conditions making it possible for a vast variety of different trees, plants and wildlife to flourish. The island's peaks, some of which are 'sugarloaf' shaped, are often shrouded with cloud and the lower valley areas remain shaded, moist, and ideal for the many native plants and wildlife.

Precious and protected

Little Barrier lies in the outer Hauraki Gulf – it is 80 kilometres north of Auckland and halfway between the mainland and Great Barrier Island, 22 kilometres east of Leigh. The island is a heavily protected nature reserve and access is by permit only.

Visiting Little Barrier is only possible via an authorised charter boat, with an accredited supervisor, a nominated group leader who assumes all responsibility for biosecurity, and with a paid-for permit from the Department of Conservation (DOC).

In order to protect the delicate environment, visitor numbers are restricted – a maximum of 20 people are permitted to land on the island each day. DOC requests that visitors arrange their charter boats and supervisors before applying for the permit. The permit can take up to 20 working days to be issued.

There is only one part of the island which is accessible to authorised vessels and their visitors. This is the area around Te Maraeroa from where there are five walking tracks, which are usually all open, that explore the surrounding bush and forest.

Because of the geography of Little Barrier, it is difficult to access, particularly in bad weather. The only landing area is at Te Tikoki Point at the south-western corner of the island – but landing can be a dicey affair. Visitors are advised to be prepared to get a dunking on arrival in some cases depending on conditions. In rough seas landing on the island may not be possible and visitors who are permitted to visit are advised to bring supplies in case they have to stay overnight if ocean conditions are rough.

There are no safe anchorages around Little Barrier and boaties are advised to keep a safe distance away both for biosecurity reasons and because the southern side of the island has many large volcanic rocks.

The surrounding ocean is rich with marine life and can be explored by experienced divers and snorkellers. The underwater terrain is diverse – huge volcanic boulders, deep crevices and kelp are ideal environments to see crayfish, sponges, angelfish, scarlet wrasse, demoiselles, red moki and John Dory. Rocky Point and Sugar Loaf Reef are both popular dive sites with dive charters run from Leigh.

Battles on Hauturu

Maori history reveals that Hauturu was discovered and settled in the twelfth century by Toi te Huatahi and his descendants. They named the island 'Te Hauturu-o-Toi' – resting place of the wind. In the fourteenth century, Ngatiwai iwi also landed and settled on the island, at about the same time as they settled on neighbouring Aotea – Great Barrier Island.

The Kawerau tribe invaded the island in the seventeenth century, landing canoes at Te Maraeroa. Fierce fighting took place on the southern side of the island and many were killed and remain buried there. The Ngatiwai people were never completely driven away from the island and, over time, the Kawerau and Ngatiwai resolved their rivalry; a number of marriages between the tribes formed connections which helped transform the conflict into a peaceful relationship.

Hauturu was spared the violence and destruction that prevailed over most other Hauraki Gulf islands in the 1820s. Hongi Hika's Ngapuhi musket raiders came to Hauturu but, on finding Ngatiwai living there and with the two iwi forming an amicable relationship, they decided to leave the island relatively unscathed. The Ngati Manuhiri and Ngati Rehua hapu (sub-tribes) of Ngatiwai are the tangata whenua (people of the land) of Little Barrier Island to this day.

In 1881, the government declared that it intended to purchase Little Barrier for military use. Fortunately, this didn't eventuate – the government changed its plans and the island was to become a dedicated forest reserve and bird sanctuary. After 10 years of Land Court disputes between the Ngatiwai living on the island and the government, an agreement was made in 1891. Ngatiwai were prepared to sell, provided they were allowed to retain a reserve and remain on the island. The government viewed their presence as a threat to the success of the island as a conservation reserve. Ngatiwai argued that the pristine natural environment, perfect for sustaining endangered wildlife and birds, was due to their careful guardianship of the land over hundreds of years. The government refused to accept the conditions and were said to have made unfair changes to the original agreement which prevented Ngatiwai from being allowed to sell the land privately. Unable to sell, Ngatiwai began felling kauri trees to make

In 1932, Robert Nelson retired after 17 years as caretaker on the island. The Auckland Weekly News *published this tribute to the work he and his wife and daughter did while living there.*

LITTLE BARRIER ISLAND 41

money. The government, concerned at the damage this would do, issued an injunction against the felling and a trespass order against the timber merchant. Ultimately, after years of dispute and agreements, which were contentious and not respected, the remaining Ngatiwai were forcibly removed from the island – a sad outcome. The land purchase disputes continue to this day under the Waitangi Tribunal claims.

In 1894 the Auckland Institute installed a ranger on the island – there have been rangers on the island, stationed at Te Maraeroa, ever since.

Until rangers were appointed to look after the island, little European meddling had taken place. In 1769 Captain Cook sailed through the Hauraki Gulf on *Endeavour*, insisting, as he did, on a naming strategy that referenced the characteristic of the land or the native people, for just about every place he discovered. Little Barrier Island became the name used for the smaller of the 'barrier isles' as he called them. He named them as he observed their benefits as buffers to the strong winds from the Pacific Ocean.

Pioneering conservation for over a century

Little Barrier was one of the first reserves in New Zealand dedicated to the protection of native flora and fauna. It is also one of the largest offshore nature reserves. The island has been described as a 'botanical paradise' – never having been spoilt by farming, grazing livestock, or extensive land clearing. Little Barrier is one of the few examples in New Zealand of primordial forest – a fascinating window into the past that allows us to see what New Zealand would have been like before human settlement.

With over 400 species of plants and more endangered bird species than on any other island in New Zealand, Little Barrier is a haven of hope for numerous threatened species of bird, wildlife and plant.

The conservation of native bird species started over a hundred years ago when the North Island brown kiwi and kakapo were first brought to the island in 1903. Saddlebacks were introduced in 1925 but they were reluctant to settle – more recently they were reintroduced and are thriving. The kakapo had to be taken off the island for a number of years whilst pest eradication programmes took place. Kakapo are critically endangered and there are thought to be only about 150 left in the world. In 2013, nine kakapo were released on Little Barrier with the hope that they would breed.

Other native species on the island include: kaka (parrot), yellow and red-crowned kakariki (parakeet), kereru (wood pigeon), korimako (bellbird), popokatea (whitehead), grey warbler, morepork (owl), North Island robin, rifleman, kokako, tomtit, tui and little penguins.

Pest eradication involved a lot of work for many years on Little Barrier. The island is now pest-free with cats having been eradicated in 1980 and kiore rats in 2006. Keeping the island pest-free is crucial to preserving New Zealand's unique wildlife, which is why such stringent biosecurity regulations are enforced.

Little Barrier is the only island where hihi (stitchbird) live without any assistance from humans. Other rare birds include the Cook's petrel and New Zealand storm petrel. The island is home to the world's largest breeding ground of Cook's petrel. The storm petrel was thought to be extinct for over 100 years but was rediscovered in 2003 in the Hauraki Gulf. The discovery was made when birds that had been tagged were traced to burrows on the island.

A CURIOUS COMBINATION OF WILDLIFE

The wildlife on Little Barrier are an ancient and motley crew. There are two native species of bats, prehistoric tuatara lizards, 12 species of gecko and skinks, wetapunga – a giant weta, and the giant earthworm, which can measure over one metre in length!

Few people realise that New Zealand does have native mammal species. Little Barrier is one of the few places in the country where both the long-tailed and short-tailed bat exist. There are two types of short-tailed bat: the greater short-tailed bat, thought to be extinct as it hasn't been seen since 1967, and the lesser short-tailed bat, which still exists in the forests on Little Barrier. Short-tailed bats are extremely rare and have very different behaviour to most other bats. Whereas most of the world's species of bats catch their prey in the air, the short-tailed bat forages on the forest floors using their folded wings as limbs to clamber around, making them an easy target for introduced predators.

*A female giant weta (*Deinacrida heteracantha*) held by researcher Mike Meades. This, the largest of the weta species, is found only on Little Barrier Island.*

There are distinct vegetation zones on the island; a variety of different forest types that provide a safe habitat for the birds and wildlife. Kauri and beech forests cover much of the mountainous terrain – some of the kauri are 30 metres tall. There are coastal pohutukawa forests as well as kohekohe, taraire and puriri forests. Ferns, giant rata and tawa grow in the valleys and lichens and moss grow on the trees where there is plenty of moisture – the ecosystems are diverse.

DOC is responsible for managing the island and works with the Little Barrier Island Supporters Trust on weed management programmes which are crucial to protecting some of the rare plants. Some 150 species of weeds once threatened the vegetation. Battling the weeds is an ongoing effort and volunteers are sometimes allowed to help but need to be super fit to manage the terrain. Experienced abseilers are required to clear weeds on some of the ridges and cliffs. The abseilers, also known as 'dopes on ropes', hang precariously in hard-to-access places whilst spraying offending weed species. The Little Barrier Island Supporters Trust, formed in 1997, also works in conjunction with DOC to assist with fundraising for projects on the island. Managing pest eradication, aerial surveys, and creating and extending tuatara enclosures are some of the other valuable work they are involved with.

LITTLE BARRIER – DID YOU KNOW?

- Little Barrier Island is one of the most important conservation reserves in the world – it is home to more endangered bird species than any other island in New Zealand.
- New Zealand does have native mammals – there are two species of bat and they can both be found on Little Barrier Island.
- Mt Hauturu on Little Barrier Island (722 metres) is nearly three times higher than the summit of Rangitoto (259 metres).
- Rats are just as happy climbing trees as they are on the forest floors – it's not just the flightless birds that suffer when there are predators like the rat around.
- A species of giant earthworm lives on Little Barrier Island – they can grow up to 1.4 metres in length!
- A giant weta also makes the island its home – the largest giant weta found on Little Barrier weighed in at 71 grams – equivalent to the weight of a blackbird.

The view across to Little Barrier Island from Tawharanui.

STEVE CLARKE — PILOT

As chief pilot for Heletranz, Steve Clarke has spent many years flying all around New Zealand, with many adventures along the way. Combining his passion for flying helicopters and his love of fishing has led Steve to a career that facilitates one of the more adventurous recreational activities within the gulf – heli-fishing.

Steve takes heli-fishing groups out regularly when conditions are good. The very best fishing locations are hidden gems along the east coast of Great Barrier or the Coromandel Peninsula. The fishing locations depend on many factors, but are often remote bays or secluded spots perched on rocks. The east coast is much more exposed to big swells and the might of the Pacific Ocean; as a result, boaties don't venture around to the eastern side of Great Barrier much – so it's relatively quiet. Much of the land is privately owned, but the fishing spots are often below the high-tide mark, which means Steve can find some pretty special fishing spots virtually anywhere there is clearance for the helicopter to land.

The experience is a real thriller for fishing enthusiasts, and for those that love fishing, flying and expansive aerial views of the Hauraki Gulf, it's probably full-scale fishing nirvana. The trips can cater to small groups of up to five people and are scheduled to be four-and-a-half hours, although Steve says the trips are often longer – particularly if the fish are biting.

When planning heli-fishing locations, Steve takes into account a long list of considerations. 'I have a bit of a formula I've worked out over the years,' he says, but, of course, won't share any fishing-related secrets! He checks seasonal considerations, fish migration routes, tides, currents, swells, weather conditions, the Maori fishing calendar, bite times, phases of the moon, and works out the best possible time and place for his clients to have the best chance of catching fish. It all sounds very scientific, but then Steve adds, 'Fishing is fishing. It doesn't always work … you get a bit of a feel for where the fish are – and I do, depending on the time of the year.' He usually has three or four spots in mind before departure, and decides upon the best location once he's had a look from the helicopter. He has a great track record – 'I've never come home without any fish,' he says cheerfully.

Some of Steve's favourite spots (the ones he's willing to talk about) are in the northern region of Great Barrier. 'There are so many special spots tucked away among the rocks,' he says.

Rock fishing has a small window of opportunity so Steve makes sure he gets the groups in position at the best bite times. 'Sometimes you'll have an hour, sometimes only fifteen minutes,' he explains – and if the fish aren't biting he'll give it a while, and then pack up and try somewhere else.

Steve stays with the group for the duration of the day's fishing and shares his expertise. 'For me, it's important to give clients that great experience.' He looks after his guests, sorts out lunch and gets bait for them (sometimes baiting their hooks), so they don't have to move much and can focus on enjoying fishing.

The heli-fishing trips catch mostly snapper, kingfish and sometimes kahawai. Steve gets a lot of satisfaction seeing his clients catch fish – 'particularly if it's a big fish,' he laughs. 'I can get quite vocal,' he jokes as he recalls catching a 12-kilogram snapper.

'I've dropped a few big ones over the years as well,' he laughs.

The biggest catch Steve has seen on a heli-fishing trip was a 13.6-kilogram snapper. He used to regularly see larger snapper over 10 kilos, but during the last couple of years there have been fewer around. 'They're coming in but not in the numbers they used to,' he says. 'I don't know if this is a seasonal thing or something more serious, I will have to consult my fishing diary in another twenty years or so to find out.' He chooses not to bring home anything over 7 kilograms – returning larger fish back into the water. 'The larger fish can be up to sixty to seventy years old … and most of them are territorial, remaining in the same region – so when they're gone, they're gone,' he says. 'I have only had one person question my decision to release a big snapper, however after a stern word and some education he understood why. I want my kids and grandchildren to be given the same opportunity to catch and release such a magnificent species.'

The Hauraki Gulf provides some of the best fishing in New Zealand and the marine life, particularly in the outer gulf, is rich and diverse. The heli-fishing clientele include regular clients who enjoy an annual trip to a new location every year; corporates who host their clients; and mostly men who have been gifted the experience by friends or family. Steve has seen a few women on his heli-fishing excursions – he's even flown one lady to Claris airfield for a toilet stop. How about that for service? Just in case you're wondering, fishing on exposed rocks presents a couple more challenges for women than men in the bathroom department.

Most of Steve's clients are New Zealanders; he estimates that less than five per cent are tourists from overseas. The experience isn't cheap; helicopters are notoriously expensive to run, and the mix of clients is often determined by the state of the economy influencing discretionary spending. A boom in the Auckland building industry has seen increased numbers of construction clients out fishing in the gulf of late.

Regardless of the type of client, they almost all ask Steve how long he's been flying. He laughs as he explains how much fun the pilots sometimes have, telling people (especially nervous flyers) that it's their first week on the job.

Steve gets a huge amount of pleasure from fishing and has done since his childhood. Always happy playing outdoors, he recalls taking every opportunity to go fishing and camping with friends. Nowadays Steve loves taking his children on outdoors adventures when he can. Steve's family are precious to him and, with a very busy work schedule involving long hours, he strives to strike a balance between work and time with family – enjoying trips out walking, swimming and boogie-boarding.

Steve's other great passion is flying helicopters. He knew he wanted to be a helicopter pilot from around the age of nine. At the age of five, he had wanted to be a truck driver but driving was quickly superseded by flying. 'It was always mechanical,' he said adamantly.

Growing up in Warkworth, he spent time around family friends who flew agricultural planes and his interest in flying developed. Another family friend, Neville Stevenson from Marine Helicopters based at Omaha, took Steve for his first flight in a helicopter at age nine. Steve remembers thinking 'this is a bit of me' and from then on he was determined to become a pilot. His first hands on flight was in 1993, and by 2001 he had his commercial pilot licence.

It is a competitive industry and Steve chuckles as he shares his thoughts about helicopter pilots: 'It's a funny industry – there are definitely a few chest-beaters!' He smirks as he assures me he is not one of them. 'Every pilot thinks they're better than the next – there's quite a lot of big egos – typical males!' he laughs.

The spirited way in which Steve talks about flying is engaging. 'The world just stops – that's what I love about flying,' he explains. 'Life can get too fast ... when you're focused on flying you can switch off and it's an escape.' It's a feeling many of his clients relish too. The novelty of being out of contact and leaving the unrelenting demands of a busy place behind, allows them a rare moment of calm and a sense of peace.

As well as flying private clients, Steve also flies all over the country; transporting tradespeople working on infrastructure projects on Great Barrier and other islands around the gulf, facilitating a range of Heletranz experiences such as trips to Waiheke Island vineyards, aerial filming projects for media, heli-golf trips at Kauri Cliffs in the Bay of Islands, heli-horse treks at Pakiri Beach – even landing on rocks perched on cliff tops in the Waitakere Ranges to enable scenic marriage proposals. Every day is different and Steve enjoys the variety.

Being a helicopter pilot sounds glamorous, and there's no doubt pilots have the very best office views and get to meet a lot of interesting people but, like any profession, there are days which hold challenges that could never be anticipated. Steve had one of those days in August 2013, when he and a group of heli-fishing clients were flying en route to Great Barrier Island. The weather conditions had been questionable and, with a large weather system on the way, Steve wasn't sure whether the trip would go ahead, but there was a window of opportunity, so he decided to go. As they flew over the chain of islands to the west of Great Barrier, Steve spotted a man waving erratically on Nelson Island, a small uninhabited rocky island in-between Kaikoura and Motuhaku islands. Steve waved back at the man as they flew past but instinctively felt that something was not right. He decided to go back and see if the man was all right. He dropped all but one of his clients on rocks nearby and flew back to where he had seen the man.

For 19-year-old Tainui Hale, who had been flipped over in his dinghy in rough seas and washed up onto the rocky coastline of Nelson Island, the sight of the returning helicopter was surreal. He thought he was hallucinating after three days and two nights stranded on the island. He had huddled up beneath a pohutukawa tree to try to keep warm. The teen had left his home on Flat Island to go pig hunting – he hadn't checked the forecast and was caught out when the weather changed extremely quickly. When Steve found him, he was dehydrated, weak and hypothermic. Wearing only a T-shirt and underpants (he had cast off his other clothes and shoes whilst trying to swim to safety), Tainui had picked kawakawa leaves and laid them out on the ground to

Like all good fishermen, Steve keeps the exact locations of his favourite fishing spots secret.

capture rainwater, which he drank. As his dinghy capsized he'd been thrown into the water, losing his dog and precious family heirlooms, and as he fought strong currents, he watched his boat and possessions disappear under the waves.

Steve approached the rocky hillside where Tainui had been waving and could see nowhere safe to land. With four-metre swells there was no way of landing further away and getting to the man on foot across the rocks. Steve could see only one option available – to try to hover near where Tainui stood to see if he could get the helicopter in close enough. Steve approached the rugged cluster of rocks and managed to find a rock just large enough to perch one of the helicopter skids on.

As he rested the helicopter precariously on the rock, his heli-fishing passenger carefully helped Tainui into the helicopter, trying to ensure he didn't move too quickly and upset the balance of the helicopter. Tainui managed to clamber aboard and was so overcome with exhaustion and emotion he couldn't speak. He just cried, overwhelmed and extremely grateful to have been rescued.

Steve flew Tainui back to Flat Island where his family had been completely unaware of what had happened. Tainui's family had not reported him missing as he often went hunting for a week at a time. The life-saving rescue was a day neither of the men will forget. 'He was a very lucky boy,' Steve says. 'The conditions were just horrendous – fifty-knot winds and massive swells ... ' In a television interview by 3 News, which included dramatic footage of the rescue taken by one of the offloaded heli-fishing clients, Tainui hugged and thanked Steve for saving his life. A real character, Tainui also described how he'd managed to survive for three days on an exposed island in bad weather and suggested 'Bear Grylls could have taken a leaf out of my book'.

Every day brings new possibilities and challenges. Steve can't imagine life without the excitement of flying and finding new places. 'I love finding new spots – that's what keeps it exciting,' Steve says. 'It's a bit like an addiction because it's such a cool place to be ... I suppose it's about being in control of a machine which isn't meant to fly – being up in the air – it's pretty special.'

Towards Little Barrier Island from the mainland.

Fishermans Bay.

Tiritiri Matangi Island

A SYMPHONY OF BIRDSONG

Tiritiri Matangi is a truly enchanting, relatively small island of 220 hectares, which hosts beautifully regenerated forests and bush as a result of many years of extremely successful conservation work undertaken by the Supporters of Tiritiri Matangi, the Department of Conservation (DOC), and an army of volunteers, known as 'the spade brigade', from all over the country – and the world.

The singing island

Tiri, as the island is affectionately known by those who visit regularly, is a scientific reserve and open sanctuary for many rare, native and endemic birds and wildlife. The island feels like a sanctuary – peace and calm emanates from the forests, bush and coastline. Although Tiritiri Matangi means 'island tossed by the wind,' Tiri has been called 'the singing island' and it lives up to its reputation; the uninterrupted birdsong is magical. Almost immediately on arrival the birdsong is entrancing and evocative of a time long ago when birds lived in forest and bush without fear of predators.

Tiritiri Matangi is accessible by ferry from downtown Auckland (75 minutes) and Gulf Harbour (20 minutes). Private boats can access the island and must comply with the biosecurity precautions. Brief offloading at the wharf is allowed, but then small craft should anchor in one of the bays. Boats must not be beached (other than kayaks or small dinghies) – this is an important biosecurity precaution. Hobbs Beach on the west of the island is the best anchorage and is closest to the island facilities. Fisherman's Bay on the east side of the island also has good anchorages and is more suitable in a westerly wind. There is a steep track up from Fisherman's Bay, which leads up to join the East Coast Track.

It is possible to stay overnight on Tiri – it is a wonderful opportunity to witness the dawn chorus, which is often described as an incredible experience. The dawn chorus on Tiri is probably one of the only places we can experience birdsong at dawn as it would have been back in times before humans cleared forests and natural bird habitats for their own uses. Beds in the bunkhouse can be booked through DOC. The visitor centre has informative displays and while the shop sells a multitude of gifts and cold drinks, visitors will need to bring their own food.

Ancestors of the land

Tiri would once have been the lush forest refuge it is for birds and wildlife today, but the island's history has not always allowed the tranquillity that existed then and now. It has a similar historic pattern to other Hauraki Gulf islands; invasions, fierce battles between tribes, and land-clearing all took place during the occupation of the first Maori settlers and left the island quite bare of native trees and vegetation.

The first Maori settlers on Tiri were from the Kawerau tribe. The island takes its name from the Tiritiri Matangi pa site, built on the western side of the island by the Kawerau people. When the Ngati Paoa tribe decided to settle on Tiri they built a pa site on the northern coast of the island, which was destroyed during the fighting that took place between the two iwi, when the Ngati Paoa were defeated by the Kawerau in around 1700. They remained living on the land until 1821 when Hongi Hika and his men invaded the island and attacked the occupants in a bloody battle. Hongi Hika's men were armed with muskets and the Kawerau people didn't stand much of a chance. Many were killed, the others fled for their lives.

In 1837, some of the Kawerau tribe returned to the island. Soon after, the Europeans started arriving and disagreements and friction about land ownership flared up. In 1867 the Maori and European claims to the island were brought before the Maori Land Court – resulting in the land title being given to the government.

In the 80 years that followed, farmers leased the land from the government and cleared more forest to plant pasture for their cattle, sheep, pigs and goats to graze. The Hobbs family farmed the land and were connected with the island for 70 years until, in 1971, responsibility for the land was granted by the government to the Hauraki Gulf Maritime Park Board.

A TOTAL MINEFIELD

In 1943, during World War II, a series of defensive minefields were laid in the ocean around the Hauraki Gulf. Two hundred mines were laid between Tiri and Motutapu, a further string of mines were laid between Tiri and The Noises, and another system was laid between Whangaparaoa on the mainland and Tiri. The mines were British MK 14 types and were laid 56 metres apart in a zig-zag formation in order to be most effective. After the war some of the mines were destroyed in controlled explosions, while minesweepers collected the remainder. Two broke free from the chain and went adrift – they were said to have been faulty!

A saddleback in full song amongst blooming pohutukawa on Tiritiri Matangi Island.

The Tiri Project

Described as 'one of the most successful community-led conservation projects in the world' by DOC, the forest regeneration on Tiri is a remarkable achievement and a beautiful one to behold.

The Tiri Project began in 1984 – a replanting programme intended to regenerate the island's forests, which had been cleared for farmland with only a few pockets of trees remaining. The 10-year replanting programme by DOC, the Supporters of Tiritiri Matangi and many volunteers was a huge success, planting 280,000 trees. Commitment to the project was so great that at times there were more willing volunteers than trees available to plant so waiting lists had to be drawn up. Due to the enthusiasm of the many volunteers, the project was completed two years early and now two thirds of the island is covered with trees, creating a rich ecosystem for birds and wildlife.

The programme of conservation work continued in the 1990s with a working plan for Tiri. This involved repopulating the island with once indigenous birds together with other endangered bird species that were in desperate need of a safe environment.

A realm of endangered species has been brought to Tiri with the hope that they would thrive – and they have. Tiri has a wonderful story to tell visitors about the successful translocated species, which are increasing in numbers. The takehe, saddleback, kokako, hihi, little spotted kiwi, North Island robin, whitehead, fernbird and pateke (brown teal), and rifleman are all doing well. Birds are often moved from Tiritiri Matangi to other Hauraki Gulf islands, and sometimes to the mainland, to increase their breeding potential and to increase genetic diversity.

It is not only birds that are benefiting from life on Tiri – shore skinks, Duvaucel's gecko and tuatara are all increasing their populations. The success story of Tiri and its unique environment is enjoyed and experienced by many visitors each year. Bird watchers and nature lovers and anyone with an interest in the island will find visiting an experience they will never forget and likely want to repeat.

Walking with birds – the original mobile twitter

There are many well-maintained tracks on Tiri for visitors to walk through the forests and bush, listening to the trills and arpeggios of the birdsong whilst watching out for the birds that flutter through the trees often right before their eyes. On a recent visit I was awestruck on seeing a couple of saddleback in flight, a couple of metres away in the trees. They landed close by, just long enough for me to get a good look at their beautiful chestnut-brown saddle markings and orange wattles. They are simply stunning – their elegant silhouette, their colouring, and the unique sound of the vibration of their wings as they fly, short distances at a time, from tree to tree.

A good friend of mine, who was with me at the time, said that as a young girl she recalled learning about native birds at primary school. The teacher had implored the class to take special note of the saddleback because, in their lifetime, it would inevitably become extinct. Thankfully, because of conservation programmes – particularly on islands like Tiritiri Matangi, Motutapu, Rotoroa and Motuora to name a few – the teacher's lesson plan will have been updated.

Looking towards the lighthouse from Hobbs Beach.

THE LIGHTHOUSE

Built in 1865, Tiri's lighthouse still stands proud today as the oldest still in operation in New Zealand. The construction of the cast iron lighthouse was an expensive and time-consuming mission. The parts were sent via a sailing ship from England to the island and then transported, with difficulty, on sledges pulled by 12 bullocks. The heavy clay soil on the island meant that digging down three metres to create the foundations of the lighthouse took four months. The lighthouse (the third to be built in New Zealand), historic signal tower, workshop and three foghorns are well worth visiting. Although visitors cannot access the buildings, they are impressive structures.

Did you know?
- At a height of 21 metres, the lighthouse stands on the hilltop at 91 metres above sea level.
- Originally red, the lighthouse was repainted white in 1964.
- The Tiri lighthouse has been powered by a variety of sources:
  – In 1865, the fixed light was fuelled by rapeseed oil
  – The light was modified to burn kerosene in 1916
  – In 1955, it was converted to diesel-generated electricity
  – Power was supplied by mains electricity from 1966 when an underwater cable was laid from the mainland
  – From 2002, solar-powered batteries have provided the light's power.
- In the 1960s, the Tiri lighthouse was the brightest in the southern hemisphere.
- Light strength is measured in candlepower and Tiri's lighthouse boasted 11 million candlepower, which could be seen up to 80 kilometres away.
- Mariners complained that the intensity of the light affected their night vision.
- Some residents of the North Shore complained that the light was so bright it kept them awake at night.
- In 1984, the candlepower was reduced from 11 million to 1.6 million.
- The last lighthouse keeper on Tiri, Ray Walter, switched the lights off manually, for the very last time, before the lighthouse became automated in 1984.
- In 2002, the light was adjusted to 1.2 million candlepower, which could be seen up to 33 kilometres away.

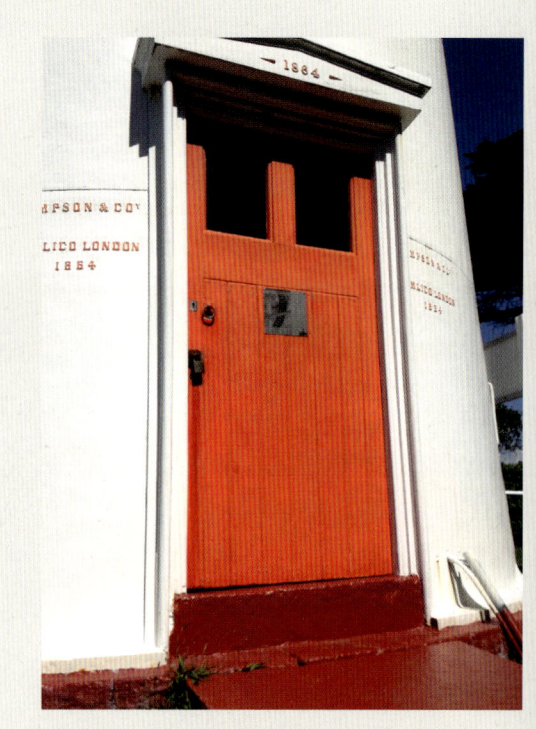

The door to the lighthouse. The red paint is a nod to the original colour of the lighthouse.

Left: The lighthouse and signal station in the early part of the twentieth century.
Right: The lighthouse as it looks today.

Endangered species, like saddlebacks, have a real chance of surviving and thriving as long as sanctuaries and environments like Tiri can be protected. It is a wonderful thing to experience the birds on Tiri – before I visited I had often heard people describe the experience as 'magical' and it really is. The challenge, as Tiri becomes more diverse and popular, will be to manage visitor numbers to ensure that the magic continues.

The tracks on the island provide a good dose of pristine nature at its best – winding through forests, bush and incorporating stunning coastal views. There are rocky bays and sandy beaches, and undulating tracks leading visitors through a variety of different terrain.

Guided walks are available on Tiri and should be booked in advance. The guides show visitors the best places to view the island's wildlife and share lots of information about the history, birdlife, flora and fauna, and conservation.

The Wattle Track is one of the best walks to see the birds as there are many feeding boxes and sugar-water stations in the area. The track leads up from the wharf to the lighthouse, through forest and bush, on gravel paths and boardwalk. Tui, bellbirds and saddlebacks are frequent visitors while kokako, whiteheads, stitchbirds and the North Island robin are a little more timid, but can also be seen in the area if you are lucky.

Hobbs Beach is short walk from the wharf and ideal for a picnic, a swim or snorkelling in its beautiful clear water. The Hobbs Beach track leads along rocky coastline with views of Whangaparaoa Peninsula and beside the track are nesting boxes for all the little penguin (korora), also known as little blue penguin. In springtime it is possible to see the penguins nesting.

Kokako on Tiritiri Matangi Island.

They are the smallest penguins in the world and have a very wide range of calls – sometimes mewing like a cat and sometimes growling deeply!

A scenic walk on the East Coast track out to Fisherman's Bay offers panoramic views from hilltops to the secluded rocky bays and out to sea. The track is undulating with a few steeps hills and leads through forest, bush and out onto more exposed hilltops with views across the water to Coromandel and Great Barrier Island. The clear water at Fisherman's Bay is ideal to cool off after the hilly walk and you can even swim and picnic without seeing another soul.

The Kawerau Track includes large and very old pohutukawa and puriri trees, some of the oldest bush on the island, and most of the birdlife on Tiri can be seen in this area. The Tiritiri Matangi pa site is a short 15-minute walk from the Kawerau track with sweeping views back across the mainland. There are a network of trails and loops that can be walked by combining tracks. The expansive views from the lighthouse across to Auckland city and Rangitoto are also superb. The city, happily for those that like to escape it, looks far away.

RAY AND BARBARA WALTER — ENLIGHTENED GUARDIANS

Ray and Barbara Walter are well known to many people with a close connection to Tiritiri Matangi Island. Ray was the last lighthouse keeper on Tiri before the lighthouse station was closed and the lighthouse was automated. Subsequently Ray trained to become a ranger and managed the Tiri Project – a 10-year replanting programme, which began in 1984 and has since successfully regenerated the island's native plants and trees to provide a rich habitat for many rare and endangered birds that have been reintroduced to the island within the open bird sanctuary.

Barbara, as well as helping Ray, has also played an integral role as part of the Tiri Project. She has worked for the Department of Conservation and the Supporters of Tiritiri Matangi, and has been crucial to the organisation and logistics of the project. Barbara took over organising the teams of volunteers who came and helped replant trees on the island. She co-ordinated school groups, hiking groups, over-60s groups and many other volunteers who helped with the Tiri Project over the 10 years it was in operation. Barbara has also worked closely with the birds, looking after their territories and welfare. As well as working as a guide on Tiri, she also started the island's shop – and still helps out there to this day.

Ray and Barbara are both still involved with Tiri despite 'having retired' 11 years ago! They're passionate about what they do, and the success of the island's conservation and open

Ray and Barbara Walter on Tiritiri Matangi Island.

bird sanctuary is a testament to them and the volunteer groups that helped them over many years.

Before taking on the responsibility for the planting programme on Tiritiri Matangi, Ray had been a lighthouse keeper for 30 years. He ran seven different lighthouse stations around New Zealand during that time.

After leaving school Ray went to sea. During a voyage to South Australia, his ship passed Kangaroo Island at sunset, and Ray caught sight of the Cape Willoughby lighthouse. The ship's crew were having a cup of tea on deck as they sailed past the magnificent view. 'That's the kind of place I'd like to live,' Ray said to his fellow crew members. His friends on board joked and bantered with him; telling tales of lighthouse keepers who had gone mad or turned to drink having lived in isolation for long periods. Ray was not discouraged – he could envisage enjoying life on an island and was determined he'd make it happen.

On the return voyage to New Zealand, the ship sailed past another lighthouse at the south-west tip of the South Island. 'Which one's that?' Ray asked the crew. 'That's Puysegur Point,' he was told, 'the bottom of New Zealand.' Ray was struck by the rugged beauty of the area and the lighthouse – his enthusiasm grew.

When Ray returned ashore to Auckland he mentioned his interest to the shipping master and inquired about the ins and outs of applying to become a lighthouse keeper. The shipping master asked Ray why he wanted to be a lighthouse keeper; Ray replied that he liked the look of Cape Willoughby and Puysegur Point lighthouses. The shipping master replied that Ray's reasoning seemed 'a bit bloody tenuous,' and explained that the New Zealand Lighthouse Service were only interested in men who were 23 years old or over, married, and with sober habits!

Ray was 17 and was not put off in the slightest. In the coming years he stopped working at sea, got married, and continued to apply to be a lighthouse keeper. Ray said, 'In 1957, they accepted my application. I was twenty years old.'

Ray explained that when you joined the New Zealand Lighthouse Service 'you had to sign a three-year bond and then they send you as far away as possible from your home – so you couldn't return home easily and had no choice but to get used to it.' Ray was sent to Puysegur Point. He was there for two-and-a-half years and then returned there for another three-year stint a few years later.

Before Tiri, Ray was stationed on Mokohinau Island, a much more isolated Hauraki Gulf island 25 kilometres north-west of Great Barrier Island. He loved his time there but was ready for a change after seven-and-a-half years. He'd been told, but nothing was guaranteed, that if he continued his service on Mokohinau he would probably be posted to Tiri next.

In 1980, Ray finally made it to manage his dream lighthouse station – Tiri! 'They used to refer to it as the lighthouse on the end of Queen's Wharf,' Ray explains. It had mains power, regular supply ships and a regular mail service. 'It was the plum station in the lighthouse service.'

I ask Ray what his main duties were on Tiri as the lighthouse keeper. He replies, 'Turning the lighthouse lights on and off,' and pauses – a twinkle in his eye. 'That's what people think – that lighthouse keepers wander around all day waiting for the sun to go down so that they can turn the lights on.'

After we'd finished laughing, he assured me there was 'a bit more to lighthouse keeping than that.' Lighthouse keepers worked seven days a week for 49 continuous weeks – and were contracted for 40 hours each week (although they couldn't get all the required work done in that time). They were allowed leave, but it was restricted to three consecutive weeks at the end of the year.

One of Ray's main responsibilities was producing meteorological reports. On a one-man station like Tiri, Ray was expected to create six weather reports each day and they had to be on time, every time. The first at six o'clock in the morning and the last one could be as late as 9pm or midnight, if requested. An exception was made for the Sunday 3pm weather report, which they were allowed to cancel if they wanted to.

Lighthouse keepers were also expected to do six hours of maintenance work each week. Ray did building maintenance, fencing and painting, while also looking after the island's tracks and roads. They were allowed 50 sheep and two cows – so there were also the animals to take care of and gardens to be tended. They were mostly self-sufficient so grew their own produce. There seemed like plenty to keep a lighthouse keeper from going mad or having time to hit the bottle.

The one aspect of the job Ray did think a little mad were the month-end reports. No details were spared in these reports, which were compulsory for lighthouse keepers. Details like: how much fog was experienced on the island, on what date, between which hours, with how much visibility, how many telegrams were sent and received – the list went on. Ray laughed as he remembered the laborious reporting process and explained that by the time the reports were sent from the lighthouse station and received in the Wellington office to be reviewed the information was often six weeks old. 'I mean what the hell were they going to do with it?' he laughs incredulously.

Despite the paperwork, Ray loved being a lighthouse keeper. 'It was a great life if you enjoyed it, but many didn't and there was a huge turnover of staff.' Ray enjoyed the routine, running his own station, getting to explore new places, and working outside. He particularly enjoyed tending to his gardens, and would always find a couple of hours every day to spend gardening. In leisure time, which was limited, he might spend time at one of Tiri's beautiful beaches, or go for a swim, or maybe head out on the water, fishing. They worked very hard, for long hours, but were happy.

I ask Ray and Barbara what it was like on the island when nobody else was around. They laugh. 'I don't think we ever had any days where there wasn't someone there ... oh, maybe there was one,' Barbara says. They never felt isolated or lonely on Tiritiri Matangi – there were always people around, especially when the Tiri Project started and teams of volunteers would spend many days helping out with planting.

Barbara explained that they also had university research students staying on the island who would be there for months at a time, and there were often deliveries, visiting tradespeople, lost boaties and lighthouse inspectors – the station was always busy with people coming and going.

On the subject of comings and goings, Ray shared a story about one particular unexpected visitor many years ago who knocked on his front door at 2am. 'I answered the door to some joker standing there in his underpants. He was soaked through and absolutely buggered.' The man had said that his boat had run ashore on the other end of the island with his friend still on it, and that it was drifting off towards Kawau Island.

The man in his underpants had wandered through the bush from the other side of the island and somehow found his way to the lighthouse keeper's house. 'How did you get here?' Ray asked. 'Did you come up the road?' The man replied that he had walked through the bush as he hadn't seen the road. The man said he'd known he was getting close to the house when he'd bumped into a letterbox. Ray was puzzled for a while before realising that the man must have walked into one of the saddleback nesting boxes, which looked exactly like an old letterbox.

Ray called the coastguard and got help for the man, his friend and their troublesome boat. Apparently the incident hadn't been enough to deter the man from returning to Tiritiri Matangi. Barbara said he had recently visited the island and recounted to Mary Ann, who had been working in the shop at the time, the story of his first visit! I couldn't help but ask Ray if he'd had many people turning up disorientated, or having been out in bad weather. 'You get a few idiots,' he says, 'you do wonder.'

Ray recalled some fun he had with his children and *Spirit of Adventure* – a large topsail schooner which was gifted to New Zealand by Lou Fisher to offer personal development courses for young New Zealanders. *Spirit of Adventure* would often sail out and back past Tiri in all her glory and would always be noticed.

One clear, sunny morning in September 1981, Ray's daughter had been milking the cows and had seen the ship sail through the Rakino Channel. They had been busy making butter and cream and had a lot of cream left over. Ray's daughter asked if perhaps *Spirit of Adventure* would like some cream. Ray thought it would be a nice thing to do and it was a lovely day, so he filled a jar with cream and wrapped it up in a mail bag to protect it. They put their dinghy in the water and started rowing out towards 'The Spirit,' as they called her. They rowed across the ship's bow and watched The Spirit change course repeatedly, so as it went past they threw the bundle up to a man standing at the bow. The man caught the bundle, looked at it and ran urgently to the stern of the boat. Ray and his children were curious as to this strange reaction, but rowed back thinking nothing of it.

The next day Ray received a telephone call from the skipper of The Spirit. 'Thank you for the cream,' the skipper said, 'you gave us quite a fright you know.' Ray was puzzled and asked why. The skipper replied, 'Well, the chap who caught it thought it was a bomb ... he bloody near threw it back at you!'

Ray was bewildered until the skipper explained that the country was up in arms about the Springboks rugby tour of New Zealand, which had seen anti-apartheid protesters disrupt the test match at Eden Park by dropping flour bombs from low-flying planes!

After Ray's first year of lighthouse keeping on Tiritiri Matangi, the New Zealand Lighthouse Service announced it would be closing down all manned lighthouse stations and transitioning them to be fully automated.

In 1984, the Tiri lighthouse became automated. Ray was disappointed – he had hoped to be a lighthouse keeper for the rest of his career. But as one door closed, another opened. The Hauraki Gulf Maritime Park Board and Auckland University announced their plans for the Tiri Project. Ray was asked if he would like the job of managing the project. Ray joked that the Maritime Park Board commissioner had seen his beautiful gardens and knew that if Ray could grow cabbages like that, he'd be good for planting trees.

Ray and Barbara were extremely busy as the Tiri Project got under way. Ray studied to become a ranger and worked, with the guidance of a landscaper, to plan and build the plant nursery buildings. During this time, some of the research students took Ray under their wing and shared their knowledge to help him with his studies.

There was never a dull moment as their lives suddenly went through a huge transition. Barbara was the organisational mastermind and co-ordinated all the volunteer groups when it came to planting. Barbara explains, 'We had walking groups, the ornithological society, the horticultural society, over-sixties groups, girl guides, boy scouts, cubs, schools, families – we even had people coming from overseas.'

When the birds were introduced on Tiri, Barbara helped out with them too. She loves working with the birds, especially the takahe, pateke and saddlebacks. Since retiring Barbara still volunteers to help with the birds and Ray hasn't missed a supporters working weekend since they started. They both laugh when they talk of their retirement, as they are still involved on Tiri and don't really feel 'retired' very often.

The Supporters of Tiritiri Matangi group was founded in 1988, partway through the initial planting programme when resources on the island were tight, and this was noticed by a passionate volunteer couple, Jim and Barbara Battersby.

One day while involved with planting, Jim asked Ray if he could borrow a rake. Ray had said no, as there was only one rake on the island. Jim was shocked by the lack of resources and decided to help raise funds to keep the project going. He asked Ray for a list of names of the 20 most dedicated volunteers. Jim contacted them and organised a meeting at St Matthews Church in Auckland city.

At the meeting the Supporters of Tiritiri Matangi group was founded and each member committed to contributing $20 annually. Since then, many more members have joined and the conservation success continues. There are now over 2000 members and some are children of the original volunteers.

Two hundred and eighty thousand trees later, the fact that the island's forests are thriving with rare and endangered birdlife is a tribute to their passion, commitment, fundraising and hard work. Today the supporters enable guided walks on the island, help maintain the tracks, continue with enhancement planting and weed management, as well as bird welfare and research. They also continue to fundraise and manage the visitor centre and shop.

Ray and Barbara said they felt very fortunate to have been involved with the Tiri Project and were so grateful for the great help and commitment of the volunteers and supporters. 'They're a great group of people,' Barbara enthuses, 'they're wonderful and a constant group who regularly come over and work hard.'

The planting work that had been planned as a 10-year programme was completed in eight years – all due to the large number of volunteers and their eagerness and willingness to help. The dedication and energy of the volunteers has made Tiri a very special place.

Whilst living on Tiri, Barbara and Ray felt privileged to have met many interesting people who visited. World-renowned scientist and broadcaster David Attenborough was one of their favourites. Attenborough visited Tiritiri Matangi to film the saddlebacks for his BBC series *The Life of Birds*. He spent several days on the island. One evening after dinner, Ray, Barbara and a group of others had been sitting around the table chatting when they noticed David had disappeared. They found him in the kitchen drying the dishes – quite the model house guest.

During the filming of *The Life of Birds*, students from Papatoetoe High School had been visiting the island. The science teacher in charge, unaware of David Attenborough's visit, had instructed the children to explore the island as if they were a scientist like David Attenborough!

When David arrived, Ray and Barbara told him about the school trip 'and of course, he's so nice, he went and spoke to them,' Barbara says, 'The kids couldn't believe it – they thought it had all been organised just for them.'

Ray and Barbara in the early days of establishing the island's nursery.

Botanist and broadcaster David Bellamy also visited Tiri. During his visit he helped plant native trees with a group of children for a TV programme called *Moa's Ark*. He described the day as 'one of the most inspiring days' he had experienced. In the foreword of Anne Rimmer's book *Tiritiri Matangi – A model of conservation*, Bellamy states that he feels Tiri is worthy of World Heritage status. He also says, 'Just as the Galapagos and the islands of the Malaysian archipelago inspired Charles Darwin and Alfred Russell Wallace to write that first paper on evolution by natural selection [a scientific paper that changed the way humankind thought about itself], so Tiritiri inspired an ever-growing bank of people from

RAY AND BARBARA WALTER — ENLIGHTENED GUARDIANS   67

One of the island's many high-profile visitors, broadcaster and botanist David Bellamy, chats with Ray and Barbara.

all walks of life to challenge the fitness of their species in the struggle for future survival.'

Prince Phillip was another memorable visitor to Tiri, and was extremely keen to see the island and its birds. Unfortunately, the people accompanying him had planned a very tight schedule, with engagements on both Tiri and Motutapu that day. When he'd finished speaking he had wanted to spend time with Ray and Barbara and see the birds. He was disgruntled when told by his organisers that he did not have time. He got quite agitated and 'marched off in quite a huff,' Ray recalls. (Prince Phillip losing his temper? Surely not!) It does seem a terrible shame to have come all that way and not be able to experience the birds and beauty of the place.

If British royalty isn't your cup of tea, Helen Clark (the Prime Minister at the time) visited Tiri on a number of occasions. A keen supporter of the work being done and avid bird watcher, Helen and her husband, Peter, had come to spend the weekend on the island, staying in the bunkhouse. They were accompanied by an entourage of security personnel who also stayed. Ray recalled quite a commotion on Sunday morning. Helen's security guards had searched the place to tell her that breakfast was ready but 'she'd gone ... they'd lost her ... and all chaos broke out,' Ray recalls. Calm was restored when they discovered that Helen and Peter had just gone for a walk to the other side of the island to experience the dawn chorus – a unique experience on Tiri.

Ray and Barbara, having moved to the mainland when they retired 10 years ago, agree that the future for Tiritiri Matangi looks great. I ask Ray if he misses island life. He says he does miss some aspects – the sound of the ocean and the birds – but he was happy to retire and that meant living on the mainland. After 48 years of managing lighthouse stations he was ready for a rest – not that he's had much! 'I had a good time out there,' he says.

Looking towards Hobbs Bay from Wharf Road.

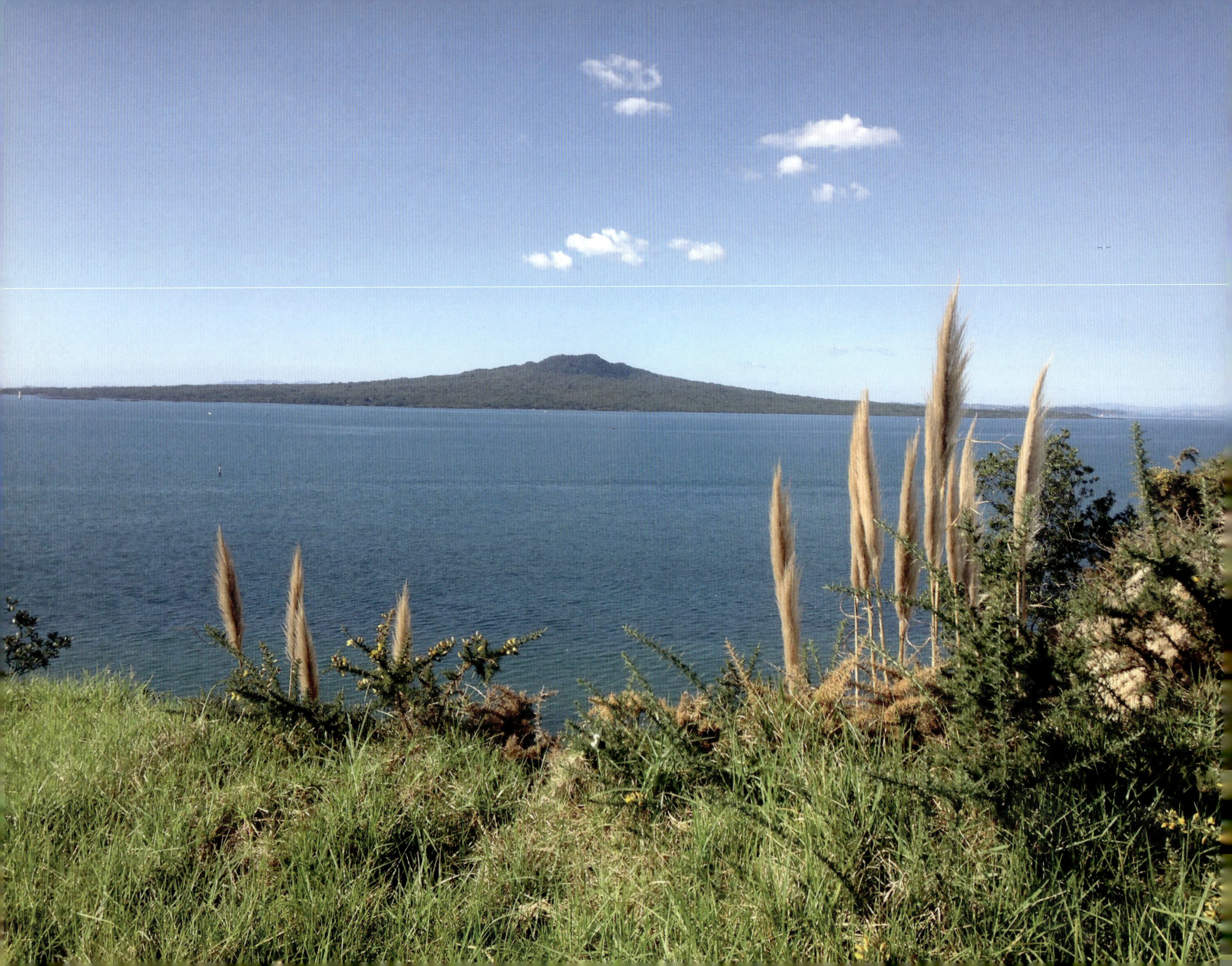

Rangitoto Island

THE YOUNG AND THE RESTLESS

Rangitoto is the youngest and largest volcano in the Auckland region. The island is 2311 hectares of basalt and scoria terrain, hosting an array of botanical gems. The volcano's summit stands at 259 metres above sea level and offers panoramic views of Auckland city, the Waitemata Harbour, and the Hauraki Gulf. Visible from many vantage points around Auckland, Rangitoto provides a natural shelter to the entrance of the Waitemata Harbour as well as some of the beaches on Auckland's North Shore.

Visiting the volcano

Situated 8 kilometres north-east of Auckland city, Rangitoto's silhouette appears the same from wherever you look at it because of its almost perfect symmetry. From the air, Rangitoto is just as spectacular. The volcano accommodates an incredible variety of trees and plants considering its rocky terrain, with a central crater which is 60 metres deep and 150 metres wide. Rangitoto is joined to its neighbour, Motutapu Island, by a thin causeway – the transition across takes you from one world to another. In a few strides you can journey from Rangitoto's 600-year-old dry and dusty volcanic rocks to Motutapu's rich, green farmland, which used to be part of Gondwanaland (an ancient supercontinent) and is millions of years old.

Conveniently close to Auckland, the island is a weekend favourite with boaties. With plenty of rocky coastline, there are good places to come ashore for walks, picnics, swimming and snorkelling, and exploring the island. Most weekends you will find a gaggle of boats anchored in Islington Bay – there is a wharf at the head of the bay and access from it to both Rangitoto and Motutapu. McKenzie Bay, on the eastern side of the island, is

Queuing for the ferry on Rangitoto Wharf.

sheltered (in all but south-westerly or north-westerly winds) and a good spot for a picnic on a sandy beach.

Rangitoto and Motutapu islands are landmarks and destinations for many yacht and boat races in the gulf. Islington Bay hosts many post-race social gatherings and barbecues as it is a sheltered spot. Islington Bay is also a convenient stop-off for yachts heading to Waiheke or north via the Rakino Channel. They bay's strategic position also lends itself well to the Auckland Coastguard, which often moors a standby rescue launch there.

The island is also a popular tourist attraction. Visitors to Auckland are often curious to know why New Zealand's largest city is situated in the middle of a significant cluster of volcanoes, including Rangitoto, which looms on the horizon from so many vantage points across Auckland. Tourists are also intrigued by the blasé attitudes New Zealanders have about living so close to volcanoes. It is a very foreign concept to many visitors, particularly Europeans. But it doesn't put them off – visitors are fascinated to explore and learn more about Auckland's most iconic volcano, its unique terrain, walks, lava caves, rich history, and panoramic views from the summit.

Visitors to Rangitoto should bring their own supplies with them – there is no food or water available on the island. During the summer months when the sun is out, the rock gets very hot. Temperatures above the rocks can reach 50 degrees Celsius, so water is essential when visiting and walking on Rangitoto. There is no overnight accommodation on Rangitoto but there is a campsite

The view from the summit of Rangitoto Island.

Looking back towards the city across the Rangitoto lava field.

at Home Bay on neighbouring Motutapu. Home Bay is a beautiful spot, surrounded and sheltered by rolling green hills.

A short ferry ride from either downtown Auckland or Devonport on the North Shore enables easy access to Rangitoto. If you're feeling more adventurous, it takes a couple of hours to kayak to the island from the North Shore but care must be taken when crossing the Rangitoto Channel, which is used by commercial shipping. Guided kayaking tours are also available if navigating the channel by yourself doesn't appeal.

The satisfaction of using your own paddle-power to get there, seeing marine life along the way, getting some fresh sea air in the lungs, and building up an appetite for a sunset-enriched beer and beach barbecue is a great way to experience Rangitoto. On the return kayak trip you may see phosphorescence – an energy-storing type of plankton that emits light as it is disturbed by movement in the water. Nature's own solar-powered underwater lighting system is a magical phenomenon.

For those who prefer ocean swimming, the Rangitoto to St Heliers Bay swim will likely be high on the bucket list. The annual event, run by Auckland Central Masters Swimming, takes place each April. It sees over 400 swimmers take on the 4.6-kilometre challenge from Rangitoto Wharf across the Waitemata Harbour to the mainland, where crowds of supporters cheer the swimmers on as they scramble out of the water to cross the finish line. Swimming over four-and-a-half kilometres is a real feat of endurance, especially if conditions are on the choppy side. The fastest man in 2017 finished in 58 minutes and the fastest woman finished in 61 minutes.

An explosive start

The Auckland volcanic field has, so far, produced over 50 individual volcanoes in the last 250,000 years. Auckland is a sprawling city and so is its volcanic field – spanning 360km^2, with the field still young and active. How many more volcanoes it will produce in the future, and when, is anyone's guess.

New volcanoes in the Auckland region are formed when molten magma, lying 100 kilometres below the earth, bubbles up through the earth's crust to the surface. The bigger the bubble, the larger the eruption. Rangitoto was a comparatively large-sized bubble in relation to other volcanoes in the Auckland volcanic field. Depending on whether the magma breaks through the surface on land or under water will affect the way the magma and volcanic rock react. Hot magma meeting cold water reacts violently.

The most recent eruption was around 600–700 years ago. The formation of Rangitoto is believed to have come about via two periods of eruptions at this time that were likely to have been about 10 years apart. The most recent of the eruptions was witnessed by Maori living on neighbouring Motutapu Island at the time.

The two most recent eruptions on Rangitoto would likely have been two distinct types of eruptions. The first would have seen lava bubbling up through shallow sea water, forming the gently sloping lower layers of Rangitoto's basalt base. The second eruption, about 10 years later, would likely have been explosive in nature and would have propelled volcanic rock and molten lava into the air, crashing down upon Rangitoto and the surrounding area. The ash cloud formed by the eruption rained down on both

Rangitoto and Motutapu – the ash on Motutapu was said to have been two metres thick.

The nature of Auckland's volcanic field (monogenetic) means that its volcanoes erupt usually only once. Recent research on Rangitoto, however, suggests that it is prone to multiple eruptions (polygenetic). In 2014, scientists drilled into the western side of the volcano revealing evidence of volcanic activity from 6000 years ago. Scientists established that Rangitoto is likely to have been a lot more active for a lot longer than previously understood.

As research provides new information, people with baches on Rangitoto and those living in Auckland and the Hauraki Gulf are, naturally, curious to know if Rangitoto is likely to erupt again. Scientists are continually monitoring Rangitoto with multiple seismographs in an attempt to try to find out.

Life among the lava

Maori settled on neighbouring Motutapu but not Rangitoto due to the latter's harsh and uninhabitable rocky terrain. The Ngai Tai iwi lived on Motutapu and consider both Rangitoto and Motutapu their ancestral home. Ngati Paoa, an iwi of the Hauraki region, also have connections with Rangitoto, even though the island was once considered by Maori to be tapu – sacred.

One of the more literal Maori interpretations of the word Rangitoto is 'sky blood', which Europeans assumed related to the red sky that the inhabitants of Motutapu would have seen when the most recent of Rangitoto's eruptions sent fiery molten lava exploding into the sky. The full Maori name for Rangitoto is Te Rangi i totongia te ihu a Tama-te-kapua – the day the blood of Tama-te-kapua's nose flowed. This relates to an ancient battle on Rangitoto between the Te Arawa and Tainui people. Tama-te-kapua, the captain of the Arawa waka, was injured in the battle that his Te Arawa people lost at Islington Bay. The Tainui people remained on Rangitoto and in the Auckland region for many centuries.

Europeans arrived early on Rangitoto – the island was bought by the Crown in 1854 and from 1898 to 1930 basalt was quarried from near Islington Bay for use in Auckland's construction industry.

In 1890, Rangitoto Island was designated a recreation reserve and became a popular destination with visitors, who sailed from Auckland by steamship, for day trips, walks and picnics. Seven years later, the wharf and road to the summit were built and visitors were charged an island landing tax as well as a summit tax.

In the early 1920s, the Rangitoto Domain Board were keen to encourage more visitors to Rangitoto and neighbouring Motutapu. They could see that there was money to be made from visitors and felt strongly that roads would be necessary to create ease of travel around Rangitoto and Motutapu. The Domain Board put in a request to the Minister of Justice, asking if a workforce of prisoners from Mount Eden Prison could be used to build the roads. The request was approved.

In November 1925, a group of prisoners were transported to Rangitoto where they assembled basic huts to sleep in for the duration of the project. The *Auckland Star* described the 'scheme' as intended 'to develop Rangitoto as a scenic asset. At the present time its full beauty is not realised owing to the inaccessibility of so much of it.'

A classic Rangitoto bach.

A path through the Rangitoto lava field.

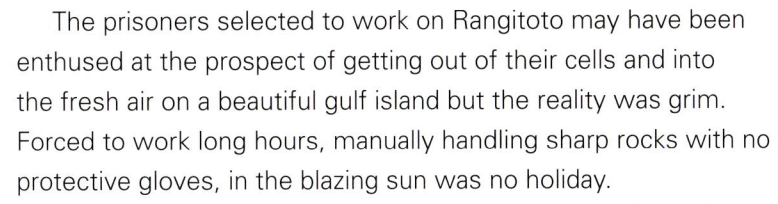

The prisoners selected to work on Rangitoto may have been enthused at the prospect of getting out of their cells and into the fresh air on a beautiful gulf island but the reality was grim. Forced to work long hours, manually handling sharp rocks with no protective gloves, in the blazing sun was no holiday.

It wasn't too long before the inevitable happened. Less than four months after the road-building started, two prisoners were reported as having escaped from Rangitoto Island. The following day, in a Press Association telegram, it was reported that two men, Charles Wahle and Samuel Rattray, had at midnight 'crept from their hut and made their way to the water's edge' where conveniently 'a bright moon had assisted them to find a dinghy, and in this craft they made good their escape. They fitted this boat with an outboard motor, taken from another boat.' The warders were a tad displeased.

A few hours later the warders, displeasure likely turned to panic as they discovered that 12, not two prisoners ' ... had been depleted'. The following morning the mainland authorities were alerted via a signal, seen by an eagle-eyed signalman on duty on Devonport's Mt Victoria, and the search began for the escapees. Two days later Press Association reports stated: 'A strong posse of detectives and police are making an exhaustive search, but so far their efforts have failed to reveal the whereabouts of the escapees.'

A week after their escape, the two original prisoners were found and recaptured at Cowes Bay on Waiheke Island. (There was no further mention of the 'depleted twelve' – probably misreported by the press.) The two prisoners captured were charged as 'incorrigible rogues' and threatened with an additional charge of theft relating to the boat they had scarpered in.

After appearing in the police court, the charge of 'incorrigible rogue' was withdrawn and they were instead charged with 'escaping lawful custody'. Records of their sentences were not available but it goes without saying that they were likely returned to their cells rather than to Rangitoto.

In May 1934, two more prisoners, Roy Taylor and James MacAndrew, escaped from the Rangitoto road-builders camp. They too stole a dinghy and managed to get to the mainland where they commandeered a car at Papatoetoe. Their escape plan seemed to be going well until the stolen car ran out of petrol on a Komakorau country road, near Ngaruawahia. The prisoners continued on foot only to be spotted by a passing constable. Exhausted and suffering from exposure, they were easily recaptured.

Subsequently, security must have been tightened up as prisoners stopped escaping and completed the roads on Rangitoto. The roads are still used today by the Department of Conservation and the Volcanic Explorer Tour – a four-wheel-drive road train which takes visitors on a guided tour of the island.

As World War II loomed, Rangitoto, with 360-degree views of the gulf from its summit, was considered a prime position to build military stations. A series of buildings were constructed, including a large camp for military personnel, an observation post, a fire command station – built of thick concrete which still exists today – a wireless station (the communications hub) and a radar station. Massive '12-pounder' gun emplacements were pointed at Musick Point on the mainland in order to defend the coastline against incoming torpedo boats. With no power on the island, a searchlight was installed with its own engine room required to power it. It was an elaborate set-up – all part of the Auckland Defence Network.

The construction on Rangitoto was particularly challenging due to the inaccessibility of the summit. A tram track had to be built in order to winch heavy materials from the road to the summit. It was an extremely expensive operation too – costing £37,000 (the equivalent of about $3.6 million today). The stations and equipment were in operation for only a year before it was decided to relocate to Devonport's North Head due to the challenges of having no power or water and difficult access to the site – a bewilderingly costly oversight for a defence system that was never challenged.

These days the guns are gone and the summit is a platform for sightseers rather than soldiers. The island is a national park and scenic reserve enjoyed by many Aucklanders and visiting tourists.

Surrounding the summit

Walking is a great way to explore the island – there are numerous tracks on Rangitoto and it is also possible to walk via the gravel roads. On a clear day, hiking up to the summit is a must for the reasonably fit. Summit Track goes from Rangitoto Wharf, traversing lava fields and regenerating forest en route to the summit where superb views make the uphill grunt worthwhile. The last section of track is a boardwalk which winds up and round the steep sides of the volcano through pretty bush and forest. The boardwalk was built in 1995 as part of an unemployed youth project; young people gained new skills and a better future as a

Walkers relax having conquered the summit of Rangitoto.

result, and visitors gained a scenic platform of 370 steps from which to enjoy the surrounding views.

Once at the summit it's the views, rather than the steps, that will take your breath away – on a clear day it is possible to see from one side of the North Island to the other. The elevation (259 metres) enables 360-degree views of the Hauraki Gulf, Auckland city and the coastal bays of the North Shore. When visibility allows, you can see as far as Great Barrier Island, Whangarei Heads, and over to the Waitakere Ranges and the Manukau Heads. It is a beautiful place to contemplate the unique geography of the region and decide what you're going to have for a snack or picnic before you walk any further. Circling Rangitoto via the Crater Rim Track is a great way to enjoy the views and the volcano's large crater, which is deep and densely clad with regenerating forest. Keen hikers can explore a network of tracks throughout Rangitoto and Motutapu.

Rangitoto has a number of lava caves which can be explored and are accessible via a walking track from the summit and also from Islington Bay Road. The caves were formed as molten lava flowed through tunnels and caves where the rock had already cooled. To explore the caves, you'll need a torch – be sure to take care as the rocky surface is uneven underfoot.

If a picnic and a swim is required after a dusty hot walk, McKenzie Bay, named after one of the old ships' captains, is the only sandy beach on the island. It is also a good fishing spot as the water current comes through a small channel as it rounds the corner of the island.

THE STORY OF THE RANGITOTO BACHES

Visitors who arrive by ferry are often surprised to see little cottages tucked in among the trees along the Rangitoto shoreline. Questions abound as to whether people live permanently in the baches, and if so, how they manage with no amenities on the island. The most pertinent question is why people have built properties on an island that happens to be of the potentially fiery and exploding variety.

The story of Rangitoto's baches goes back to 20 years before the first bach was constructed. Rangitoto Island was owned by the Crown and administered by the Lands Department (later to become the Department of Conservation) in Wellington. The Lands Department felt Rangitoto was too far away to manage from Wellington so requested that Rangitoto Borough Council (Rangitoto Island Domain Board) administer the island on their behalf. The Rangitoto Island Domain Board agreed, but no clarification was provided as to exactly what the council were to 'administer'.

In 1910, in an attempt to generate income from Rangitoto, the Domain Board responded to longstanding requests from fisherman, keen to be able to camp on the island over weekends, by offering them the chance to lease campsites. The fishermen were delighted and over 100 of them took up the offer. Within a year it became clear that camping wasn't sustainable as there were no toilets or sanitary arrangements. In 1911, the Domain Board agreed that the campsites could become shack sites – with some form of toilet (probably just a hole that could be dug in the lava but better than nothing). The fishermen were encouraged to construct one-room shacks or sheds, which they did. The fishermen were happy and the Domain Board were making money – all seemed well.

As the years passed, the shacks evolved into larger and more solidly constructed dwellings becoming holiday homes used by the families of the fishermen. Small baches were built with timber and materials brought over from the mainland. Many families with children spent their summer holidays enjoying the natural playground with all the fun of the outdoors. The long summer holidays were full of fun for the kids on Rangitoto, with plenty of organised activities to keep them occupied. There were swimming galas, fishing competitions, boat races and possum-catching competitions – all the carefree characteristics of an idyllic childhood with plenty of time spent outdoors.

In 1936, 26 years after the first shack site had been leased, representatives of the Lands Department visited Rangitoto Island for an inspection and were horrified to discover 140 baches, some of them permanent residences, built on public land.

The bach owners were ordered to leave the island but they protested; they had legally signed lease documents for their sites and felt justified in their right to remain. The blunder made by the Lands Department was clear for all to see. They had handed over the administration of Rangitoto to the Domain Board without defining clear guidelines, and had neglected to inspect the island for 26 years. The Domain Board had issued lease documents that they weren't permitted to issue and the lease owners had signed them in good faith – both parties believed the documents to be legally binding agreements. The Crown considered the situation and admitted their unreasonable stance. To resolve the situation they offered leaseholders a 20-year moratorium to remove the baches, which the bach owners considered reasonable.

Over the next 20 years the bach owners took care of their baches and the island; they kept things clean and tidy, put out fires, and stopped people cutting down pohutukawa trees. They were protecting the island in a way that a ranger would (there were no rangers on Rangitoto in those days). Their guardianship was noticed by Forest and Bird and the Botany Department of Auckland University, who were researching and working on the island and could see the value the bach owners were adding. In 1957, the government, having been made aware of the benefits, issued the bach owners lifetime leases. There were conditions associated; bach owners were not permitted to rent or sell the baches and they were not allowed to extend them in any way. A significant number of baches were pulled down in the 1970s and 1980s, but there are still 34 baches remaining on Rangitoto today. The decline of the traditional Kiwi bach in the 1990s highlighted the importance of preserving Rangitoto's quintessential Kiwi baches as part of New Zealand's history.

Top: People enjoying a swim in the historic saltwater swimming baths on Rangitoto Island.

Bottom: A quintessential Kiwi bach surrounded by pohutukawa.

The Dual

In March each year, usually on a scorching-hot sunny day, Rangitoto and Motutapu play host to a unique event – The Dual. Organised by Total Sport, an Auckland-based event production company, The Dual started as a trail half-marathon and marathon encompassing both gulf islands – hence the name. In more recent years, The Dual has grown into a series of races; participants can tackle the courses on legs, mountain bikes or in the water – or all three if they're a triathlete. For the last couple of years, The Dual has included walking, running and mountain-biking races as well as an off-road triathlon. The Dual is the only opportunity to ride mountain bikes on the islands – they are strictly forbidden outside of this event for biosecurity reasons. The organisers work closely with the Department of Conservation and the Motutapu Restoration Trust to ensure that all equipment brought over to the island is clean and pest-free.

The event courses are hilly and sometimes rugged and take participants on a scenic journey through lava fields, rolling hills, forest, private farmland, around stunning coastal trails and culminate in what must be one of the most beautiful race finish lines you're ever likely to cross, at Home Bay on Motutapu. The scenic downhill finish, for many of the races, is breathtaking – both because of the preceding hills and the captivating panoramic views across Home Bay. The finish chute is a dream – flanked by a sandy beach on one side and rolling green hills on the other. A race finish line with a sandy-beach swim within staggering distance is a very happy ending – as is the post-race relaxation. Concerts and prizegiving take place on a centre-stage whilst tired but happy athletes, friends and families enjoy tucking into some post-race fuel and perhaps a celebratory beer or glass of wine before being transported by ferry back to Auckland.

The Dual event assists with conservation efforts on Motutapu, contributing to the Motutapu Restoration Trust, which is currently working towards replanting large sections of the island with native trees over the coming years.

Runners completing The Dual, which is run on both Motutapu and Rangitoto every year in March.

A botanical enigma

Rangitoto is a botanical enigma – despite having no natural source of water or soil, the island sustains a surprising number of flowering plants and trees considering the conditions. There are over 200 species of trees and plants on the island, including over 40 species of fern and many rare and native orchids. Plants have cleverly adapted to the volcanic landscape – lichens that usually grow in alpine terrain have adapted to grow at sea level on Rangitoto, and mangroves have adapted to grow where their usual muddy conditions are replaced with lava. The unique ecosystem exists because, during the 6000 years of eruptions beneath the ocean and Rangitoto, many layers of rock and ash have been formed, and the layers of nutrient-rich ash absorb rainwater and moisture from the atmosphere allowing small trees and plants to grow. What looks like dry, inhospitable scoria and basalt rock somehow hosts the largest pohutukawa forest in the world. The pohutukawa trees provide a sheltered habitat for smaller plants and trees to grow, and scientists are intrigued to learn more about the types of vegetation that grow naturally and develop on a newly formed piece of land.

The bird populations on Rangitoto are smaller than on other Hauraki Gulf islands as there is no soil for burrowing land-based birds and there isn't much food or water for the birds either. With no marshlands or soil for worms or rotting trees with bugs, their habitats are limited. Birds that can be seen on Rangitoto usually nest on Motutapu including tui, fantails, bellbirds and kaka as well as endangered saddleback, which were introduced in 2011.

DID YOU KNOW?

- Rangitoto represents almost 60 per cent of the volume of all material that has erupted within the Auckland volcanic field.
- Wallabies and deer used to roam on Rangitoto. They must have had very hot feet in summer! The rock absorbs the heat from the sun and it isn't uncommon for temperatures to be in the high 40s or early 50s.
- Rangitoto's eruption (about AD 1400) was witnessed by Maori living on Motutapu at the time. Human and dog footprints were found on Motutapu, which proves this.
- There were once 12 quarries on Rangitoto. Before the island became a scenic reserve, scoria was quarried for use in the Auckland construction industry.
- Rangitoto was bought by the Crown in 1854 for £15!
- Salt works were built on Rangitoto in 1892 – salt was produced by evaporating the sea water.
- Islington Bay used to be known as 'Drunkards Bay'. Ships' crews were notorious for getting drunk whilst on shore, so when a ship left the port of Auckland it would often stop at Islington Bay to allow the crew to sober up before venturing out to open seas.
- If you dug straight down from Rangitoto's cone through the earth you would come out in the south of Spain not far from the city of Ronda.

JOHN WALSH — BACH OWNER

Bach owner John Walsh.

Family, friends, and the close-knit Rangitoto bach community of good sorts are close to John's heart and have been throughout his life. John has an enduring connection with Rangitoto Island – it is a special place, a haven of calm, abundant with cherished childhood and family memories.

John has retired after 40 years as a park ranger in Auckland's Waitakere Ranges. As a ranger, John was involved with search and rescue, law enforcement and fire control – his role was often stressful. His bach was his bolt-hole and happy place. 'After my fortnightly shift I would come here and unwind ... it is very calming here – it doesn't take long to relax once you're here.'

John's family bach, Heartsease, was built in 1936 by two brothers who were bach owners on the island at the time. They also built two other baches close by, one identical to John's, and one closest to the wharf which is now the museum bach, restored and run by the Rangitoto Island Historic Conservation Trust. Coincidentally, the identical bach is also owned by a Walsh family – but there is no family connection.

John says he could walk around this bach blindfolded as it's exactly the same (not sure if he has ever tried this!), and all three are beautifully built from kauri. The timber for his bach was transported from the mainland by barge, all carefully planned to arrive at high tide in the little bay opposite to allow the barge to get close enough to the island.

There are three bach communities on Rangitoto: one situated

at Islington Bay, one by Rangitoto Wharf (where John's bach is located) and one on the western side of the island. Of the 143 baches that were originally built, only 34 remain today. The baches are all built close to the water's edge allowing easy boat access; some of the baches have little boat sheds perched on the rocks close to the water.

The first bach was built on Rangitoto in 1911 and, as the bach community grew, many families, and sometimes neighbours, would build baches next to each other. John's family owned three baches close together. John's grandfather, his two uncles and their families (each family with three children) enjoyed holidays and long weekends on Rangitoto for many years together.

The view from the table and chairs in front of Heartsease is framed by trees and looks across the water towards Auckland city, which appears through the haze as a soft silhouette tucked behind the grassy volcanic cones of North Head and Mt Victoria. John and his wife often have breakfast here or sit with a glass of wine in the evening. It's a peaceful spot, and partly shaded by trees; even with visitors to the island walking along the path in front of the bach, it feels tranquil. John has crafted and built cleverly designed outdoor spaces to relax, barbecue, and eat and drink outside in the shade (it gets hot in summer with the rocks absorbing the heat), and a neat formation of benches to accommodate larger gatherings – the happy hour congregations on Rangitoto are legendary!

The bach interior is unchanged from the 1930s – a time capsule and fascinating window into the past. 'Welcome to 1936,' John says proudly as we walk in. The bach is cosy, calm, and brimming with character. Black and white photos of John's grandparents,

John's bach, Heartsease.

The outdoor dining area at John's place.

parents and his family adorn the walls and portray numerous family activities: boating, fishing, family portraits and groups of children playing together. Everyone looks blissfully relaxed and happy – the images are heart-warming.

The living room is alive with family history – photos, maps, ornaments, and bits and pieces from the island – everything has a meaningful story attached. The bach is like a family jewel – a locket of living history. A fishing rod belonging to John's uncle is mounted on the wall, while the mantelpiece is adorned with kina shells, ammunition shells from the old Rangitoto military base, pieces of wood and rocks – all reminding them of times gone by.

'I couldn't bring myself to change anything,' John says, and it is easy to see why. The space exudes personality and a sense of humour that is obviously a family trait. There are two clocks in the living room – both convey the family's belief that time, when you're on holiday, is irrelevant. The clock on the wall above the main window has no hands, and a label across the clock face which says 'Who cares?'; the other clock sits, inactive, on the mantelpiece and remains at 9.15 – as it has throughout John's lifetime! Time is not important – unwinding, relaxing and enjoying yourself, most definitely are.

John recalls, as a child, being told after breakfast to 'go out and enjoy yourself and don't come back 'til dinner time.' Rangitoto is a safe place for children to roam and explore (scrapes from the rocks aside) and the kids often play together, exploring the island, its lava caves, boating and fishing, and generally revelling in a carefree, outdoor playtime amongst the unique Rangitoto landscape. 'It's just a kids' paradise,' John says. 'The kids today do the same sorts of things that I did as a child – exactly the same things.' Whenever Rangitoto children have friends to stay, John explains, 'The friends are gutted there's no TV for the first night, but after that they're absolutely fine. The second day they're out there fishing, turning rocks over and exploring caves. It's cool to see, and quite encouraging actually.'

The children learn boating and fishing skills very early on. When John was a young boy every child had a boat. 'My childhood was boating, fishing and botanising!' John says, recalling his childhood adventures. 'I had a dinghy at the age of seven. I'd sail it to Rakino on my own, tip it upside down, sleep under it and come back the next day,' he laughs. 'You wouldn't be allowed to do that these days!' He also recalls taking his boat to Browns Island and camping there. 'It probably wasn't permitted, but they were a bit more lenient in those days,' he chuckles. John remembers his uncle and one of his uncle's friends – both had a huge knowledge of the island and were superb mentors for many of the children. The men took the kids under their wing and taught them a great deal about the island, boating, and invaluable life skills.

There is a saying on the island that 'every child has 30 mothers.' With around 30 baches still occupied, all the adults look out for and look after the children. It is a friendly, welcoming community with strong family values, a lot of heart, and an unwavering community spirit that extends to all the blokes knowing where each other's toolshed keys are hidden!

John explains that they all help each other out because that's the kind of people they are, and because living on an island with no electricity, reticulated water or supplies often means collaborating makes life easier and more enjoyable. It is not uncommon to find a birthday card tacked to your front door from all the neighbours, or to be offered fresh snapper if someone has some spare, or even (as one of John's neighbours recently did) to receive a batch of freshly baked scones because your neighbour knows you have guests visiting. And baking without all the mod-cons makes it even more of a kind gesture.

During the holidays, when everyone is on the island, the community gets together in the late afternoon and early evening for 'happy hour'. There are a few baches that are able to host larger gatherings or sometimes they assemble at 'the green', which is the large grassy area near the swimming pool by the wharf. 'Everyone turns up with their ancient wheelbarrows loaded up with deck chairs, snacks and chilly-bins. The tourists love it,' John says. John's wheelbarrow has a sign which says 'Party Bus!' Often the neighbours will be gathering in the late afternoon sun as the visitors are all making their way to the wharf for the last ferry back to Auckland. 'When the ferry captain toots the horn as they pull away we all raise our glasses.' The adults arrange their chairs in a circle and get settled in, whilst the kids all play together. I ask John how they organise the happy hour logistics. 'Sometimes someone will send their child round as a messenger, but mostly it's just an organic thing, I've never worked it out – you just sort of turn up,' he says laughing.

The neighbours enjoy socialising in the amber glow of the evening sunset and then gradually head home to barbecue some snapper they caught earlier. The evenings are spent chatting, playing cards, board games or reading. 'We don't do loud parties on the island,' John states. The art of conversation, as opposed to staring at screens, is alive and well among the Rangitoto bach folk. Visitors sometimes struggle at first without the modern conveniences and multiple devices – but it doesn't take long to discard them and revert back to more traditional and meaningful

Two huts out the back of John's bach. The names and initials of prisoners who worked building roads on the island can be seen carved into the door of the one on the right.

values. When John packs up to return to the mainland he admits, 'I always have a pang of regret when I leave.'

I've often wondered what happens when visitors miss the last ferry. It must happen quite often, I surmise. 'Fairly regularly,' says John. He recalled the most recent occurrence, which happened during Easter weekend. Happy hour was under way at 'the green' and the bach gathering had all just toasted the last ferry on its way and were enjoying the peace.

About 20 minutes later, a couple in their sixties, and a little girl of about five years of age appeared. The group immediately knew they'd missed the ferry – they all know each other and recognised that these were strangers. The little girl was crying, having taken a tumble on sharp rocks and cut her knee. The girl's grandparents were stressed, they had an injured granddaughter and no way of getting home. John remembers knowing exactly what would happen next – and it did. One of the mums called her daughter over and asked her to run to their bach and bring back a first-aid kit; within minutes the little girl's knee was being tended to. Another of the bach owners sent her son off to get a couple of deckchairs. Grandma was swiftly issued with a glass of pinot gris and Grandad with a cold beer. Before long they were seated with the group, having been assured that someone had called the ferry company who were going to swing a ferry by the wharf in 40 minutes' time. The eldest boy of the bach children, who looks after the children, instinctively took the little girl by the hand and introduced her to the rest of the island kids who then played together happily. When the ferry captain tooted his horn on his approach to the wharf, the little girl's grandma called her over to tell her they were going to get the ferry home. The little girl, who had been enjoying the company of her new friends, burst into tears. 'I don't want to go home!' she cried. Grandad was then heard crying, 'I don't want to go home either!' The grandparents and little girl left the island, relieved and grateful for the help they had received and, no doubt, touched by the friendliness and kindness of the group.

'Falling on lava really hurts ... and we don't like seeing people have bad experiences on the island,' John says. There are often incidents which require 'a sticking plaster and some magic lollies.'

For those who might like to experience a 1930s bach there is a chance, in the near future, that three of the baches on Rangitoto may be rented out to the public. In the late nineties three baches were handed in – the next generation didn't want to use or maintain them! The baches have been carefully renovated and could likely be enjoyed by visitors soon. The Rangitoto Island

Historic Conservation Trust is working through the rental logistics with the Department of Conservation. One of their challenges is ensuring the safe use of open fires, gas, candles, and kerosene lamps – all second nature to bach owners and their children, who are taught very early on, but not for visitors who are unfamiliar with the old-school lighting, heating and cooking methods. Like many gulf islands, fire is a significant risk on Rangitoto as it would be almost impossible to put out, with extremely dry conditions and no water pumps or fire brigade. John has buckets of salt water outside his bach, should anything catch fire.

Luckily for Rangitoto, keeping warm by the fire when it does get cold isn't difficult. John explains, 'Firewood is free on Rangitoto – it is delivered twice a day by the tides ... and I'm lazy, I only pick up timber that's the right length. I don't believe in chopping firewood.' There certainly is a surprising amount of timber and driftwood of all shapes and sizes which gets caught on the rugged rocks as the tides rise and fall.

When it gets hot in summer the temperatures over the rock can be around 50 degrees Celsius. The locals sometimes swim, but only with shoes on – the rocks are too sharp for bare feet. Most baches have outdoor areas where they cook and eat during the summer, as it's too hot to be inside during the day.

John has on his property a historic hut which was part of the camp built for inmates from Auckland Prison. The prisoners came over from Auckland to build roads and other facilities on Rangitoto. On close inspection of the hut door, it is possible to see prisoners' names and initials carved into the wood.

John remembers his mother telling him about the harsh conditions the prisoners endured. Despite not being incarcerated in a prison cell, the prisoners had some tough undertakings on Rangitoto. Building roads by moving volcanic rocks around by hand to create a flat surface would have been slow and back-breaking work; and handling sharp lava for up to 10 hours a day without gloves would have been excruciatingly painful on the hands. John's mother told him that the prisoners were expected to work in extremely hot temperatures with no sunscreen, hats or water bottles. 'They wouldn't be allowed to treat prisoners that way now,' John says. The prisoners would spend two or three months at a time on Rangitoto, involved in the road building, before being returned to serve the remainder of their sentence in prison. Many prisoners volunteered to return to work on Rangitoto, which made John and his family wonder what the conditions must have been like in prison.

In those days the baches were never locked, and some of the bach owners were concerned that their baches may get interfered

The back of John's bach, Heartsease.

with. John's father and other bach owners built a rapport with the prisoners – they would calculate the distance of road the prisoners would complete every day and hide cigarettes or packets of tobacco for them along the way. The system was successful and there was never any trouble between prisoners and the bach community. The roads stand up to a significant amount of traffic to this day – four-wheel-drive vehicles used by the Department of Conservation, and two tractor trains operated by Fullers to transport visitors around the island on the Rangitoto Volcanic Explorer tour.

John works one day a week as a driver and guide hosting the Volcanic Explorer tour. Visitors get a guided tour of Rangitoto on a four-wheel-drive road-train with an entertaining and informative commentary about the island's history and geology. The tour takes visitors to the base of the summit were they can take a short walk to the summit and enjoy the 360 degree views of the gulf and across Auckland.

Tourists sometimes ask John why the bach community chose to build on a volcano which has proven not to be extinct. His response is accompanied by a nervous laugh. 'I try not to think about it!' he says.

John sums up the significance of his family bach and time spent on Rangitoto, 'It's a huge part of my whole existence. It's probably shaped the person I am actually.' John's father used to say, 'Rangitoto is four miles and forty years away from Auckland.' For many, who value the simpler pleasures in life, they'll hope it stays that way.

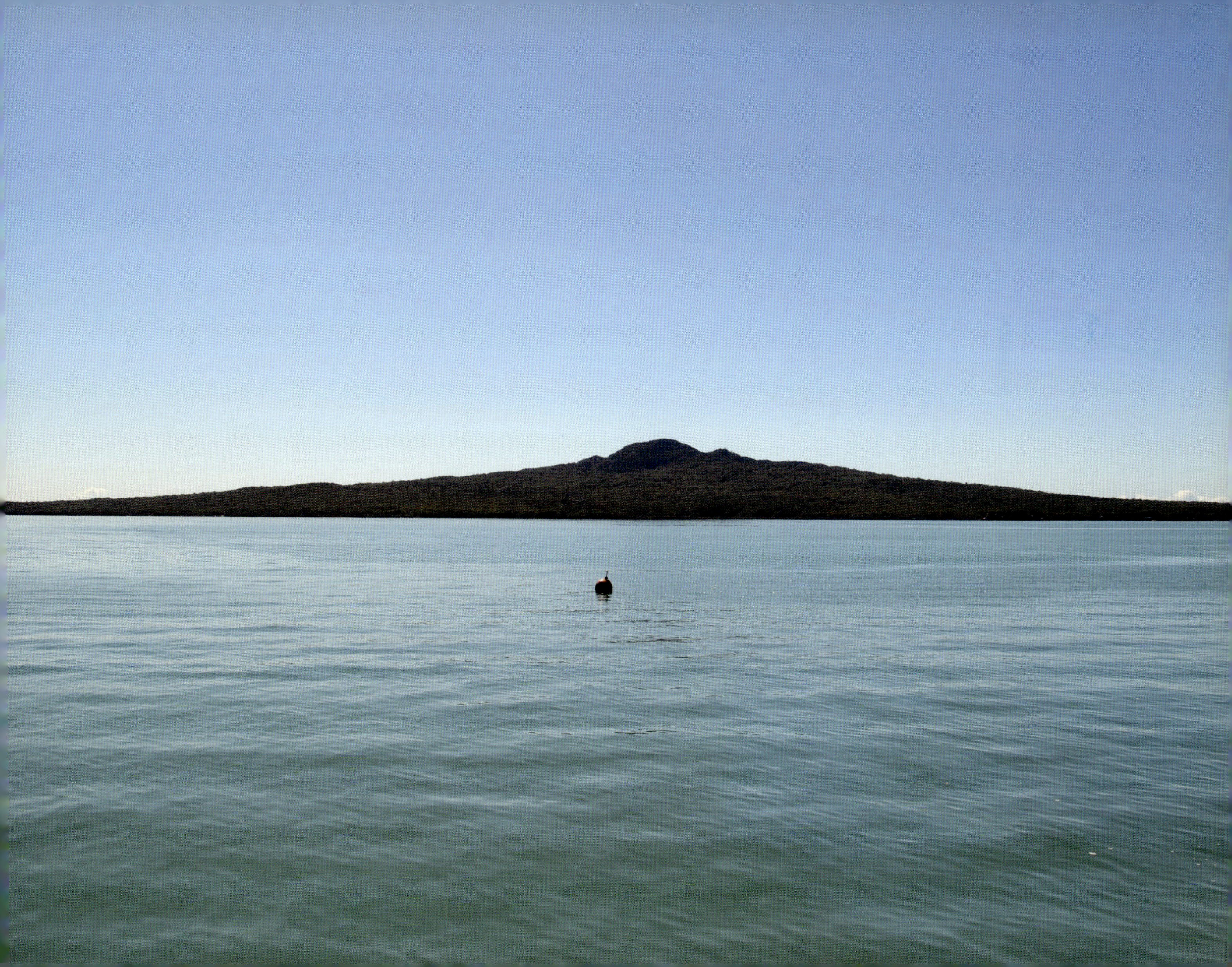

Motutapu Island

Motutapu Island

AGE BEFORE BEAUTY

With gentle rolling hills and sandstone cliffs, the inner Hauraki Gulf island of Motutapu sits alongside its more rugged and potentially noisy neighbour, Rangitoto. Today the islands stand side by side, but they weren't always neighbours. Motutapu stood alone for 180 million years until around 600 years ago, when a series of volcanic eruptions under the seabed forced volcanic lava high into the night sky. The island we know as Rangitoto surged up out of the gulf waters in a pyroclastic display of fireworks right next to Motutapu.

Close but contrasting

Motutapu and Rangitoto are joined by a causeway, which was built in 1941 to link the islands as part of the Auckland defence network. The contrasting terrains of the two islands are very different – harsh, jagged volcanic rock juxtaposed with grassy and fertile farmland. The volcanic ash cloud formed during the pyroclastic eruptions rained down a black blizzard onto Motutapu, smoothing out the island's contours and destroying forests, as a thick layer of ash smothered the island's surface. The ash enriched the soil and the deforestation that occurred acted as a catalyst for a change in land use making it easier to cultivate.

With the shelter from the south-west wind provided by Rangitoto, a warm and settled climate was perfect for working the land. Farming on Motutapu has been a historical constant; other than wartime interruptions when defence systems were built, beef cattle and sheep have grazed there. The farmland that exists on Department of Conservation land, as part of a pest-free environment, is unique and so are the challenges. Apart from the obvious demands that come with being surrounded by water and having to transport animals to and from the island by barge, the farms also have to work in with the conservation and heritage restoration efforts undertaken on the island.

A complex array of objectives exist for the land, and various groups and organisations work together to ensure heritage, cultural, restoration, education and conservation objectives are met – a formidable collaboration.

Magical motu

Motutapu is easily accessible with fast ferries to the island through the summer months running from downtown Auckland directly to Home Bay – the journey time is 35 minutes. With a safe swimming beach and basic facilities at the Reid Homestead, which is also a visitor centre, it is a lovely place for a picnic (continuing the traditions from Victorian times!) or a family day out.

Overnight camping is available – there is a beautiful campsite at Home Bay with water and barbecue facilities. The campsite is right by the picturesque sandy beach and is a stunning spot, great for a cooling swim after a long walk. Good swimming spots can be found at any of the beaches on the island and there are plenty of them. Snorkelling and diving around Motutapu are popular activities as is kayaking.

Kayaking from the mainland to Home Bay takes around three hours and is suited to the more experience kayaker. Kayakers also paddle across to Home Bay from nearby Waiheke and Motuihe islands. For those who are keen, but would benefit from some instruction, there are guided kayaking tours from Auckland which include trips around the Hauraki Gulf islands.

Fishing off the rocks or beach from Motutapu is allowed. There is a voluntary no-take fishing area at Administration Bay, next to the Motutapu Outdoor Education Centre – so best to catch your snapper anywhere but there.

Motutapu is a very popular gulf island for boaties. Access by private boat to Motutapu is best via Home Bay or Islington Bay on Rangitoto, which is close to the causeway access to Motutapu – both are safe anchorages. There are also anchorages, depending on wind conditions, at Station Bay, Mullet Bay, Waikalabubu Bay, and Administration Bay (although care should be taken as there are rocks separating Administration from adjacent Sandy Bay).

Traversing the island's 15 square kilometres is a network of walking tracks; walking is a rewarding way to explore the island. The five main tracks navigate the main features of the island: coastal views, military bunkers and installations, native forests, wetlands, restoration planting, historic Maori pa sites, sandy bays and beaches and the chance to see native and endangered species of birds. Most of the walks are between one and two hours long but there are plenty of options to create longer walks by combining or looping tracks together.

Life on the sacred island

As one of the first islands settled by Maori, Motutapu was considered sacred. In Maori, motu means island and tapu means sacred. The Maori people who settled on Motutapu did so in great numbers – they knew they were on to a good thing with a strategic position in the gulf, fertile land, and excellent fishing.

The causeway between Motutapu and Rangitoto islands as seen from Motutapu.

Hundreds of archaeological pa sites have been discovered on Motutapu, where the remains of villages, gardens for growing food, kumara storage pits, and middens (food refuse deposits) are still evident. Carved tools made from stone for gardening, hunting and fishing have also been found. Evidence of oyster shells, fish bones, bones from many native species of birds and even fur seals are evidence that they had plenty of food options to choose from and lived well.

Maori settlements on Motutapu pre-date the most recent series of eruptions on Rangitoto, and there were inhabitants living on Motutapu who witnessed the eruption in AD 1400. Proof of this was discovered at a Maori site at Sunde, on the western side of the island, where both human and dog footprints were found embedded in the volcanic ash. Those who were able fled the island in waka (canoes) to escape the exploding fiery furnace of the volcano. The eruption blanketed the surrounding area with a thick layer of ash and the footprints are thought to have been made when people returned to Motutapu, quite soon after the eruption, for reasons we will never know. The ash solidified over time and the footsteps of the inhabitants were recorded, immortalised, within the rock. (When the footprints were discovered a cast was taken, and it can be seen at the Auckland Museum.)

Following the eruption more settlers arrived on the island. The Arawa and Tainui canoes were said to have visited Motutapu, and Tainui ancestors of Ngati Tai settled. They inhabited the island peacefully until Hongi Hika and Ngapuhi arrived in the 1820s armed with muskets. Forced to evacuate for a number of years, some inhabitants returned in the mid-1830s. Ngati Tai remained on Motutapu until a northern section of the island was sold in 1840.

European settlers purchased a section of the island in 1840 and continued to farm the land that Maori had cultivated before them. Motutapu was bought in its entirety in 1857 by Auckland politician Robert Graham who was Superintendent of the Auckland Province (1862–66). An eccentric and fun-loving character, Graham welcomed groups of people to the island, hosting parties and picnics. Motutapu became the most popular destination for day trips in the Hauraki Gulf and frequently hosted 10,000 visitors in a day.

The fun and frolics organised for the Motutapu champagne picnics included activities for everyone: for the gentlemen there were races across several distances as well as a tug-of-war, with trophies for the victorious; there were ladies' races – including different categories for married and single ladies; children's races with toys as prizes for the younger ones; employee races, with medals for the fastest employees; committee-men's races (mustn't leave the organisers out!); and top of the bill, a 'greasy pig chase.' The ensuing hilarity of Auckland's great and good chasing a greasy pig must have been something to behold.

Graham was quite the entertainer and manufacturer of fun. His eccentricities, soon to be mirrored a few years later by Sir George Grey, manifested in the creation of a substantial menagerie of exotic animals on the island, which included emu, ostrich, buffalo, deer and wallaby.

A day out on Motutapu Island at one of the reputable 'premier picnics' was an exhilarating adventure for families and organisations. The excitement of boarding a steamship in the early morning, with a party atmosphere already under way, would have been an adventure in itself. And the chance to enjoy a cruise out into the Hauraki Gulf, with views of Auckland and Rangitoto to take in along the way – what a novelty!

Once on the island, picnickers could relax, socialise, and choose to take part in any of the orchestrated larking about that had been planned. A bonus attraction was the chance to watch and learn about animals they would never have seen before, from all over the world. Fresh air, a blat out on the water in a steamship, a pot of tea and a good feed with a jolly afternoon of sports and fun and a mini-zoo to investigate – what more could you want from a jovial day out in the Hauraki Gulf?

Robert Graham hosted reputable picnics for 10 years during his ownership of the island. Unfortunately for him, his fun on Motutapu came to an end when he was forced by the bank to reduce his overdraft. He sold Motutapu to Scottish farming twins James and John Reid in 1869.

The Reid brothers had taken a shine to Motutapu a few months earlier. They had been travelling through Australia and New Zealand searching for the perfect place to set up a farm and identified Motutapu as their ideal island. They submitted an offer of purchase to Robert Graham which was initially rejected.

Heading next to Melbourne they continued their search for good-quality land to farm. On arrival in Australia they were informed that their offer for Motutapu would be accepted after all, so they returned to New Zealand, bought their dream island, and began clearing the manuka and scrub before employing local Maori workers from Waiheke to help build fences. The farm, once established, was substantial. The stock included 5000 sheep, 4000 cattle and around 50 horses.

The Reid brothers, close friends of George Grey who had bought Kawau Island seven years earlier, were both avid collectors of exotic animals. They created unusual menageries and sometimes collaborated on importing animals – bulk buying wallaby (buy-one-get-one-free!) from New South Wales.

Visitors were invited to the island to shoot deer and 'other game,' presumably the wallabies. James brought in fallow deer from Kaipara Heads and went to great lengths to import red deer from as far away as the grounds of Windsor Castle in England. The deer were shipped out from England, transported 18,000 kilometres or more to a small island to be shot and killed. Quite an extravagant and expensive journey for the deer to ultimately meet their maker. The return on the ship-them-out-then-shoot-them investment can't have been a particularly lucrative one.

At their peak population, there were over 1000 deer on Motutapu. The population was readily reduced by small invitation-only hunting groups – if you can call shooting deer kept enclosed in fenced fields hunting.

Top: A picnic at Home Bay in 1907.
Bottom: Auckland Butchers' annual picnic, 1901.

As well as bringing in animals from all over the globe for shooting, the Reid family also ensured that the picnic traditions continued. They hosted warmly in the spirit of their predecessor, even upping the stakes with brass bands, cash prizes and trophies for race winners, along with horse and pony rides for children. The fun, games and hilarity continued to be an attraction of the island and the Reids' praises were sung heartily in the newspapers of the day for their generous hospitality.

When James Reid passed away on 21 January 1908 (having outlived his brother by seven years), the *Poverty Bay Herald* printed very high praise. James 'honourably sustained the reputation of the lairds of Motutapu for graceful and unstinted hospitality, with a liberality so distinguished that his name was held in the highest respect by every individual in Auckland, and by large numbers of world tourists, who on their visit to Auckland, experience the unaffected graciousness with which Mr Reid fulfilled the duties of host and master of his island kingdom.'

It would take more than organising a few epic picnics to obtain the highest respect from every individual in Auckland these days. (Not to mention pleasing a large number of tourists.) The offering of such an accolade by journalists today seems extremely unlikely. The opposite sentiment perhaps – but 'master of his island kingdom' doesn't sound like a phrase we're likely to read in the news any time soon. Hats off to James Reid – the prince of picnics, whose act would not be followed.

OUTRAGE AS DELINQUENTS CAUSE 'THE INNOCENT TO SUFFER FOR THE GUILTY'

Not everyone appreciated the hospitality – in 1891 the gulf picnic destinations were reducing in numbers as 'reckless pleasure-seekers' ruined the occasions for many. In December of that year, the *Auckland Star* in an article headlined 'The Destructive Hoodlum' expressed anguish that a deliberate act of arson had 'most ruthlessly destroyed' Mr Reid's property. Picnickers arriving at Motutapu by boat were horrified to see thick smoke rising from behind the Reid residence. It was understood that the criminals had arrived on the island before the picnics were due to begin, setting fire to the surrounding trees and home. This destructive act put a sharp end to the hospitality shown: 'The islands of the harbour abound in bays of exquisite beauty, and they are owned by gentlemen who, unlike English landlords, are courtesy and kindness itself to pleasure-seekers.' Unfortunately, due to the damage to Mr Reid's property 'one of the most beautiful, if not the most beautiful resorts in the harbour, Putiki Bay (Waiheke Island), will now be closed to boats' crews.' In response to the damage, 'Mr Kennedy has made visitors free of his bay, and in return they [hoodlums] have destroyed his property and burned his pohutukawa trees.' Rewards were offered for any information as to the persons who had committed these crimes. (The Reid homestead that remains today in Home Bay on Motutapu Island was built in 1901.)

Defending the empire

Many of the picnickers would return to Motutapu in years to come with very different roles to play. The real threat of invasion during World War II meant that Motutapu became host to army soldiers rather than picnic revellers.

In the lead-up to World War II, Motutapu was called into service as part of the Auckland Coastal Defence Network. The perceived threat of attack from German and Japanese enemies was considered to be very real. The Auckland Coastal Defence Network was designed and built to defend New Zealand's largest city from possible attack. Motutapu was also designated as a fallback location for ammunition storage to assist the United States' defence of the Pacific.

The defence structures were intricate and included a gun emplacement with three gun pits; a large underground ammunition storage area; a battery observation post with multiple pillboxes to protect the battery from a commando attack; many underground shelters and stores for fuel, generators and radar; plotting and communications equipment; an observation post; an engine room for anti-submarine defence; a search light emplacement and many tunnels and quarries.

Roads were built where needed to link the defence system network and the wharves and personnel camps were set up at Administration Bay. Fortunately there were not required.

The remnants of some of the defences are well preserved and can be visited to this day. When the barracks were decommissioned by the military they were handed over and used to assist the development of young New Zealanders.

Members of the territorial army training on Motutapu in 1910.

The barracks are a listed historical site, but have been upgraded and converted into an education centre that has been operational since 1966.

Learning through adventure

The Motutapu Outdoor Education Camp is located in its own private valley at Administration Bay and encompasses five hectares. The centre offers both instructor-lead and self-supervised activities enabling groups or corporates to design their own programmes if they wish. The Motutapu Outdoor Education Trust, formed in 1991, is the current operator of the camp and works with the Department of Conservation, the Motutapu Restoration Trust, and Motutapu Farms, to ensure that the unique environment, land and sea, is preserved and protected.

The sun rising across the gulf from Motutapu Island.

The range of activities offered by the education camp is extensive. Orienteering, tramping, raft building, dinghy sailing, kayaking (sea or flat water), canoeing, archery, climbing, abseiling and bouldering are some of the many activities available. There are also programmes that focus on environmental studies, keeping the coast clean, studying birds, flora and fauna exploration, and conservation efforts. Opportunities to play indoor and outdoor sports are also part of the offering. There are facilities where volleyball, basketball, soccer, table tennis and cricket can be played.

Looking after the land

The importance of the environment is high on the agenda of the conservation, education and farming groups and trusts that work on Motutapu. Conservation has made some great gains on the island in recent years. Trees and endangered plants that were destroyed by possums and wallabies and have been replanted and are now a growing ecosystem for native birds. The successful eradication of all pests from Motutapu and neighbouring Rangitoto in 2011 means bird habitats have improved considerably. Endangered species have been successfully released including Coromandel brown kiwi – which have been seen on footage captured by video cameras set up to monitor takahe feeding hoppers. Takahe have been doing well since being introduced, although in 2014 a blunder set them back considerably when four takahe were shot dead. Sadly, the takahe were mistaken for pukeko, which were being culled due to their penchant for eating the seeds that are sown as part of the replanting programme and the risk they pose to endangered bird species.

Other birds doing well as a result of rodent eradication on Motutapu are shore plovers, which lay eggs and raise their chicks on the beach and in the sand dunes, saddlebacks, tomtits, tui, kakariki, and the endangered New Zealand dotterel. The wetlands on Motutapu are a crucial foraging ground and environment for kiwi and takahe. The wetlands on Motutapu make up six per cent of all the wetland area in the Auckland region.

Within the Home Bay forest, birdwatchers can enjoy glimpses of saddlebacks, tui, and kakariki. Takahe can sometimes be seen around the Home Bay vicinity. Also in the forest are bellbirds, whiteheads, kingfishers and spotless crakes. Brown kiwi can be heard at night in the forest during mating season. Brown teal can also be seen on Motutapu – this native species has returned to the island (self-introduced) since the replanting and conservation work has created safe habitats for them.

The shorebirds are more likely to be found at Gardiner Gap – New Zealand dotterels, shore plovers and Caspian terns are seen in larger numbers during winter. It is best to avoid the beach during nesting season (August–September) to avoid crushing their eggs, which are often hidden in the sand or gravel.

KIWI CHICKS TRAVEL BY WAKA TO NEW HOME ON MOTUTAPU

In April 2016, three Coromandel brown kiwi were released on Motutapu. The birds are so endangered that it is thought there are only 1700 remaining in the world. Their story is remarkable and demonstrates the enormous efforts made by many people and organisations to save these precious birds. A partnership between Motutapu Restoration Trust, Rotoroa Island Trust, the Department of Conservation, Auckland Zoo, Ngai Tai Ki Tamaki, Ngati Paoa, Ngati Tamatera and the Coromandel Kiwi Collective worked together to establish a sustainable population of the birds on Motutapu. The delivery of three new kiwi chicks brings the number of kiwi on Motutapu to 25. Ultimately they hope to build a population of around 40 birds.

The eggs originated from a community-led project in Te Mata, part of the Thames Coast Kiwi Care project. They were taken to Auckland Zoo where they were incubated and hatched as part of Operation Nest Egg. The chicks were then transported to Rotoroa Island where they grew to a safe size and weight, as part of the kiwi crèche environment. They were then taken by waka to their new home on Motutapu. James Brown, Chairman of Ngai Tai ki Tamaki, said 'transporting our taonga by waka hourua to their new home signified traditional protocols and rituals. We have been entrusted as guardians of these birds by our Ngati Paoa brothers in the Coromandel and we wanted to deliver them safely in the way our ancestors would have. The four-hour journey was a time for us to honour these beautiful and special birds as part of our duty of care.'

The Motutapu Restoration Chair welcomed the birds on their final leg of an incredible journey and thanked the trust and 'the thousands of volunteers who were involved in restoring the forests so that kiwi could live safely there.'

Sunbathers and swimmers making the most of a summer's day on Rakino Island.

Rakino Island and The Noises

FISHERMEN'S FRIENDS

The relatively small island of Rakino is separated from Motutapu by the Rakino Channel. The 146 hectares of land are mostly privately owned and the landscape a mix of rolling green hills, similar to those on Motutapu, and pohutukawa-lined bays with lovely sandy beaches. The Noises, a group of smaller islands, extend out to the north-east of Rakino and are all privately owned.

A world away

From the water it is clear to see that Rakino has an eclectic collection of houses – some sleek, glass-fronted modern mansions, others older wooden baches and villas – which can be seen dotted around the island. Many are perched in elevated positions affording extensive sunrise and sunset views across the sparkling ocean and surrounding gulf islands. There are fewer than 20 permanent residents on Rakino, as the majority of properties there are holiday homes.

During the America's Cup races in the Hauraki Gulf in 2000 and 2003, Rakino's location made it a natural grandstand from which to watch the races. Many wealthy international sailing enthusiasts rented properties on the island to watch Team New Zealand battle it out successfully against Italy's Luna Rossa in 2000 and not so successfully in 2003 against Switzerland's Alinghi. Rakino is a popular sailing destination and many Auckland and North Shore yacht and boat clubs enjoy regular races or trips out to Rakino. It is also the start line for some of the Auckland Regatta keelboat races.

In summertime, the quiet island is a secluded and peaceful world away from the Auckland busyness; the surrounding waters are an inviting playground for outdoor fun and relaxation. Kayaking, snorkelling, diving and swimming are all popular pastimes.

The area is also a popular fishing ground. The surrounding waters are known for good snapper and kingfish, particularly around the neighbouring Noises.

Sheltered bays and good anchorages can be found at pretty Woody Bay and West Bay on the western side of Rakino. Home Bay in the south has rocks right in the middle of the bay and so isn't considered a good overnight anchorage. Sandy Bay has a passenger wharf and adjacent Home Bay has a wharf suitable for freight. Maori Garden Bay on the eastern side of the island is open to the east and flanked by steep cliffs.

The island's clay soil base sits atop greywacke rock. After the eruption that created Rangitoto, the island received a dusting of ash which has helped create a more fertile soil and vegetation.

The island is self-sufficient: residents collects their own water and solar power is the main source of energy. In fact, Rakino claims to have been the first place in the world to have a solar-powered public telephone – it still stands proudly at the centre of the island and free calls to Auckland can be made from inside the red phone box.

Small island; big vision

Rakino's history is less troublesome than many of the Hauraki Gulf islands. Used as a place to intern prisoners during the Waikato wars in the 1860s, the island avoided the significant devastation caused by fighting that other islands suffered.

In 1862, Governor George Grey bought Rakino Island and started building a house at Home Bay. Building a house on Rakino was no easy feat, with kauri logs rafted in from Mercury Bay in the Coromandel. When Kawau Island came up for sale, Grey was immediately smitten with the place, and he abandoned Rakino although retained ownership of the land. In the 1870s, Grey leased Rakino before eventually selling it to Albert Sanford, a fisherman and entrepreneur.

Albert Sanford moved from Pakatoa Island to Rakino in the hope that he'd find better snapper fishing close by. He did, and he became well-known in Auckland for the kauri-smoked snapper which he would sell from his cutter *Foam*, moored at the steps of the old Queen Street Wharf. The demand for Sanford's snapper grew and in 1894 Albert established a fish market on the corner of Albert Street and Customs Street West. The Sanford business expanded and in 1900 Albert bought a schooner, *Minnie Casey*, which became the first trawler based in Auckland to fish out in the Hauraki Gulf. Sanford's business continued to grow and eventually extended to other parts of the country. Sanford Limited is now New Zealand's biggest seafood company.

The island was bought in 1963 by Doctor Maxwell Rickard, who was president of the United Peoples Organisation (UPO). An interesting character with rather a lot on his plate, Doctor Maxwell was a clinical psychologist, a hypnotherapist who toured as 'The Great Ricardo', an Auckland nightclub owner, as well as president of the UPO. He had a vision for Rakino which would see it become a philanthropic community developing facilities for those in need. His plans included a clinic for 'disturbed and nervous' patients, an international orphanage and a refuge for unmarried

Boaties at anchor in one of Rakino Island's many bays.

mothers. His plans never eventuated as his business failed and he was forced to pass the island to the receivers who sold it to North Shore Ferries. The island was then subdivided and sold in 1965. The land was divided into 25 blocks of 10 acres (four hectares) and other smaller pieces of land. The island remains a peaceful and undeveloped gulf jewel with few residents – and that's the way the locals would like to keep it.

The Noises

When French explorer Dumont d'Urville sailed the *Astrolabe* from Toulon to the South Pacific in 1826, his intention was to finish off the explorations that Captain Cook had started. His voyage of exploration included the Hauraki Gulf and along the way he named the islands north-east of Rakino the 'Noisettes' – hazelnuts. It seems that months at sea had left the European explorers really low on imagination. The islands were later renamed The Noises by New Zealanders who either didn't like or couldn't pronounce the nutty French name.

The Noises, a group of smaller islands, extend out to the north-east of Rakino Island and are all privately owned. The main islands are Otata (21 hectares), Motuhoropapa (9.5 hectares), Orarapa – 'the haystack', and David Rocks. The waters around The Noises are home to extensive reefs and are a popular fishing ground. Snapper and kingfish are commonly found in the area. The reef systems are also popular with divers. There are no suitable overnight anchorages or wharves.

ANDY LIGHT — SKIPPER

Andy Light has been working with Auckland Whale and Dolphin Safaris since its inception 16 years ago. Prior to skippering their 65-foot (19.8-metre) power-cat *Dolphin Explorer*, Andy ran his own fishing charter boat in the Bay of Islands and was a skipper for Dolphin Discoveries in Paihia where he worked with Stephen Stembridge.

Stephen founded Dolphin Discoveries, the first dolphin-watching experience in the North Island, in the early 1990s before coming to understand (from PhD research that was conducted on his boat) that commercial and recreational boating traffic was having a negative effect on the dolphins and other marine life in the area. Passionate about dolphins and whales, Stephen didn't want to operate under those circumstances. He pulled out of the Bay of Islands and started Auckland Whale and Dolphin Safari, in partnership with Mark Draskovich, and asked Andy to come and work with him in Auckland.

Tragically, not long after, Stephen suffered a cerebral haemorrhage whilst driving the boat and was taken by helicopter to hospital. Unfortunately, there was nothing that could be done to save him. He died, leaving his wife and a young family behind. The guys who had worked with Stephen were determined to carry on his business – they knew how much it meant to him and they have continued the business as a successful research-led safari experience ever since. 'Steve's passion was always whales and the research,' Andy explains. 'He always wanted this boat

Andy Light aboard Dolphin Explorer.

[*Dolphin Explorer*] to be a research boat and to do some good out there in the Hauraki Gulf, as opposed to just being a commercial boat putting pressure on animals.'

Respecting the marine life that they take people out into the Hauraki Gulf to see has always been a priority for Auckland Whale and Dolphin Safari. As a research-led operation they work closely with the Department of Conservation and several universities. Taking people out to see whales, dolphins and other marine life goes hand-in-hand with the marine biology research that plays an important part in understanding and protecting the gulf and its marine life. Andy explained that the Hauraki Gulf covers an area far larger than the Bay of Islands and the animals they are looking for are completely different. They are searching for common dolphins, whose populations are large and are found in many different areas of the gulf, and whales, of which there are a variety of species that spend time in the gulf.

The crew are all experienced researchers and marine biologists. Rob, the other skipper, has been with the company for over eight years and is a marine biologist. Andy has 25 years of experience running whale-watching boats in New Zealand. They have a high success rate; finding dolphins on over 90 per cent of trips and whales around 75 per cent of the time. Andy also worked on humpback-whale watching boats in Tonga – taking people swimming with humpback whales 'was a bit different,' he says.

I ask Andy what he loves about his job, because it's very clear he does love his job. 'It's a pretty nice office when you live in the middle of a city and get to spend every day surrounded by dolphins and whales!'

A Bryde's whale seen on an Auckland Whale and Dolphin Safari.

He tells me that half of Auckland don't realise that there are whales and dolphins out in the Hauraki Gulf. In fact, he recalls multiple occasions where he has talked to Aucklanders about what he does and they've confidently declared that there are no whales or dolphins in the Auckland region. He has conversations that end something like this quite frequently: 'I've just told you I run an Auckland-whale watching boat, and have done for sixteen years, and you're telling me there are no whales in Auckland.'

Every day is different, which Andy likes, and each day he

A bottlenose dolphin seen from Dolphin Explorer.

meets many different people. He especially enjoys his work when he gets a group on board who are really keen to engage, ask questions, and find out more about the gulf and the marine life they are searching for. He says it's really rewarding when he sees people learn more about the ocean and marine life as part of their safari experience. He especially likes chatting to kids who are enthralled by dolphins and whales and who are eager to find out as much as they can. He has a great rapport with his customers and speaks passionately, answering all sorts of questions, and delighting them with stories about the Hauraki Gulf, the ocean and its precious marine mammals.

Andy provides an informative commentary during the safari, making people aware of what the crew are searching for and what to look out for. He asks questions that encourage people to really think about the importance of the ocean and the life it sustains. He enjoys sharing his knowledge and says sometimes people are astounded by what they learn. 'A lot of people don't realise that our oceans provide most of our oxygen, all of our water – and therefore all of our food, and our climate. The four things we all need to survive!' Another great 'did you know?' fact that often gets raised eyebrows is that the atmosphere was created by plant plankton and algae in the ocean long before trees existed. He laughs as he tells me how amazed people often are. He makes the learning process fun as his commentary has plenty of good Kiwi humour interwoven. He says it's quite challenging trying to get messages across to a diverse group of people from different countries and cultures, all with different expectations and levels of knowledge about the Hauraki Gulf — but he seems to manage this effortlessly.

Throughout the safari experience you can see Andy and the crew live and breathe the company's mission statement: 'the preservation of species and environment through research, education, and awareness'. Andy says, 'We're not there to eco-bash people ... just to make people aware of how important the oceans are.'

With each day being different, every safari presents its own challenges. Andy and the crew have to ensure that everything runs smoothly on the boat and often have to look after passengers, particularly in rougher weather, who don't handle the conditions well.

The biggest challenge for Andy is trying to meet the wide-ranging customer expectations on a daily basis. Many passengers are happy be out on the water exploring the gulf and learning more about marine life — if they see whales and dolphins they are thrilled and feel privileged. For many, seeing whales and dolphins is a treasured, once-in-a-lifetime experience. Others have more demanding expectations and might ask questions like 'How long until we get there?' and 'When are we going to see the whales?' and, of course, it's not about 'how long' and 'when.'

Often if the crew find a whale that is sounding (which the mammals do when communicating or feeding) and the whale's behaviour is evasive, as it is engaged in important survival business, the crew won't pursue it. They recognise the behaviour and respect that the animal needs to be left alone.

Andy explains it can sometimes be difficult to get that message across to passengers who are intent on seeing a whale and perhaps haven't considered that for whales, just as with people, there are convenient times and not so convenient times to interrupt or visit them.

As part of the approach to education, the crew continually myth-bust and dispel misconceptions that people have, inspiring them to find out more and be mindful of the effects humans have on the marine environment. Some people, obviously, 'just don't get it,' Andy tells me, 'Mother Nature can be exploding right in front of them and they're fixated on their cellphones.' You can't win them all!

The crew don't use any location equipment to track the animals — it is a safari, after all. Each day they plan an approach: they look at the sea state, establish a search area, monitor water temperatures, look at scattering layers of plankton, and observe what the seabirds are doing. Andy explains that the birds are the biggest indicators of what's going on in the food chain. By understanding the bird's behaviour, they get a good sense of whether there might be predators associated with them in the area. They investigate nature as a means of discovery, and the process is fascinating.

During the safari, Andy pointed out hundreds of fluttering shearwaters on the surface of the ocean in the distance; their presence likely indicating marine mammals in their vicinity. The majority of people on the boat would not have seen or known the birds were even there — they appeared like a haze on the horizon in between patches of reflective light glistening on the ocean's surface. The birds led us to a group of common dolphins that chased and played on the bow wave, delighting everyone with their playfulness, speed and agility. The crew explained that the dolphins are often inquisitive about the people on the boat and will sometimes swim on their sides to get a better look at the people watching them. The passengers noticed the dolphins taking an interest in them and were captivated. To be made aware that the dolphins might be enjoying the encounter as much as they were was thrilling. A mother and calf swam speedily alongside the boat and leapt together, out of the water, for a brief moment; everyone instinctively reacted with joy at seeing the mother with her little calf. It felt like nature was putting on a show and it was wonderful to witness.

The most common animals seen on Auckland Whale and Dolphin Safari trips are common dolphins, Bryde's whales, penguins and orca – over 23 species of whale and dolphin have been seen in the gulf including bottlenose dolphins, humpback whales, and southern right whales. Seabirds commonly sighted include Australasian gannets, shearwaters, petrels and little penguins.

The Hauraki Gulf is one of the most biologically and geographically diverse marine parks in the world and, lucky for us, it is visited by a third of all marine mammal species. The Auckland Whale and Dolphin Safari team and research students collect data on every trip, making this data available to the Department of Conservation. Andy explains that, over time, the data builds an important picture of the health of the marine life in the gulf. He has been collecting and collating data for 15 years and has customised a mobile app which the crew use to record what they see each day. The information is transferred to a database, which is shared with research students and DOC. They also assist research students and marine biologists by taking them out into the gulf, and the result is a valuable contribution to the research and conservation potential of the region. Andy showed me a big drawer full of PhD theses that have been conducted aboard *Dolphin Explorer* – an impressive collection containing a wealth of vital insights.

Andy loves fishing and is an experienced diver but currently works most days so can't get out to enjoy the gulf in his own time as much as he would like. 'The only diving I get to do is under the boat!' he laughs. He has a network of friends and contacts who run fishing vessels and they keep in touch and often share fish-finding tips or whale sightings.

I ask Andy when the best time to go out dolphin and whale watching is, half-expecting it might be a silly question – it turns out winter is definitely best. In the winter months, when the temperatures are lower, the marine mammal food-chain activity changes and whales and dolphins are seen in much larger numbers. He said sometimes, in the winter, *Dolphin Explorer* might be the only boat out there for miles and they can sometimes be surrounded by large groups of dolphins – groups of between 2000 and 4000 have been seen! The surrounding waters can be a mass of magnificent marine mammal activity as far as you can see in all directions.

One of his favourite spots in the gulf is Great Barrier Island, 'Whangaparapara – such a stunning spot, and Port Fitzroy …

you can't beat Fitzroy Harbour,' he enthuses, 'it's such a nice environment and so sheltered.' He also especially likes The Noises and Otata Island.

As Andy is out on the Hauraki Gulf every day, I ask him if he has any concerns or things he would change to improve it. He feels strongly that there are a lot of boaties out there who need to learn more about boating. His views echo many others I have spoken to. 'There are a lot of idiots out there. One of the things I'd like to see is more boating education … you shouldn't be able to just go out there and buy a boat without educating yourself, people do stupid things, not just from a safety and environment perspective but they do stupid things around dolphins, around rocks, and they do stupid things with their rubbish.' Andy has seen people drop bags of rubbish from their boats – the ignorance is appalling.

'People go out there putting their own families at risk, other people at risk and the marine environment at risk – it's frustrating when you're a commercial skipper operating out there every day and a boat comes screaming across your bow with their kids sitting up front bow-riding and they've got no lifejackets on.' He cites the irony that a boatie requires a licence to operate a VHF radio but not a vessel. It does seem ludicrous. Andy says the solution lies with 'focusing on education and trying to get people to take Coastguard courses, like a day-skipper or boat-master course – just the basic stuff. It's available, it's cheap and it's brilliant, but should be compulsory.'

Andy also identifies the pressure being put on the Hauraki Gulf by both commercial and recreational fishing. This is currently a hot

Common dolphins.

topic as the government has proposed plans to change the way New Zealand's marine environments are managed. A recreational fishing park has been proposed for the inner Hauraki Gulf where commercial fishing would be banned. The conversations and negotiations with the multitude of stakeholders are ongoing and the future outcome is unknown, but Andy's view is clear: 'If they were to ban commercial fishing it would be great for the marine life in the Hauraki Gulf – if they could reduce recreational fishing, that would be good too.'

Despite the challenges that are beyond his control, Andy loves his job and being out in the gulf every day. He loves seeing people leave the boat after a safari 'knowing that they're leaving with a much better understanding of the ocean and its marine life. And kids, who have asked lots of questions, will go back to school and tell all their mates about it.'

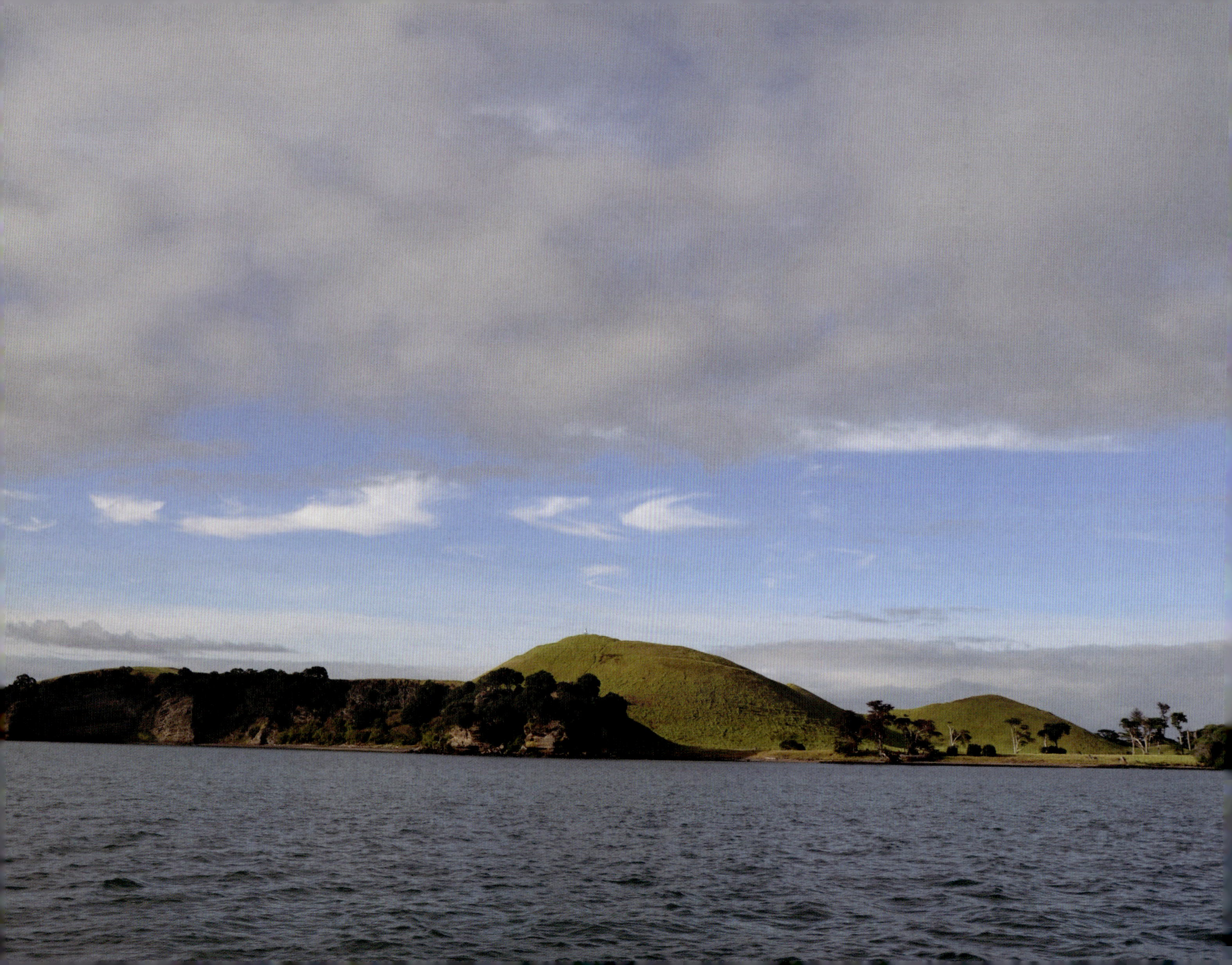

Browns Island

FLYING, PIGS AND CLASSIC CONE

Situated close to Auckland's eastern suburbs, Browns Island is easily accessed and is a handy destination for family picnics, swimming, fishing, walking or just taking time out to relax on the beach. The island is a small but perfectly formed recreation reserve of 59 hectares and can be comfortably explored within a day.

Background on Browns

The island was named Motukorea – the island of the oystercatcher – by Maori after the oystercatchers that have nested on its shores for hundreds of years. In later years the island was also named after wily Scotsman William Brown, who purchased the volcanic island in 1840 to farm pigs and grow produce in the fertile soil to feed the country's new capital city.

Visitors to Browns Island will need their own waterborne means of getting there. Access to the island by boat, depending on wind conditions, is best via Crater Bay on the north-east side of the island or West Bay. Care must be taken on approach as there are rocks and reefs surrounding the island. Anchorages are safe in good weather during the daytime but not recommended overnight.

Kayaking to Browns Island is possible from the eastern beaches of Auckland and is recommended for intermediate to advanced kayakers. It's about a 5.5-kilometre paddle one way from St Heliers and the best place to land is Crater Bay. It is also possible to kayak from neighbouring Motuihe or Rangitoto islands. For those without their own kayaks, Auckland Sea Kayaks offer guided trips to Browns and Rangitoto islands. Browns is also a destination for windsurfers – experienced windsurfers can be seen dodging sailing craft whilst catching a westerly wind straight out of the Waitemata Harbour.

A visit to Browns Island usually means a picnic and a walk to the summit to check out the best-in-class volcanic cone and crater. (The walk from Crater Bay to the summit takes about 45 minutes.) Then, perhaps, explore the Maori pa site at the summit and seeking out the remains of stone-walled gardens from hundreds of years ago. If the weather is good, make tracks to the beach at Crater Bay for the best place to swim on the island. It is possible to swim at other beaches on the island but they are rockier. Whilst enjoying views of the crater, spare a thought for the Barnard brothers who built an elaborate double-decker glider only to slam it into the hillside.

Rich in resources

Like neighbouring Rangitoto, Browns Island was formed by a series of multiple eruptions over a long period of time. The most recent volcanic activity is believed to have occurred between 10,000 and 20,000 years ago. The initial eruptions formed a large tuff ring (a raised rim around an explosive volcanic crater) of which some remains can be seen on the eastern side of the island. Subsequent eruptions and lava flows formed the main cone which exists today – the most perfectly preserved volcanic cone in the Auckland volcanic field, standing 68 metres tall. The island has an invisible tail – long trails of lava flow that extend out beneath the ocean for two kilometres to the south.

There is evidence of settlement on Motukorea for over 600 years – archaeological sites date back to the first Maori migrants. The Ngati Tamatera iwi cultivated the rich volcanic soil and created complex garden systems, growing produce which they later traded with European settlers. Stone-tool manufacturing sites have also been discovered on the island – the Maori who cultivated the land built their own tools from stone. The remains of a complex system of stone walls and middens was also found on the island, indicating gardening systems for growing food and farming.

The marine resources were also exploited on Motukorea and evidence of old fishing traps have been discovered by archaeologists. The remains of the three pa sites can be found at the summit of the main volcanic cone, on the eastern side of the island, and to the west of the main volcanic cone. The archaeological sites, of which there are 68, show layers of complex gardening, stone work and fishing systems.

In the 1820s the first European visitor to the island was Richard Cruise, closely followed by Samuel Marsden and John Butler. They reported small numbers of Maori living on the island at the time. By the time French explorer Dumont d'Urville visited the island in 1827 there were no reported island inhabitants – presumably because of the musket wars.

In 1840, William Brown, a Scotsman looking for land to farm, purchased the island from Ngati Tamatera chiefs. Brown and fellow Scot Logan Campbell, who he had met by chance in the Coromandel, wasted no time in beginning work, farming produce to trade. Brown took quite a risk with his investment, believing that Auckland would soon become the colony's new capital and that he could make his fortune as a merchant trading vegetables and pigs.

Brown's risk paid off. In March 1841, Governor William Hobson was offered land in the Auckland region by several Maori chiefs who were keen for Hobson to declare Auckland the new capital of New Zealand. Hobson obliged, relocating to Auckland from the previous capital, Russell, in the Bay of Islands. Russell had been established as New Zealand's capital after the signing of the Treaty of Waitangi in 1840. One year later that all changed and William Brown and Logan Campbell did very well as a result. Their partnership endured more than 30 years and, as an astute businessman, Brown went on to expand his business ventures.

As Auckland developed into the political hub of New Zealand, Brown, ever the opportunist, kept an eye on the administration and wasn't afraid to oppose them at a moment's notice should he disagree with any plans or developments. He frequently opposed the administration and challenged Governor FitzRoy and Governor Grey over their policies and their management of the country. Viewed as a troublemaker by some and a critical thinker and leader by others, one thing was certain – Brown spoke his mind like a true Scotsman.

To make completely sure that his voice was heard, Brown purchased the best platform of the day via which he could air his views. He bought Auckland's first newspaper – the *Southern Cross*. He was proud of his public media vehicle and he wasn't afraid to use it. Aware of the cutting critiques coming their way, Governor FitzRoy and Governor Grey tried to keep Brown on side by inviting him to contribute to the legislative council. Their tactics were in vain; Brown deliberately gave bad advice to FitzRoy and upset Grey so much that he claimed that Brown's 'hateful sentiments' caused him so much anguish that it was with feeling of 'sorrow, rather than of pleasure and pride, that he every day entered this council'.

Brown sought political status of his own and was elected a Member of the House of Representatives in Auckland. After further scrapping with the Grey administration his ambitions to become superintendent were realised in 1855. But his reputation preceded him and the provincial council made his life very difficult. Karma was quick and unrelenting.

The council made Brown's working life as miserable as possible, denying him the resources he needed to do his job well. Later that year Brown resigned from his position, and he and his family moved back to the UK with a tidy pot of earnings.

On leaving New Zealand, Brown employed a local manager to take over his business interests whilst he was overseas.

A graveyard of old paddle steamers on Browns Island.

This didn't work out and in subsequent years Brown and Logan had to take turns to return to New Zealand to sort out issues. Eventually Logan became fed up with this arrangement and asked Brown if they could dissolve their partnership. Brown wasn't prepared to give up his London life to return and so agreed. In 1873, Campbell bought out Brown's share of the company and Browns Island, which he went on to sell in 1879. Since then the island has had many different uses.

In 1906 the Devonport Steam Ferry Company, a family-run business, bought the island as a destination for Auckland daytrippers and picnickers. Browns Island became a very popular picnic destination, particularly because of its proximity to the mainland. The competition among ferry companies to get the punters on their boats was fierce and the public were spoilt for choice with a range of beautiful Hauraki Gulf island excursions to choose from. A few years later the Devonport Steam Ferry Company abandoned four of their obsolete vessels on the shore at Browns Island, creating an unsightly 'ferry graveyard'. The remains of several of the ferries can still be seen to this day at low tide.

In 1909 Browns Island became the site of a historic and short-lived moment of glory – a New Zealand first and last! The '15 minutes of fame' occurred when two brothers from Auckland embarked on a top-secret experiment, raising little more than a few eyebrows at the time.

Alex and Claude Barnard used the relative seclusion of Browns Island to squirrel away their carefully crafted invention until the day it would be unveiled. Safe from the prying eyes of the public they had designed and built a prototype flying machine. Inspired by the Wright brothers in the United States, the Barnard brothers had been intent on flying their double-decked glider from the top of the 68-metre volcanic cone. Where they had hoped to fly

The Barnard brothers attempting to fly on Browns Island in 1909.

to (and land) is unknown, but they successfully flew their home-built machine from the top of the cone for a brief moment before the wind blew them crashing into the crater slopes. A notorious day for the island – a short but historic flight for the Barnard brothers.

In 1946, the fate of Browns Island took a dark turn when the Auckland Metropolitan Drainage Board purchased it with the intention of building a sewage treatment plant. Fortunately, the public were not impressed that such a historic island should be spoilt and opposed the idea. The plans were scrapped and the plant was built on the mainland instead.

The island was then bought by Sir Ernest Davis in 1955, who gifted it to the people of Auckland. The island is still owned by Auckland Council and is now a public reserve managed by the Department of Conservation.

Native nesting

The island is uninhabited apart from a couple of resident bird species. The rare New Zealand dotterel can sometimes be found nesting on the shoreline and the oystercatcher, after which the island takes its name, is also keeping up appearances. The oystercatchers are shorebirds and remain on the island's coast to breed – usually between September and December. Their diet is more interesting than their name suggests – they are seafood connoisseurs, dining on mussels, crabs, oysters and limpets. Their nests are shallow and often just above the high-tide mark. Often, if you are walking near their nests, they will tell you about it – squawking loudly and running or flying towards the potential egg-crushing perpetrator – showing aggression. They were once at risk due to hunting but have flourished in recent years and are no longer on the threatened species list. They are regulars at beaches and shorelines around the gulf.

INGRID VISSER — SCIENTIST

An orca approaches Ingrid's boat in the gulf.

Doctor Ingrid Visser needs little introduction to many New Zealanders who will be familiar with her work and research with orca in New Zealand and around the world. A finalist for New Zealander of the Year in 2010 and a globally respected scientist, Ingrid is passionate about protecting orca and their natural environment – one of which is the Hauraki Gulf.

Often asked if she has always wanted to work with orca, Ingrid says that she knew she wanted to work with whales and dolphins from about the age of six. Having grown up in rural New Zealand on farms and around animals, her interest in, and respect for, the animal world flourished as a child. Always hungry to learn and a voracious reader at school, Ingrid would get involved on the farm with her father, saving birds or mice and collecting frogs. When her father decided to retire from farming the family moved to Tutukaka, Northland. Ingrid would go out fishing with her father and put all her knowledge to use, identifying many different species of whale and dolphin whilst out on trips.

In her teens, Ingrid sailed around the world with her mum, dad and sister, spending four-and-a-half years circumnavigating the globe during which time her passion for cetaceans (whales and dolphins) was amplified. With her unique life experience came incredible self-discipline and independence. There wasn't much Ingrid and her family didn't experience on that trip. Ingrid describes it in her book *Swimming with Orca*: 'The story of our lives aboard the boat and our experiences sailing around the world would fill at least another book ... the journey was everything I could have dreamed of, and much, much more.'

The trip instilled in Ingrid a formidable determination, resilience, and self-reliance, which she immediately put to good use when she returned to New Zealand and relentlessly pursued her dream to study cetaceans.

After many years of study Ingrid obtained a zoology degree, a masters and a PhD. During her studies she set up the Orca Research Trust – a not-for-profit organisation reliant on donations from the public. The Orca Research Trust's mission statement is 'To protect orca and their habitat, through conservation, education and scientific work.'

Ingrid, working primarily by herself, but occasionally in collaboration with others, continues to discover more about orca and their behaviour, which helps to understand

Top: Orca pass by Rangitoto Island.
Bottom: Rocky breaching.

Spy-hopping orca.

them and improve their protection. Ingrid writes articles which are published in international journals, along with publishing her research on the Trust's website. She also gives talks all over New Zealand and at international conferences. By making the science available and easy to consume by non-academics, she helps people understand and be more mindful of orca and other marine mammals. She also helps people to comprehend and consider the impact humans have on the orca's environment, their health and wellbeing, and ultimately the future survival of the species. Ingrid and her team at the Orca Research Trust also assist with rescuing and re-floating stranded whales, of which New Zealand has the highest rate in the world, some of which are mass strandings.

I ask Ingrid what her work means to her. 'It's my world. It's literally everything,' she explains. She cares intensely for orca and tells me about a recent trip she had taken to an event where she found a mother orca mourning her calf, which had been hit by a boat and killed. Ingrid's dedication to her work saw her there for two nights where she slept in her small boat, out in the rain, in a body bag that she had brought with her for the dead whale. Her devotion is unfaltering and her passion and enthusiasm is inspiring.

Ingrid relies on the public and anyone out on the water to report orca sightings. She has a freephone number (0800-SEE ORCA) and is responsive to call-outs which can happen at any time. From day to day Ingrid never really knows where she's going to be or when she'll be back. Her time isn't her own – it's dedicated to orca and their protection. Ingrid says a typical day will see her in her office at around 5am and she'll often still be there until 10.30 at night – with trips out to see orca if she has been alerted.

When Ingrid first began her research, she spent the majority of her time in New Zealand working with orca up and down the country. She still does, but more recently Ingrid has found herself spending a significant amount of time on anti-captivity work. As a leading expert on orca, she is called upon to assist with court cases all over the world. In her efforts to free orca held in captivity and inform the public of the real suffering the animals endure, she has set up two websites to help debunk the myths and spin published by such organisations as SeaWorld in the USA and Loro Parque in Spain, which try to convince the public that it is acceptable to keep whales in captivity. As Ingrid's work shows, it is not okay, in fact, it is far from it. Orca, without exception, suffer greatly in captivity and many die as a result.

Ingrid tells me that orca have similar characteristics to humans – they are a highly intelligent, family-orientated species. They hang out and socialise in groups and they work together in teams. Often when someone asks Ingrid a question about orca, she tells them that the human answer to the question will apply. Yes, they grieve for the loss of their friends and family, they look after each other, and they communicate with each other constantly.

The tough parts of Ingrid's job are outweighed by the good times, she assures me. 'Working with the New Zealand orca is incredibly rewarding.' Recently whilst in the Hauraki Gulf, Ingrid was thrilled to be reunited with an orca she had first known as a young calf in Whangarei Harbour. Ingrid recalls it was Anzac Day and the poor calf had war wounds from being run over by a boat

Ingrid and 'Sam', eye to eye.

so was named Anzac. About six months ago, while Ingrid was out in the gulf, Anzac approached her boat and stayed for a while, letting Ingrid rub her down like you would a horse or play with a dog. 'I had sore cheeks from smiling all the way home,' Ingrid recalls.

Through her many years of experience researching orca in New Zealand, Ingrid has photographed orca around the North and South islands, also capturing data on behaviour, location, social groups, travel patterns, feeding techniques and communication. Her research has led to many world firsts and discoveries that were so surprising even other whale scientists doubted her findings. Some of these were in the Hauraki Gulf and in regions just outside the gulf.

After about eight years of research, Ingrid was able to determine the number of New Zealand orca – slightly less than 200. On discovering the small population, she made great efforts to get legislation changed so that orca in New Zealand were categorised as endangered 'nationally critical' rather than 'common', their previous categorisation because no one knew how few of them there were.

Ingrid's work determined that there are different groups of orca and that, although they are family-orientated animals often travelling in groups for long periods, they do sometimes venture out of their groups and socialise with other individuals or groups. This style of orca society wasn't understood before Ingrid made this discovery. Her detailed studies of orca and their social networks and how they interact are fascinating (and available in detail on the Orca Research Trust website).

She also takes hydrophone recordings of the orcas communicating – squeaks, clicks, shrieks and whistles. Scientific research conducted in the United States and British Columbia, Canada determined that orca populations have particular calls that are unique to that population. It has also been proven that smaller groups within these larger populations use dialects to distinguish themselves from other groups. Scientists believe these dialects have evolved so that orca can identify with their groups, and possibly to avoid inbreeding. So, effectively, New Zealand orca do have a New Zealand accent!

Ingrid was the very first scientist in the world to discover that New Zealand orca feed on rays. There are four species of ray which the orca dexterously hunt and eat: the short-tailed stingray, long-tailed stingray, eagle ray, and electric ray. No other orca being studied in other parts of the world have been known to consume rays to the extent that they do in New Zealand.

Orca are often seen in the Hauraki Gulf herding rays in shallow water. By diving down in muddy areas or driving the rays into the shallower water of coves and bays, the orca often use teamwork to track and hunt their prey. Their methods and dexterity are impressive – often an orca will pin the ray down whilst another goes in for the kill. The orca have cleverly worked out methods of hunting to avoid the dangerous stingray barb. They have been observed flipping the rays up out of the water by the tail, or lifting them gently in the water so that another orca can bite and kill them. Their foraging for food in shallow water is, however, unfortunately linked to their high rate of stranding.

On a visit to Kawau Island I was told by one of the ferry staff that he had recently witnessed orca hunting rays in North Cove, Kawau. A group of around five orca had been seen by many who were travelling on the ferry. The whales were 'going bonkers' in the shallows, and 'the rays were flying out of the water and onto the beach to try and escape'.

Ingrid first discovered that New Zealand orca hunt rays when she began to swim with the orca and was able to observe this in action. She is the only orca scientist she knows of that regularly swims with orca. I ask why other scientists did not, whether it was a courage thing – she says no, explaining that in places where other orca populations are studied, like Norway, where the water is only three degrees Celsius and there are only three hours of daylight, or in the Antarctic where the air temperature is, at times, minus 31 degrees Celsius, 'the conditions are not really conducive to putting on a swimsuit and plopping over the side.'

The crew of Phocoena *spy orca just off Browns Island.*

She recognises that she is lucky to be based in Tutukaka where it is warm enough to get in the water. To Ingrid, it is logical to swim with the orca – they spend less than 10 per cent of their lives on the surface. 'If you want to understand the behaviour you've got to understand it in the context of what is going on underwater.'

New Zealand orca have a number of different methods they use to hunt rays and sharks that haven't been described anywhere else in the world. Feeding on the bottom (benthic foraging) is unique to the New Zealand orca. Also karate-chopping sharks with their tails is a hunting technique not observed previously. A shark may take a big hit from the orca's tail rendering it immobile long enough for them to get hold of it in their teeth. Orca also use ambush attacks when hunting. Ambush attacks have been observed around the world but New Zealand was the first place orca were observed feeding on common dolphins. All of the above hunting techniques are prevalent in the Hauraki Gulf.

As well as shark- and ray-eaters, Ingrid has identified a group of orca she has named the 'marine mammal munchers.' This is a particular population that comes in from offshore – from north of New Zealand. They travel down the coast of the North Island to feed (have a munch on a few marine mammals – namely bottlenose dolphins, common dolphins and false killer whales) and then they leave. The mammal munchers have been seen in the Hauraki Gulf. 'They're big orca,' Ingrid tells me, 'big girls … and they're covered in cookiecutter shark bites.' This indicates they travel long distances as cookiecutter sharks aren't prevalent in New Zealand coastal waters – they prefer deep, offshore and typically warm waters, with the southern-most record of this tiny shark being found off the East Cape.

'The Hauraki Gulf is unique – there is nowhere else like it in the world,' Ingrid says. She has seen some incredible sights there, even the world's largest animal – a blue whale – sighted between Great Barrier and Little Barrier islands. The blue whale was inquisitive and lifting her head out of the water in a behaviour termed spy-hopping, in order to take a look at her boat. Ingrid was mesmerised; the whale's head alone was bigger than her boat. The gulf is a popular feeding and mating ground for orca as well as many other marine animals, like the common dolphin, bottlenose dolphin, penguins and turtles.

The gulf is an exceptionally special place. But when we look at the clear blue water and the islands with their beautiful coves and beaches, we also need to be mindful of things we perhaps can't see or don't notice. Ingrid constantly strives to publish information and give talks to educate the public about the dangers and threats that exist, with the hope that people will become more aware and become stakeholders of the precious marine environment. Although the Hauraki Gulf is already a designated marine park, there are many threats to this environment: pollution (chemicals and fire retardants that get into the food chain), rubbish (especially plastic), shipping noise (at times deafening for marine mammals in busy areas), agricultural run-off, boat strike (10 out of the 200 New Zealand orca – that Ingrid knows of – have been injured by ships and boats; three of which she knows happened in the Hauraki Gulf), debris and pollution from aquaculture farms. The list goes on and the threats to all marine life are very real.

Orca in the gulf with Auckland city in the background.

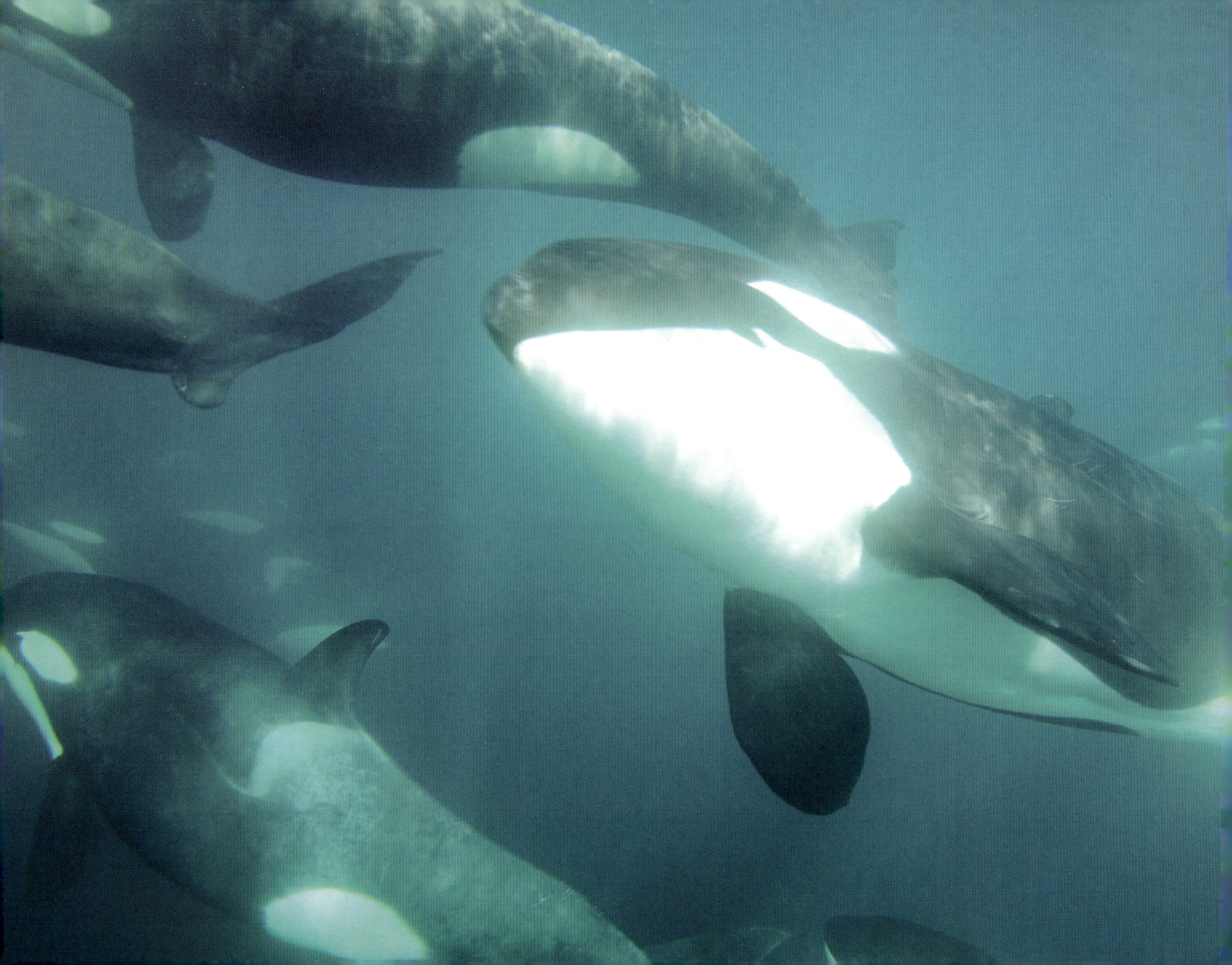

New Zealand orca have the highest recorded levels of toxicity in any animal so far measured in the southern hemisphere. As apex predators (at the top of the food chain) orca consume, without realising it, toxins that exist in high levels in the food they eat. Ingrid has observed that New Zealand orca seem to have a penchant for eating the livers of rays, which exacerbates the problem as the liver, being a filtering organ, contains high levels of toxins. The dangers and threats are everywhere so it is our responsibility to take the time to consider them, and do our bit to reduce them wherever possible.

Boat strikes could easily be reduced or avoided if ships and boats slowed down, Ingrid explains. She has seen people drive boats at reckless speeds around whales and dolphins. The animals don't stand a chance of getting out of the way quickly enough. People should drive boats around any marine life – dolphins, whales, penguins, turtles – as if they were driving around their own pets. It comes down to respect and giving marine life the consideration, appreciation, and space it deserves.

Ingrid tells me more about what happened the night she slept in the body bag while attending to the orca whose calf who had been hit by a boat and killed. As if this horrific situation couldn't get any worse, a reckless boat driver, travelling at great speed, approached the mother orca – trying to get close enough to take a photo on his phone. The orca was in the location where her calf had died and remained in the area, carrying her calf and grieving for her loss. The boat drove the mother away thereby preventing her from finishing the mourning process for her calf. Heartbreaking stories like this are not rare and as such Ingrid sees it as part of her role to educate the public so that they understand these beautiful creatures better in order that they can offer them the respect they deserve.

Ingrid has many hopes for the future of the gulf. She would love to see a ban on commercial fishing and the entire area turned into a marine reserve, which would actually increase fish stocks for the fishermen. She would also love to see the public take personal responsibility and take only half their allowed quota when fishing. She would be thrilled to see a marine sanctuary for marine mammals set up where there is more education available for the public.

When she's not working 17 hours a day Ingrid's favourite places in the gulf to spend time are Tiritiri Matangi Island, The Noises and the Tamaki Strait. She sees lots of orca in each of these locations and loves the area.

I ask Ingrid if there was one thing she'd like people to understand better about orca. Her response is heartfelt: 'People have to realise that these are incredibly intelligent family-orientated animals and that we have to give them the respect they deserve. It's not all about how close you can get to them, it's about watching them in their natural environment and not crowding them. The reward will be even greater if we let them do their own thing.'

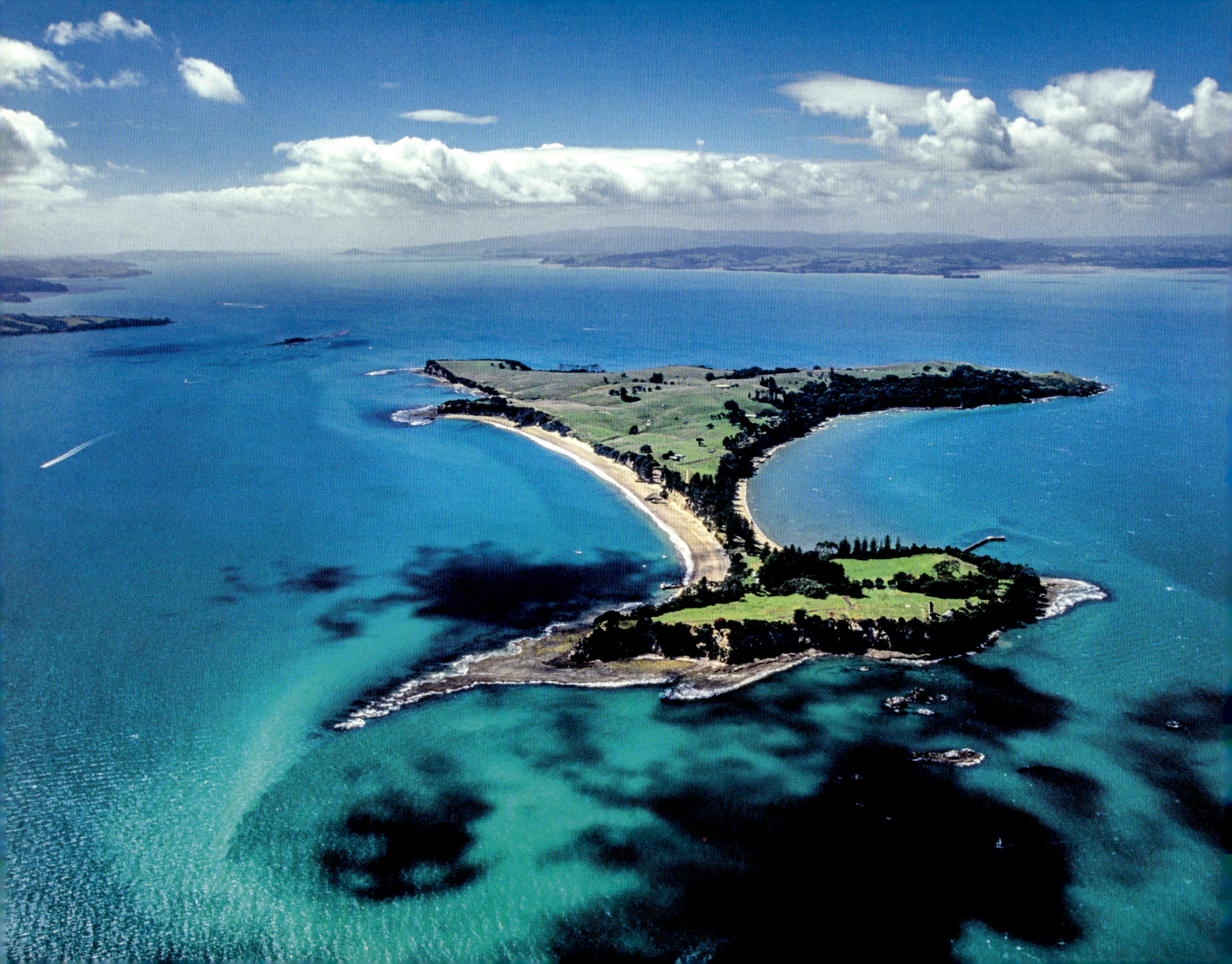

Motuihe Island/Te Motu-a-Ihenga

BEAUTIFUL BEACHES, FAVOURABLE FISHING AND TUATARA TRAVELLING BY HELICOPTER

Motuihe Island is so close to Auckland, many boaties regularly take the opportunity to head out there of an evening to fish, relax, shake off the city stresses, and enjoy the sunset. The unique environment and natural beauty are almost impossible to take for granted. Cruising away from the mainland with the salt spray and fresh air clearing the head, the experience induces relaxation. Having the gulf islands so close to New Zealand's largest city is a blessing and a welcome antidote to the frantic pace of city life.

Safe anchorage

With picture-perfect beaches, clear water and safe bays for swimming and snorkelling, Motuihe is a favourite inner-gulf island with visitors and boaties. The anchor-shaped island, only 16 kilometres from Auckland, lies sheltered between Motutapu and Waiheke islands, with Browns Island just 4 kilometres away.

The island is a recreation reserve frequently visited by Aucklanders and visiting tourists for picnics and lazy days on the gorgeous beaches.

Ferry services operate in summer months from downtown Auckland to the wharf at the north-west side of the island. Larger boats can also land at the wharf for drop-off and pick-ups.

Private craft can easily find sheltered anchorages around Motuihe in just about any weather – Wharf Bay, Ocean Beach and Calypso Bay are all sheltered, and small boats can also land at each of these spots.

Motuihe is within reach of the mainland by kayak. Recommended for more experienced kayakers, the paddle takes a good two-and-a-half hours.

Fishing is popular around the bays on Motuihe and from the rocks around the island's coastline. The Motuihe Channel is a fishing ground favoured by many as the currents provide good opportunities for snapper, kingfish and, recently, gurnard have returned in larger numbers to the area. Fishing competitions and corporate fishing days are often held at Motuihe with prize-giving parties on the island afterwards.

Events, weddings, barbecues, corporate and club team-building days and large family gatherings can be held on Motuihe. A permit for these events can be obtained from the Department of Conservation, and the Motuihe Trust hire barbecues, tables and chairs.

There is a campsite located on the north-western headland, minutes from a beautiful sheltered beach and the wharf which has good anchorages close by. Campers and picnickers should bring their own food and drink as there are no shops on the island. During the busier weekends in summer there is a kiosk on Ocean Beach selling drinks and ice creams.

Exploring Motuihe's history and beaches is easily done in a day. There is a network of walking tracks that take in different aspects of the island. The walks explore historical features: Maori pa sites, the quarantine station, a cemetery, gun emplacements, some of the naval base buildings, the water tower (which is quite a well-known landmark for boaties), and the natural environment: the old olive grove, native wetlands, forest and coastline.

Beauty and despair

Evidence of Maori settlement on Motuihe Island has been discovered at the northern headland where two pa sites were constructed. An important battle took place on the headland at Mangoparerua, which means 'two hammerhead sharks' – the shape of the headland resembles the head shape of a hammerhead shark. The Maru iwi were thought to have inhabited the island first but were invaded by the Te Arawa tribe in the fourteenth century. In later years Ngati Paoa took hold of the island and were the last known Maori tribe to have ownership of the land.

Now the island is recognised to have 13 collective iwi and hapu of Nga Mana Whenua o Tamaki Makaurau. Interestingly, Motuihe is the only Hauraki Gulf Island with two Maori names – Motuihe and Te Motu-a-Ihenga. The question was asked as to why, at a meeting in 2014 where official Maori names for Auckland volcanic cones and gulf islands were discussed. Ngarimu Blair, one of the 13 members of the co-governance authority, answered that 'the first was simply a misspelling of the second.'

Motuihe has a colourful past. The land was discovered and cultivated by Maori, then farmed by Europeans for over 100 years. John Logan Campbell and William Brown (of Browns Island) owned Motuihe for a time and farmed the land. An olive grove planted during the Logan Campbell and Brown era still exists today and is believed to have been the origin of New Zealand's olive-growing industry.

The island is now an open and generous host to nature, birds, wildlife and visitors but was once a hub of disease, containment, incarceration and secrecy. Not all at the same time, but mostly in the same location – on Motuihe's northern headland.

A quarantine station was built and operated there between 1872 and 1941. The station was intended to contain diseases carried by immigrants arriving on ships. Smallpox, scarlet fever and Spanish flu were some of the nasties that immigrants arrived with. Some of the sufferers died of their illnesses and were buried in a small cemetery at the northern tip of Motuihe, on the way towards Te Tumurae Point. There was also an animal quarantine station situated separately further south on Motuihe.

During World War I, an internment camp was established on the island for Germans and Austrians who were living in New Zealand at the time. The camp was also used to house prisoners of war from Samoa, a German territory at that time, which New Zealand seized and occupied at the request of the British. The Motuihe camp, which was relatively comfortable, housed German and Austrian dignitaries, including consuls and a number of German businessmen. The lower-ranking prisoners were sent to a more forbidding camp on Matiu/Somes Island in Wellington Harbour.

In 1914, when New Zealand occupied Samoa, the German Governor of Samoa was captured and interned on Motuihe. The camp was relatively civilised and conditions were unlike many other war-time prison camps. Historical photos show the prisoners were not confined. The internees had the freedom to roam around the island and, astoundingly,

Count Felix von Luckner in full military regalia.

were sometimes granted the use of the prison commandant's launch to take supervised trips to Auckland. Their freedom was curtailed after the antics of a particularly colourful character, a German count, nobleman and naval officer, who was brought to the camp after being captured in Fiji.

Count Felix von Luckner, also known as 'The Sea Devil,' was a German naval captain in charge of a ship called *Seeadler* (Sea Eagle). He and his crew were raiders, charged with the responsibility of disrupting supplies by raiding allied merchant shipping. He was good at it too – von Luckner and his crew destroyed 64,000 tonnes of shipping and, while doing so, maintained a surprising and humane silver-lining to their story of destruction. Von Luckner prided himself on ensuring the safety of all ships' occupants before destroying the vessels. Even the ships' cats were safely extracted from the vessels before they were blown up and sunk. Unfortunately, von Luckner didn't have a completely clean scorecard. There was one fatality as a result of his raids but it was reported to have been accidental. He gained notoriety and a reputation as a folk hero – a man who chose not to be as dreadful as his role gave him scope to be.

Once captured and brought to Motuihe, von Luckner spent little time assessing his escape options before promptly taking off on board the prison commandant's launch. He escaped and made his way towards Mercury Island where he commandeered another boat (*Moa*) before sailing north towards the Kermadec Islands.

Once news of his escape reached the mainland a New Zealand ship was launched in hot pursuit of von Luckner. He was eventually captured during a brief stop-off in a Fijian port to let some of his crew ashore. His mistake led to his return to New Zealand where he eventually ended up back at Motuihe. Von Luckner was not one for accepting his fate. On his arrival back at the internment camp he resumed scheming for a second escape. His plan was never executed as news that the war had ended broke just in time for him to leave the island by the official route and transport.

In the 1930s, Motuihe was used to house a children's health camp. Children were evacuated to the camp after the Napier earthquake in 1931.

As World War II approached, Motuihe was prepared to defend New Zealand from potential invasions. Gun emplacements were installed at the northern headland as part of

A yacht at anchor at Motuihe Island.

the Auckland Coastal Defence Network. Motuihe was also the location of a naval training base – HMNZS *Tamaki*. Although the Royal New Zealand Navy did not have a large fleet of ships to engage in the war at sea, it did have men and women who could be trained and serve. By 1945, 6000 navy recruits had trained at HMNZS *Tamaki* – representing 60 per cent of the New Zealand Navy involved in World War II.

The navy sold the site to Auckland City Council in 1963. Before they left the premises they stripped and dismantled much of the site – much to the disgust of the council, who called their actions criminal. The navy's rationale for this destruction is unclear.

A forest in a day

Motuihe Island is a recreation reserve jointly managed by the Motuihe Restoration Trust and the Department of Conservation. Since 2000, the island has received lots of tender loving care from hundreds of volunteers who have replanted more than 300,000 native trees and plants. Their vision to restore, enhance and protect the indigenous flora and fauna for future generations is being realised. The record number of trees planted in one day was 22,400, planted by 350 volunteers. That sounds like a forest in a day!

An indicator of the success of the island's rejuvenation is the variety and volume of native wildlife that now thrives on Motuihe. It is a magnificent success story. Since the island's plants and native forest have been replenished, many endangered species have been released on the island. There are New Zealand's smallest kiwi species, the little spotted kiwi, saddlebacks, kereru, dotterels, kakariki, blue penguins, oystercatchers, whiteheads, moreporks, tui and fantails – the island's bird populations are flourishing.

TUATARA ON MOTUIHE

Motuihe is one of a few Hauraki Gulf islands home to the endangered and prehistoric tuatara. The tuatara (which means 'peaks on the back') was once prevalent on the mainland until foreign pests were introduced and the population was decimated by rats.

Tuatara are the only surviving species of a prehistoric era 200 million years ago when dinosaurs walked the earth. It is incredible to consider that all other species of that time became extinct about 60 million years ago – except for this resilient reptile.

The species is of great interest to biologists and scientists around the world, and conservation efforts to create safe habitats for these reptiles are ongoing. For now, pest-free island habitats are working well for tuatara. They benefit from co-habiting on islands where colonies of seabirds exist, as the seabirds help fertilise the plants that tuatara need to survive.

In 2012, 60 tuatara were flown by helicopter to Motuihe, having been gifted by Ngatiwai to the people of Auckland. A ceremony was held to officially hand over the precious reptiles. An elder from Ngatiwai accompanied the tuatara to Motuihe and blessed their arrival. The ceremony was attended by 320 people – many of whom were volunteers who had assisted with replanting, weed control and pest-eradication from the island.

Looking across Owhanake Bay towards Oneroa.

Waiheke Island

FROM QUIET BACKWATER TO GLOBAL GLAMOURPUSS

Waiheke is a feast for the eyes with 40 kilometres of sandy beaches, rocky bays and clear blue water lapping every promontory and cove – for people who love being by the water it's nothing short of seventh heaven. Despite the increasing urbanisation and number of visitors to the island, Waiheke's laid-back character remains intact. The beauty of the wide open spaces, gently rolling farmland, forest, and deserted beaches has not changed. But now the natural landscape plays host to some of New Zealand's finest wineries, restaurants and olive groves – each offering adventures for the taste buds.

Spoilt for choice

Recently recognised as the world's fifth-best region to visit in 2016 by global travel guide *Lonely Planet*, Waiheke Island's profile continues to build. Listed by the *New York Times* as one of 'The 46 places to go in 2013' and one of the reasons 'why Auckland is worth travelling 25 hours for' by the *Telegraph* in the UK in 2015, the island's popularity seems to be on an unstoppable stratospheric trajectory. Also described as a 'playground of the gods' and 'the island of wine', it's easy to see why Waiheke's population explodes from around 9000 in winter to up to 50,000 in summer.

Waiheke Island is the second largest (after Great Barrier Island) and by far the most populated and urbanised of the Hauraki Gulf islands. Waiheke lies 17 kilometres from Auckland and 21 kilometres from the Coromandel Peninsula. Its position in the gulf is sheltered from the westerly winds by a double buffer: the Waitakere Ranges on the mainland as well as Rangitoto and Motutapu islands.

The island is said to have its own microclimate, although there is no scientific proof of this. However, sunshine hours don't lie and Waiheke gets more of them than the mainland. Waiheke also gets 30 per cent less rainfall and lower humidity than the surrounding Auckland region. Often likened to a Mediterranean climate, it's clear Waiheke's reputation for grape growing didn't happen by accident.

Getting to the island from Auckland is easy. Ferries for Matiatia leave from downtown Auckland, while ferries for Kennedy Point set off from Halfmoon Bay.

For yachties and boaties visiting Waiheke, there is a limitless supply of picturesque bays providing safe anchorages. With 40 kilometres of beaches, it is usually easy to find sheltered bays depending on the prevailing weather conditions.

For those who don't have their own yacht but are keen on sailing, there are trips to Waiheke that leave from Auckland's Viaduct Harbour. It is possible to participate in sailing under the guidance of an experienced crew. On arrival to the island, lunch and wine-tasting awaits at a vineyard restaurant and the return journey is, wisely, by ferry.

A good diving spot can be found at Gannet Rock, which is a kilometre north of Thumb Point at Hooks Bay on the north-eastern side of Waiheke. There is a large sea cave for divers to explore and the area is teeming with kingfish. Gannet Rock is one of a small number of gannet colonies in the gulf and the super-speedy seabirds also like diving there and are frequently seen propelling themselves into the surrounding bays like missiles.

Visitors can mix and match their Waiheke experiences, choosing from a variety of activities and pastimes: sightseeing, visiting art studios and galleries, a walk through sculpture gardens, vineyard tours, cellar-door tastings, sampling local olive oils, shopping or dining at a local café or vineyard. For those who enjoy guided tours, there are operators running sightseeing and wine tours around the island.

For the more adventurous on land you can try archery, clay-pigeon shooting, mountain biking, hire a scooter, or even see the island from a flying fox zip-line high above the forest canopy. For those wanting adventures in and out on the water there's snorkelling, diving, sea kayaking, surfing, fishing charters and endless beautiful swimming beaches to choose from.

The laid-back vibe on Waiheke is a reminder that taking it easy is as good a plan as any. Taking a picnic to any of the island's beaches, or to the top of a secluded grassy headland overlooking one of the many beautiful bays is a fine way to relax and make the most of the magnificent coastal views.

For a quiet picnic spot away from it all, head to Whakanewha Regional Park on the south-west of the island. The park has a beautiful, safe swimming beach and you can walk up to the top of the bluff and picnic with views out across Rocky Bay and towards Auckland city. The park has a campsite and there are picnic and barbecue facilities along the foreshore. Swimming, kayaking, horse riding and mountain biking are popular pastimes in the park

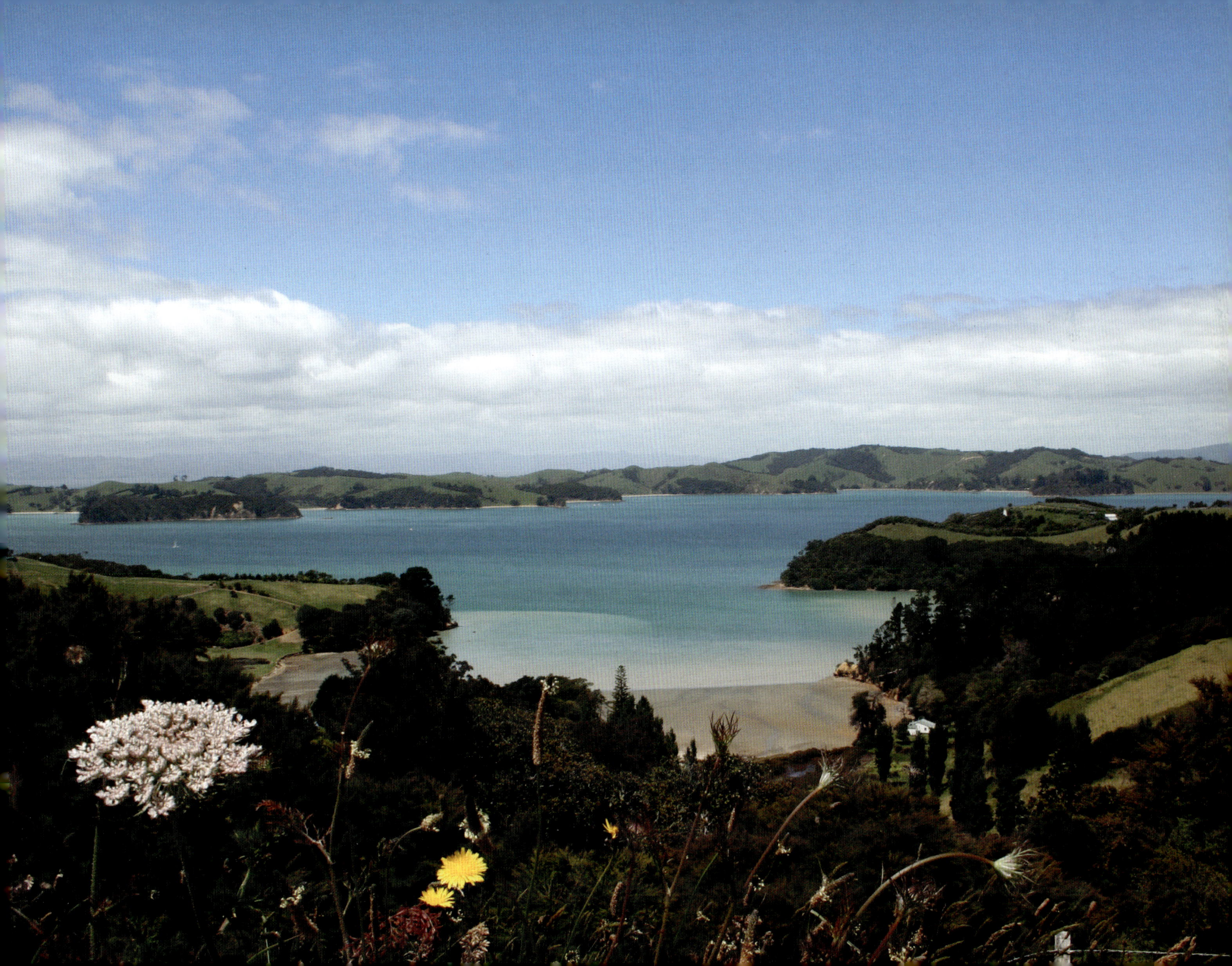

A ship at anchor in Man o'War Bay in 1905.

and there are walking trails through the park and surrounding mature coastal forest.

If a village wander is more your thing, a relaxed amble around the shops and art gallery at Oneroa is a pleasant way to while away an hour or two. Oneroa village has a number of small shops with art and craft, clothing, gifts, souvenirs and beachwear in good supply. Basic groceries, fruit and vegetables, beer and wine are all available from Oneroa. There is also a pharmacy, delicatessen and a number of cafes for those essential coffee stops. For those staying on the island for a few days there is a large supermarket at Ostend where visitors can buy just about anything they may need.

Visitors are spoilt for choice as far as places to stay are concerned. Spending a few days on the island is definitely recommended and the variety of accommodation options from backpackers to five-star luxury, many with elevated coastal views, will suit all tastes and budgets. Whether you're there to relax and unwind or fit in as many of the sights and activities that you can manage, the island life offers a multitude of experiences to enjoy.

Island of cascading waters

Like Great Barrier and Little Barrier islands, Waiheke was once connected to the Coromandel Peninsula before the land subsided, creating valleys that were then flooded after the last ice age.

When Maori first occupied the island around AD 950 the landscape would have originally been completely covered with forest and bush. Tall kauri forest was predominant on the island – rimu and totara also thrived. Rich with natural resources and with plenty of freshwater streams, the island was an attractive settlement proposition for the first inhabitants of New Zealand. Maori built many pa sites high up on headlands safe from any coastal invasions. The Hauraki and Te Arawa tribes ensured good vantage points from which to keep watch for incoming danger, particularly from the Tamaki Strait.

The ancient Maori name for Waiheke was Te Motu-arai-roa, 'the long sheltering island'. It was so named as the island sheltered canoes travelling along the Tamaki Strait from any bad weather coming in from a northerly direction. In the early 1800s, when the first Europeans started arriving, the name of the

THE HAURAKI GULF

island changed to Motu-wai-heke, 'island of cascading waters'. It has been suggested that the change in name occurred when Europeans mistook the name of a stream for the name of the island.

Maori settlers used fires to burn off areas of land to clear them and enrich the soil for cultivation and food production. It is thought that fires intended to burn off smaller areas of land may have become uncontrolled on the western side of the island, destroying large areas of forest.

Whilst anchored off the east coast of Waiheke in 1769, Captain Cook made note of the dense kauri forests and remarked on the 'noble' trees that he imagined would make excellent masts for the man-o'-war battleships of the Royal Navy. With battleships on his mind he named the nearby bay Man o'War Bay.

When European settlers arrived they logged the forest aggressively. Kauri logging on Waiheke was big business, as it was on many of the gulf islands. Kauri timber was shipped to Britain and used to build masts – Cook had not forgotten his idea. The timber was also used locally for construction in Auckland as well as overseas in Sydney and Melbourne. By the 1950s Waiheke's kauri trees had almost been logged to extinction. As with many other Hauraki Gulf islands, the only kauri that remained survived because they were impossible to get to.

The Reverend Samuel Marsden visited Waiheke in 1820 and reported it being 'as large as the Isle of Wight and contained much good land.' He was right. The land was so good that in 1821 the Waiheke inhabitants were invaded and attacked by Hongi Hika and his Ngapuhi tribe at a big battle at Onetangi beach. (Onetangi means 'weeping sands'.) Those who were not killed or taken captive fled the island escaping to the Waikato region.

When European settlers arrived in the 1830s they bought land and quickly got to work ensuring the island's natural resources were being monetised. Mining for manganese, timber logging and kauri gumdigging were all unsustainable in the long term. It was only when all of the natural resources ran out that they started more sustainable agricultural work, farming sheep and cattle. Farming didn't come without its problems on Waiheke; the hilly terrain meant grazing sheep and cattle caused erosion of the light soil. The erosion led to silting in the estuaries – a problem that still exists today.

As the European communities grew in size, amenities were established – the first post office was opened in 1876 and in 1882 the first school was opened at Te Matuku Bay. The island's population was around 160 in the early 1900s, although many people visited from the mainland for day trips, picnics and regattas. The first regatta was held at Huruhi Bay in December 1883. The SS *Coromandel* was chartered to bring in spectators from Auckland to watch the races and enjoy the scenery. The *New Zealand Herald* put a cheerful spin on a wet-weather day regatta in their race reports: 'Although the day was most unsuitable for a regatta ... a great number of Auckland people took advantage of seeing the beautiful scenery and sandy bays ... the only inconvenience to visitors was the absence of any refreshment booths.' Friendly locals remedied the inaugural event hiccup and brought food and drinks from their homes to cater for the visiting crowds.

The first cruising races of the season are always a cause for celebration. Seen here are revellers in 1937.

As infrastructure continued to be developed in the Auckland region, resources were shipped in from surrounding areas. Large quantities of Waiheke sand and shingle were removed from Hooks Bay on the north-eastern side of the island in the early 1900s. It seems a strange location to be exporting sand from, as there doesn't appear to be a shortage of it on the mainland coastlines, but large quantities were transported to Auckland to assist with building Grafton Bridge and other Auckland construction projects.

More building of the concrete variety began on Waiheke as World War II threatened New Zealand. The gulf islands were strategically placed to host components of a large coastal defence system and Waiheke's north-east coast was a chosen site. At Stony Batter, a high point littered with huge volcanic rocks, a top-secret defence complex consisting of an underground fort, gun batteries,

THE HAURAKI GULF

extensive underground tunnels and buildings, offices and camps were built. Work continued on the bunkers, tunnels and gun emplacements for many years with over 200 men secretly toiling away, using local rock to produce concrete. The walls of the fort at Stony Batter are 3.7 metres thick; the construction was a gargantuan effort – one that engineers still marvel at.

The guns at Stony Batter were the biggest the New Zealand Army or Navy had ever had command of. At 120 tonnes each in weight, with barrels that were 23.4 centimetres in diameter and 11 metres long, they were capable of firing 172-kilogram shells to a range of 32 kilometres. Two guns were installed, whilst the order for the third gun was cancelled after the war. The guns were never used, not even tested, until 1951, long after the war had finished.

In 1960, despite requests from local residents to keep them for historical reasons, the government scrapped the guns, ironically selling the scrap metal to Japan – one of the countries they were intended to defend against. The fort, underground tunnels and gun emplacements still remain and are worth a visit – but don't forget to take a torch.

After the war, the island remained a quiet and secluded backwater with around 800 residents. Waiheke continued to grow in popularity as a destination for tourists and visitors, which didn't go unnoticed by Auckland City Council who attempted to assume control of the island. The inevitable rejection of this idea from residents was accepted and independent island life continued under a local council of sorts.

Between 1948 and 1958 the island changed considerably. The first residents sought work on the mainland and ferries began daily trips to Auckland. The services were on old, slow ferries that took well over an hour. The infrastructure developed; roads were gradually improved and some were tarsealed. Electricity was installed across the island by 1957, and the first hotel at Onetangi – The Beach House – opened its doors. By the end of the 1950s Waiheke's population had grown to over 2000.

In the 1970s, improved infrastructure, electricity and cheap housing in a semi-rural paradise attracted more people to move to Waiheke. A proper local government was established in 1970 and the Waiheke County Council governed the island until Auckland City Council eventually managed to amalgamate Waiheke in 1989. Fast ferries were an accessibility game-changer for Waiheke; these started running in 1987, and accelerated the growth of the population, economy and real-estate prices.

Waiheke's wine-growing was pioneered in 1978 with the establishment of the then Goldwater Vineyard (now called Goldie Vineyard). Stonyridge Vineyard was the next to set up in 1982 and Te Motu Vineyard followed in 1987. There are now over 20 vineyards in operation on Waiheke – some of which have produced internationally recognised, award-winning boutique and artisan wines.

Life on the island

Waiheke Island was once a quiet peaceful retreat; a backwater without many roads or amenities – it happily shunned the busy city din and embraced a private, independent way of life. There were no fast ferries and the beaches were very quiet, if not deserted. It was a place to escape city life, rules and ideologies – and many people moved there to do precisely that.

As Auckland's more affluent bought up property on Waiheke the population mix changed. Previously described as a 'hippy haven' or, more scathingly, as 'beneficiary island', Waiheke's community evolved into something quite different.

Waiheke is often described as a hub of diversity. This may be true when talking about the people, their skills, creativity, characteristics and lifestyles, but not the population mix. The population of Waiheke has a unique make-up: predominantly of European descent – approximately 90 per cent, according to the 2013 census, compared with 59 per cent in Auckland. Overall, those living on the island are older – the average age on Waiheke is 45 years. (Waiheke is second behind Great Barrier, which has an average age of 58 years.) Waiheke also has a third of its population who live alone, compared to 19 per cent in Auckland. That's a significant sector of artistic and creative hermits. Luckily, that's just the way they like it. (The Waiheke population figures are from the 2013 census and include surrounding islands – Rangitoto, Motutapu, Motukorea, Motuihe, Ponui, Rakino, and a number of smaller islands.)

Socially, Waiheke is diverse and is renowned for its creative community. There are many artists, designers, carvers, painters, weavers, musicians, sculptors, writers, poets, actors, chefs, winemakers and scientists living on Waiheke, making it a hothouse of art production in many forms. The happily isolated, bohemian lifestyle that characterised Waiheke in the sixties, seventies and early 1980s is still evident, but has been diluted as the island has become more accessible and the population has grown.

The island has seen significant change in the last 20 years with more people living on the island and over 2000 residents commuting to Auckland every day. The Waiheke economy grew rapidly when the fast ferries services started in the late eighties and more people moved to Waiheke as daily commuting became feasible. Local businesses and artists suddenly had a bigger market to sell to. Horticulture (including wine, olives and livestock), tourism, restaurants, retail, construction and real-estate markets all boomed – with prices to match.

Waiheke, with its secrets now well and truly out, still retains its charm, relaxed way of life and community focus. Long live the proud claim that there are no traffic lights or fast food restaurants. Stay classy, Waiheke!

One day on Waiheke

Tourists often ask, 'If I only have one day, what should I do on Waiheke?' There are myriad possible answers to this question.

If you have an interest in wine and food the answer is easy: visit the island on the one day each year when many of Waiheke's vineyards get together at the old Onetangi airstrip (owned by Te Motu Vineyard) for the Waiheke Wine and Food Festival, which is usually held in late March or early April. In previous years, visitors travelled between vineyards on buses tasting wine and food at various locations as they went. In 2016, for the first time, all the goodness was concentrated at one location accompanied by live entertainment throughout the day. The opportunity to taste a range of Waiheke's boutique wines accompanied by locally produced food is one that many foodies and wine enthusiasts will be extremely excited about. The vineyards host additional events

Crowds enjoying one of Waiheke Island's many festivals at Rangihoua Estate.

around the time of the festival; there are talks given by Waiheke winemakers, concerts, lunches, wine and cheese matching events – visitors can even pick grapes and stomp on them at Passage Rock Vineyard.

For music lovers, the Waiheke International Jazz Festival is likely to be a hit and is held over three days at a variety of venues on the island. The event is nicely timed for Easter – making the most of the four-day weekend. Local and international acts bring something for a wide variety of musical tastes. The line-up is not limited to jazz; the festival includes bands and artists playing blues, funk, soul, pop, gospel, fusion – you name it, you're likely to hear it.

Combining art and the outdoors is a genius combination which can be experienced each year at Sculpture on the Gulf – a sculpture trail located close to Matiatia Wharf. A regular shuttle bus runs from The Pavilion (which overlooks Matiatia Bay) to the the start of the trail whilst the exhibition is running during February each year. Works of sculpture from New Zealand artists are created especially for the exhibition and visitors can enjoy the sculpture installations along the headland between Church Bay and Te Atawhai Whenua Reserve. A stroll along the two-kilometre stretch of hillside, whilst soaking up sunshine and intriguing contemporary sculpture as part of the stunning coastal landscape, is a unique experience. The trail brings you back to the Pavilion, where local food, wine, craft beer, entertainment and a sculpture gallery shop await.

Another popular annual occasion on the island is the Onetangi Beach Races. This exciting day of horse races takes place in February on the golden sands of the longest beach on the island. In the last few years the horse-racing schedule has broadened – the event now includes fun activities and races for kids as well as a craft market, corporate hospitality tents, local food trucks and coffee carts. Local families as well as visitors join in the fun as horses, ponies and their jockeys race through the surf at one of the most glorious of race settings.

The races first began in 1883 when Maori and European settlers gathered together to pit their horses against each other, testing their riding and racing skills. Spectators would enjoy the thrill of the chase as well as betting on the horses as part of the experience. In the mid-1920s the races were banned as the focus on gambling had become too consuming for some and was too big a problem to be ignored. In 1938 the races were reintroduced with a more responsible approach; punters could still gamble but there was a cap on how much could be bet and won.

Nowadays, the races are a fun family day out and have expanded to include tractor, Segway and wheelbarrow races, as well as races for hospitality staff and a uniformed services race including members of the Police, Fire Service, Coastguard and St John Ambulance services. The Onetangi Beach Races are run by Waiheke Rotary as a fundraiser for local community initiatives and projects.

For an island that boasts a laid-back vibe, they like their races on Waiheke. If you're a runner or a walker, the Wharf2Wharf fun run and walking event held every year in mid-January is a great way to experience Waiheke's scenery and meet some of the locals. A real community event, the Wharf2Wharf race was started in 1992 by the Waiheke Harriers Club in order to raise money for local organisations. The temperatures are usually at the scorching end of the spectrum for this event, so volunteers from the island dress up in fancy dress and ensure there's plenty of water, fuel and entertainment at the aid stations along the route. The course takes in quite a few hills and in the heat they definitely seem bigger than they probably are. Possibly the biggest challenge for some will be running past signposts to vineyards and shady outdoor vineyard cafes and restaurants. A special ferry service for the event drops the runners off at Orapiu Wharf on the eastern side of the island and the race ends at Matiatia on the western side where the regular ferry service runs from. There are a few distances to choose from so if the full 25 km is not your bag, 13 km, 12 km, 5 km, a kids' dash and a family bear hunt are all on offer.

If running and racing across the island sounds too athletic, there are plenty more sedate ways to experience Waiheke. There are scenic walks on well-maintained tracks centred around many of the island's beaches and bays. Some of the best are: a circuit around Church Bay (the walk begins at Matiatia Wharf); Oneroa village to Oneroa Beach; Hekerua to Palm Beach (both are popular places to swim); and Onetangi Beach – Waiheke's longest sandy beach. There are also guided walks or cycle tours (including wine-tastings) with Maori guides for those who would enjoy exploring Waiheke whilst learning about the Maori history and culture.

PENNY WHITING – SAILOR

Penny Whiting has an inordinate number of sailing accolades and life achievements to her name. How on earth she has crammed it all in only she knows. Successful yachtswoman, owner and operator of the Penny Whiting School of Sailing, MBE, mother of two, America's Cup and Whitbread race commentator, author, speaker, rugby coach, city councillor, chairman of the Auckland Zoo Charitable Trust, founding trustee of the Auckland Maritime Museum and Sea Cleaners NZ ... the list of achievements continues.

When Penny was in her teens she qualified to swim for New Zealand at the Commonwealth Games in Jamaica. She also surfed competitively, coming fifth at the World Championships in Puerto Rico. As well as spending time in the water, Penny has enjoyed ocean racing and cruising yachts all around the world and has multiple ocean races under her belt. She works hard and loves what she does. She is passionate about her boat, *Endless Summer* – a 50-foot yacht named after film-maker Bruce Brown's 1966 surfing film of the same name. The film follows two surfers as they follow the summer season around the world, surfing in many beautiful locations along the way. Penny was a surfer in the film – and so, she explains, her 'summers really are endless.' She's managed to continue to live that dream and avoid the New Zealand winter for the last 19 years; teaching at her sailing school for four months during summer and travelling to the United States to work and sail in Maine during the southern winter.

In 2016, Penny celebrated 50 years of success, having taught more than 33,000 people to sail or crew a yacht. She loves sharing her knowledge, skills and experience and helping people learn. Her sailing courses are very hands-on and students learn to sail on *Endless Summer* in Auckland Harbour, between Westhaven, North Head and Kauri Point. 'I never get sick of the harbour ... I see turtles out there, dolphins and orca, it's wonderful,' she enthuses. She loves the great feedback she receives when people complete her courses. They frequently tell Penny how thrilled they are that they were able to learn to sail – especially when they didn't think they'd be able to master the skills required.

I ask Penny about the Hauraki Gulf and her sailing experiences there. 'The Hauraki Gulf is a special place for me – I love it ... it's the jewel in Auckland's crown – a real treasure,' she beams.

Penny then tells me about a family trip out to the gulf with her son, his wife and their three children a couple of years ago. One of Penny's grandchildren was just two years old; and determined to ensure he felt part of the fun they brought his car seat along and strapped it to the stern of the boat. Whilst they sailed the boat, wrapped up warm, the little one was a part of the team and included in the sailing experience. He loved seeing what was going on, watching his siblings steer the boat and the waves crashing. Penny herself had been sailing with her father when she was two – they start young in the Whiting family!

When Penny's children were small she took them on similar trips out in her boat all the time. She recalls a day sailing with her daughter, who she carried in a child's harness on her back. They were having a lovely time out on the water and spotted dolphins chasing the boat.

Top: Penny sailing with her young son Carl in the backpack.
Bottom: Fishing in the gulf on Endless Summer.

Penny gives a sailing lesson on Endless Summer.

Penny leaned over the side so that she and her daughter could see the dolphins and they called out to them and squealed with excitement. The dolphins raced under the boat and chased the bow and then promptly disappeared. Five minutes later they returned and were chasing the boat as before. She leaned over the side of the boat again and as she did, the dolphin flipped over on its side to reveal a baby swimming with it. Penny was really surprised and said the experience 'was a bit spooky!' The dolphin had sensed that Penny had a baby on her back and had brought back a mother and calf. 'No matter how many times you see dolphins, you always get excited,' she says.

Penny remembers great times sailing in 'his and hers' races with her husband. These races were fairly long and navigated all around the Hauraki Gulf. All boats had one-man, one-woman teams and Penny enjoyed the challenge of sailing the boat 'with all the big gear on, out the bottom of Waiheke and out round Gannet Rock – fabulous memories. It was great to get around the gulf in a different environment – not just cruising.'

Penny raced frequently with her father – they used to race in the Balokovic Cup and Gold Cup races in the Hauraki Gulf. She took part in many Auckland Anniversary Regatta races too – she was destined to be a yachtswoman given she was born on Auckland Regatta day!

The opening chapter of her book *Endless Summer – The Penny Whiting Story* tells her father's amusing tale of the day she was born. He had gone to visit his wife and new baby daughter in hospital before rushing down to the marina to race his boat in the Auckland Anniversary Regatta. Hilarity ensued as he climbed up onto a roof to get in through a window and sneaked through the wards in the early-morning semi-darkness. He managed to find a lady and baby he had believed to be his wife and baby, and kissed the lady he'd thought was his wife, only to switch the light on to see his newborn baby girl, and realise he'd got the wrong ward!

Penny inherited her parents' energy, determination, work ethic and sense of fun. At 16 years of age, she was adamant she was going to sail her little OK dinghy to Kawau with all the big yachts on squadron weekend. She'd been invited to sail with a crew on one of the larger yachts but had declined – she was determined to get to Kawau by herself. She did so despite difficult conditions in the Tiri channel and the sad loss of a bacon and egg pie her mother had made for her trip. 'Ah, my little OK dinghy – the damn thing kept falling over,' she says. But, after getting her boat back up in the water about five times along the way, she made it to Kawau and was greeted with the congratulations and recognition she deserved.

In her teens Penny's racing frolics saw her challenging the commodore of the Royal New Zealand Yacht Squadron (RNZYS) to a race against her and her all-girl crew. She had been told that she would not be able to challenge the commodore, as women were not allowed to be members and therefore couldn't skipper boats in RNZYS races. Of course, Penny had researched the constitution and found no such legal ruling. The commodore accepted the challenge and the girls made the most of the racing experience starting with their team uniform – they wore navy blue shorts, pleated mini-skirts, pink bikini-bottoms and pink shirts. Penny remembers her mum had made them all pink lace hats – 'Ah, they were terrible,' she says and laughs. 'It was priceless.' They raced the commodore in the squadron race to Kawau – and won.

Penny was later to become the first woman member of the RNZYS – but not without the backing of a couple of very prominent Auckland businessmen to nominate her as a potential member. Penny recalls the meeting where it was proposed that she become a member. She said one of the squadron chaps stood up and asked, 'Will she use the urinals or does she expect us to build her a toilet?' (Penny's impersonation of the man was quite something to behold.) The rest is history – they built her a toilet and she happily became the first lady member – all she really wanted was to be able to race her beloved boat. Penny assures me there are now plenty of women members at the club these days.

I ask Penny what inspires her to get out on the water and sail. 'I just love it out there, being at one with my boat. My boat's lovely and I cook and bake and just have a wonderful time!' I ask her if she gets cranky if she can't get out on the water. 'Oh yes, one hundred per cent,' she confirms. 'Any time is a good time ... if I've ever got a house full of people I'll go and sleep on the boat.'

Her favourite places to sail in the Hauraki Gulf are at the bottom end of Waiheke Island. She loves the coastline there and there is shelter in all sorts of winds. It's a great place to paddle a kayak, swim or fish.

Recently, Penny took a Swedish couple out into the gulf for several days. She provedored the boat and the guests sailed as much or as little as they wanted to. They had a wonderful time, seeing orca just off Matiatia and visiting lovely restaurants for lunch and dinner. The Swedish couple couldn't believe the Hauraki Gulf had so many beautiful places to visit – all hidden away amongst the islands.

I ask Penny where she'd go if she had a few days off and could head out sailing in the gulf. She says, 'A weekend sailing around Waiheke Island, or across to Te Kouma (Coromandel), or up to Kawau and the islands up there – we just have the most amazing playground on our doorstep.'

Sailing with grandsons Crue and Ryder.

Endless Summer *with Auckland Harbour Bridge in the background.*

Looking towards Home Bay, Rotoroa Island.

Rotoroa and Pakatoa islands

FROM REHABILITATION TO REGENERATION

Rotoroa Island is a green, peaceful island with secluded sandy beaches, scenic walks and a newly created wildlife sanctuary. Rotoroa is situated off the east coast of Waiheke and the northeast coast of Ponui Island. The views of the Hauraki Gulf from all around the 500-hectare island are spectacular.

Sanctuary and shelter

Rotoroa is a popular Hauraki Gulf destination for visitors who can enjoy walks through the bush or on scenic coastal tracks around the island. The island is relatively small so it's easy to walk around and see everything in a day. The island's four beautiful sandy beaches are perfect for picnics, relaxing, swimming or snorkelling. Ladies Bay and Mens Bay offer sheltered swimming and views of the Coromandel Peninsula. Cable Bay and Mai Mai Bay look out to Waiheke, Pakatoa, and Ponui islands and are equally pleasant swimming spots.

Access to Rotoroa is easy. A 75-minute trip by ferry from downtown Auckland or 10 minutes from Orapiu Bay on Waiheke Island. For private craft, the bays and beaches offer plenty of sheltered anchorages. Home Bay and Ladies Bay are favourites. Home Bay has a wharf (for ferries only) and offers the closest access to the facilities on the island as well as the exhibition centre and museum.

The sheltered and shady picnic area alongside the exhibition centre and museum is welcoming – it is a nice place to relax and

This Chris Booth sculpture, inspired by pohutukawa trees, was unveiled in 2011.

take in the view of Home Bay through the avenue of palms and Norfolk pine trees that escaped removal during the native plant restoration programme. There are barbecue facilities at the picnic area and at Ladies Bay, which is an ideal spot to anchor your boat, come ashore and sizzle some sausages with surrounding views to rival any beach barbecue spot! There is no food available on the island, so visitors must bring their own. There is a water fountain at the exhibition centre for filling up water bottles.

If a day doesn't sound like enough, visitors can stay overnight on Rotoroa. There are three boutique accommodation options to choose from, each with views of the island and the gulf, or there's dormitory-style accommodation in the old Superintendent's House.

Rotoroa rehab

Until recent years, Rotoroa served as an alcohol and drug rehabilitation centre run by the Salvation Army. The centre was set up after the New Zealand government passed the Habitual Drunkards Act in 1906, which allowed magistrates to declare someone a habitual drunkard (if convicted of inebriety three times within a nine-month period) and commit them to an appropriate institution as an alternative to a prison. Such an institution did not exist in 1906, so the government asked the Salvation Army if they could establish one.

The Salvation Army took on the responsibility and opened the first institution on Pakatoa Island on Christmas Eve 1907. The timing was intended to assist families by removing alcoholic family members at a time of year when excessive drink-related violence and crime was common.

In the first three months of opening, the facility housed 24 men but the numbers quickly grew too large for the Pakatoa facility. In their search for a larger site, the Salvation Army negotiated the purchase of neighbouring Rotoroa Island in 1910. The new facility was developed and opened in 1911. The men from Pakatoa were transferred to Rotoroa – the Pakatoa Island facility remained operational for women.

The methods used by the Salvation Army to treat the alcoholics were not scientific in nature. They believed that by removing 'inebriates' from their usual environment to experience sobriety they would be able to instill new values and help addicts decide to stop drinking; at the same time as reasoning with them and imploring them to see the error of their ways.

Those who were sent to the institution were treated as criminals for their addictions. Indeed, some of them had committed serious crimes and were violent as a result of their addictions, but the underlying health issues were not addressed because they hadn't been identified. Alcoholism was not understood to be a disease or illness, but was considered a choice that people consciously made to drink to excess. The Salvation Army, and society in general, believed that alcohol and drug addicts could be made to change their ways with moral guidance, religious influence, fresh air, hard work, and activities to keep them busy. Those who were able were expected to work for six hours a day. There were various opportunities to do so including a working farm and an extensive vegetable garden on the island.

Many of those committed to the facility were locked up in the jail house on arrival if they were particularly drunk and disorderly. They were effectively imprisoned until they 'dried out'. The inmates were confined to the island for various periods of time ranging from six months to two years.

Eventually, the effectiveness of the institution was questioned as many addicts were sent back to the facility repeatedly – one was reported to have returned 27 times. As many as 12,000 admissions were recorded at Pakatoa and Rotoroa centres in their 93 years of operation. Sadly, there were many repeat visits.

The well-meaning and extremely resilient staff at the facilities did their best to help the addicts, some of whom were successful with many embracing sobriety, particularly the women. More than 70 per cent of the women who spent time at Pakatoa did not return. The women's facility closed in 1942 and Rotoroa was adapted to house both men and women.

As medical advancement revealed addiction to be a disease rather than a crime, the government responded to this new information with a shift in funding (funds would be sourced from the Health Department rather than the Crime Department). Unfortunately, a response to the approach and treatment of addiction, from a health perspective, took a lot longer. It was recognised that addicts weren't getting the help they needed and the institution entered a period of great change.

In 1982, Rotoroa was amalgamated with the Auckland Bridge Programme and opened itself up to private clients. By the early 2000s, the ineffectiveness of the centre was well-known; the rising costs had become a problem, and more modern, medically orientated alcohol and drug rehabilitation centres had been established on the mainland.

In 2004, the decision was taken to relocate the treatment programme to the mainland. The facility on Rotoroa was closed down in 2005. It remains the longest running drug and alcohol treatment centre in New Zealand, and as such has significant historic and sentimental value to the staff who worked there, the families of the addicts who were treated there, and some of the addicts themselves who remember being there.

Restoration and replanting

After the closure of the Salvation Army facility, the island's future was uncertain – but not for long. Philanthropists Neal and Annette Plowman stepped in and purchased a 99-year lease on behalf of the Salvation Army. Their vision was to see a significant restoration programme carried out and to open the island up to the public as a heritage and conservation area. In 2006, they set up the Rotoroa Island Trust, and began work to restore, replant and re-envision Rotoroa. The trust is a registered New Zealand charity and proceeds from the island's landing fee go towards the upkeep of the island as well as towards the continuing work of the Salvation Army. An additional income stream for the Salvation Army, proposed for the future, would be the stuff of dreams for a number of lucky home owners – there are plans for 10 lifestyle blocks, which will be available for sale on a licence-to-occupy basis. Never mind 'California dreaming' – this is an idyllic island paradise we're talking about.

Back to the here and now: Rotoroa is a blossoming arts, heritage and conservation estate. Since caretakers of the island Phil and Ginene Salisbury were employed in 2006, over 400,000 native trees and shrubs have been planted, creating a new and pest-free environment for birds and wildlife. In 2012, a partnership with Auckland Zoo and the Department of Conservation saw the development of a wildlife sanctuary on the island. The sanctuary is going from strength to strength with takahe, saddlebacks, kiwi, pateke ducks, and skinks all taking to their new environment. There are only around 250 takahe left in the world – so there are high hopes that the Rotoroa pair will breed in the future.

Shorebirds are being encouraged to the island with the creation of fake colonies. As on other gulf islands such as Motuora, pretend nests, plastic decoy gannets, and a sound system broadcasting gannet calls (put in place in 2014) have successfully enticed a couple of Australian gannets to nest. Hopes for the future are that a full gannet colony will form. The progress to date is very encouraging.

Looking south across Rotoroa Island.

As with other Hauraki Gulf islands, the restoration of native plants and trees combined with the elimination of pests has meant that the island can act as a crèche for kiwi and other endangered birds. The birds are relocated as youngsters so that they can grow to a certain size in a safe environment before being relocated to other areas of New Zealand. The future looks extremely bright for Rotoroa as a safe haven for endangered birds. The Rotoroa Island Trust also has plans to bring and encourage other species of birds and wildlife to the island once the habitat conditions are right.

A small cemetery stands elevated on the island's north-east shoreline – those buried there include Salvation Army staff and inmates of the centre. There are expansive views across the Hauraki Gulf from the cemetery. It is a quiet and peaceful hillside spot.

At the southern end of the island there is a walk to a large sculpture by New Zealand artist Chris Booth. Inspired by the pohutukawa trees that cling to the island's shores, it is a large and impressive sculpture with a stunning backdrop of views of the Coromandel and Ponui Island. The sculpture was commissioned in memory of Jack Plowman, the father of island benefactor Neal Plowman.

Education is a valuable part of the trust's work and they offer educational field trips for schools – teaching children about the importance of conservation. The interactive learning experiences were designed in conjunction with Auckland Zoo and engage children by demonstrating conservation efforts and techniques. Their programme has a point of difference; children don't just go on a nature walk on the island – they get hands-on experience with conservation techniques, like learning to use GPS to find tracking tunnels across the island and identifying animal tracks.

The award-winning exhibition centre and museum is well worth a visit. The story of the Salvation Army's alcohol and drug rehabilitation centre is sensitively told. The museum has historic photos, artefacts, and audio and visual recordings relating to all aspects of the Salvation Army and the rehabilitation centre. The cool air-conditioned museum is a short walk from the wharf. Heritage buildings which have been restored – the chapel, jail house and tea house – are all close by. The overall historic experience is sombre in nature. The suffering and torment that the addicts endured is evident throughout the museum's narrative and a deep sense of empathy is evoked within visitors as they contemplate the very different role the island played for nearly a century.

'A bold wildlife experiment'

In 2015, Rotoroa Island received keen international media coverage in response to their unique approach to wildlife conservation. By bringing birds and wildlife to the island that wouldn't naturally have existed there, and by letting the public roam around the conservation island freely, Rotoroa was breaking all the rules of what would be considered a conventional approach to conservation. Described as 'radical' and 'a bold wildlife experiment' by the *Guardian* newspaper in the UK, and as 'an ambitious wildlife experiment' by *The Travel Show* (which came from Britain to film on the island), Rotoroa was punching way above its weight in the global conservation news category.

Once thought to be extinct, takahe now make their home on Rotoroa Island.

This statement by the Director of Auckland Zoo, Jonathan Wilcken, surprised scientists and conservationists: 'We are deliberately aiming not to recreate an ecosystem, but to create an ecosystem anew ... we don't frankly care very much whether those species existed on Rotoroa Island ... nor do we care very much if the species could sustain themselves if we weren't there to manage them.'

The radical experiment seems to have already proven its worth. The progress and success on Rotoroa, so far, speaks for itself. There are tuatara lining up at Auckland Zoo looking forward to their new island paradise. It shouldn't be long now.

Pakatoa Island

One of a group of gulf islands often described by boaties as 'out the back of Waiheke Island', Pakatoa lies 3 kilometres off the east coast of Waiheke Island and 1 kilometre north of neighbouring Rotoroa Island. Pakatoa is a small (24 hectares), privately owned island and access to the public is prohibited. But – for a mere $40 million – it could be yours. Pakatoa is currently for sale, listed on local and international private island real-estate websites as well as Trade Me, should you feel your bank account bursting at the seams.

It may not be affordable for the majority of Kiwis, but it does have some attractive coastline to admire from the water. Care should be taken when boating in the area as the island has many surrounding reefs. Boaties can anchor close by and take their chance on the good fishing that the Pakatoa waters offer. The reef at the northern end of the island is supposedly good for snapper, kingfish and scallops.

The island has an interesting history. In 1907, Pakatoa was closed to the public and a rehabilitation centre for alcohol and drug addicts, run by the Salvation Army, was established

Mens Bay, Rotoroa Island.

there. When the facility first opened it housed up to 50 men. As the demand for space increased, the men were moved to neighbouring Rotoroa Island and Pakatoa operated as a rehabilitation and treatment centre for women.

The success of the institution was questioned early in its existence by Member of Parliament Mr C.H. Poole. In June 1910, Mr Poole commented in the *New Zealand Herald* that the centre was not worth the money that was spent on it, on account of the low levels of success the facility had with 'cures' regarding inebriates. The article stated, 'Mr Poole also observed that if he had his way he would send to Pakatoa the people who were responsible for the liquor traffic.' His feelings were shared by many who were opposed to the liquor trade and the damage they believed the trade was directly responsible for.

The women's centre eventually closed in 1942 and the women who were housed there at the time were transferred to join the men at Rotoroa. Pakatoa was then used as an 'Aged Men's Retreat' until it was sold in 1949.

The island has passed through a number of owners since then. Sir Robert Kerridge, better known for his cinema and theatre empire, bought the island in 1964 and built a holiday resort complex on Pakatoa. The resort comprised numerous buildings and facilities including 62 accommodation units, a conference centre, squash courts, a gymnasium, a couple of swimming pools and a spa, and a nine-hole golf course. The resort didn't survive the market crash of the 1980s but the buildings and the golf course are still there today and are all included in the $40 million price tag.

In 1991, a German conman, Ralf Simon, moved to New Zealand and attempted to buy Pakatoa Island. His criminal past was quickly uncovered; he had been in prison in Germany for investment-related fraud and was wanted in his home country on further charges of money-market fraud. He left New Zealand in 1992 having been accused of giving false information to the immigration authority and for forging his passport. Not long after his departure he was arrested in Malaysia and returned to Germany to face 18 other fraud charges. Needless to say he was convicted and sent back to prison where he remained until 1997. His behaviour prompted the New Zealand government to change the laws regarding foreign investment. The new laws stated that foreign investors with criminal records could not own more than a 25 per cent stake in any New Zealand investment.

The current owner of Pakatoa, businessman John Ramsey, bought the island in 1994 for $4.25 million. The Ramsey family ran the hotel and resort for a while in the 1990s but eventually closed the business, leaving the place looked after by a resident caretaker. The Ramsey family no longer live on the island; it is uninhabited apart from a caretaker.

In 2000, Pakatoa Island was used as a venue for a number of 'night-till-dawn' dance parties. The *New Zealand Herald* described one particular evening, in March 2000, as 'one of the best dance parties Auckland has seen.' An elaborate set-up was put in place to host the 500 partygoers who arrived on a flotilla of vessels from Princes Wharf in Auckland. Two dance floor areas were constructed, one on the resort tennis court by the beach and one by the swimming pool. The party featured eight guest DJs and was described by the *New Zealand Herald* as having '... great music, impressive light shows, dancing, drugs, a good vibe in the air ...'. The party was halted at around 2am when a young man from Northland collapsed and sustained head injuries. He remained unconscious, despite attempts to revive him, and later died. The coroner found extremely high levels of Ecstasy in his blood. Surprisingly, the tragedy did not stop another dance party going ahead the following night.

Any future owner of Pakatoa will have to deal with a lot of run-down resort buildings, but if tarting up a *Hi-de-Hi!* scenario is their bag – it would be a dream come true. Otherwise, no doubt, some rich tycoon from offshore will probably snap it up for a rainy day, or for the day when the super-rich need a place to hide to escape civil uprising. I know I shouldn't read the British tabloid the *Daily Mail* but they reported in January 2015 that, 'As world events threaten the comfortable lifestyles of the west's super-rich they have begun buying up fabulous "bolt hole" properties in the far-away safe haven of New Zealand ... Interest in pricey land and homes in the North and South islands has soared in recent years following terrorist strikes and civil disobedience in North America, the UK and Europe.' Pakatoa Island was mentioned and marketed in the article. We have been warned.

Pakatoa Island, with Waiheke Island in the background, as seen from Rotoroa Island.

ALAN GOOD — BOATIE

Alan is an Auckland-based entrepreneur and boatie who enjoys trips with his family out to the Hauraki Gulf and beyond. He and his wife, Nicky, enjoy escaping the city and heading out onto the water to explore new places and meet new people, a frequent occurrence while they're out boating.

Alan and Nicky regularly venture out on their boat for day trips and sometimes overnight trips or long weekends. Each year they also plan an extended holiday for two or three weeks during the summer months. Often taking friends and family out for adventures, they enjoy the variety of island destinations that the gulf offers within close reach of Auckland. The appeal is not limited to just getting out on the water and enjoying their classic boat, it's also about escaping the city bustle; feeling the stresses of daily life melt away once they're out on the ocean; and visiting beautiful bays and anchoring to explore the islands, going for walks and maybe having a picnic or barbecue and relaxing. They also enjoy swimming and snorkelling, particularly in rocky bays; and the rewarding experience of exploring the underwater world.

Alan grew up around boats. Having been a competitive water skier and triathlete, he is very at home on or in the water. He used to have an aluminium runabout on Lake Taupo, which he enjoyed going out on alone or with family, sometimes fishing for supper. He became more interested in boating through talking with friends and colleagues who were keen boaties. He decided he'd like to go and have a look at some boats, do a bit of research and see what the options were, so he and his wife visited the Auckland On Water Boat Show.

Alan originally thought he was looking for a planing launch but, having been told by a friend who had one that they often followed displacement launches when the sea got rough because they travelled more smoothly through the water, he kept his mind open. (A planing launch is lighter and built for speed. It has a flat hull that enables it to skim over the water. A displacement launch pushes through the water with its round-bottomed hull shape. The design is sturdier and more economical. Conventional sailing boats, rowing boats, tugs, trawlers and ships all have displacement hulls.)

At the boat show, Nicky spotted a Logan 33 – a semi-displacement launch, which she immediately liked the look of. They checked out the Logan 33 and were enamoured by her uniqueness and classic design. She had stacks of character, old world style and charm, a comfortable interior with period features and a sleek kauri finish. They met boat builder Eric Knight and got talking – immediately they got on well. After talking to Eric and finding out everything they could, they were both so impressed they put down a deposit. 'I was given the deposit as a birthday present,' Alan explains.

From inception to finish the boat took three years to build. Master craftsman and boat builder Eric Knight and his team built the Logan 33 from moulds which he took from an original 1912 Arch Logan design. In the 1990s, Eric had been looking for a semi-displacement launch that would be well suited to cruising in areas like the Hauraki Gulf. He discovered the *Coquette* – a 33-foot semi-displacement launch from 1912 that had been designed and built by Archibald Logan, whose father Robert Logan was also a boat builder. Arch Logan was considered the very best yacht and launch designer of his time, and *Coquette* had been designed and built for his brother Robert.

After cruising around the Bay of Islands in *Coquette* and receiving many inquiries about her, Eric decided to try to clone the Logan 33. He believed there would be a niche market for replicas – and he was right. He cloned the *Coquette* successfully by taking moulds from her every last detail. His first boat was named *Dolly*, after the first sheep to have been cloned!

Back to 2004 and Alan and Nicky's clone was complete and *Lucille* was ready to launch. 'It was a big deal,' Alan explains. 'I was so nervous I couldn't eat … the nerves were worse than my wedding day!' They launched *Lucille* at Whangarei Harbour and celebrated with an excited throng of people who had been involved in the design and build process. After a short run out in the harbour, Alan and Nicky spent a long weekend on *Lucille*.

Their first proper run out on *Lucille* was spectacular. They navigated their way out of Whangarei Harbour, 'a bit nerve-wracking if you've never done that before,' and slowly cruised down the coast to gently run in the engine. Before they'd gone far they noticed a huge boil-up of fish and stopped to watch – it was a mesmerising sight. A pod of about 40 dolphins then appeared, rounding up the fish and causing quite a fish frenzy. They couldn't quite believe what happened next. An orca appeared before diving down beneath the surface. It was quite a marine party going on and it wasn't finished yet. About 100 metres away from the boat

Alan and Nicky were thrilled to see Bryde's whales – a mother and calf this time, then another whale surfaced not far from the boat. To say it was a special first voyage was an understatement. *Lucille* had been blessed, was Eric's response when Alan called him to tell him what had happened.

Their first stop was at Mansion House Bay for lunch at Kawau Island. Alan and Nicky remember pulling into the bay and passing another vessel, taking care to give way and give it plenty of room. The skipper of the boat, on observing *Lucille*, opened his door, stepped out of the cabin and doffed his cap and bowed. A very civilised and good-natured crowd, these boaties!

Alan and Nicky keep *Lucille* at the Outboard Boating Club in Auckland and are members of the Classic Yacht Association (CYA). They regularly take part in trips and events organised by the CYA – the events are mostly about having fun and socialising rather than hard-core racing. 'Although there are some serious "slow" races,' Alan assures me.

They recently took a trip up to Fairway Bay at Whangaparaoa with a group from the CYA – they cruised on up to a fair at the bay and then had drinks and dinner and were entertained. It all sounds very civilised. They've taken part in log races – which they reckon are great fun: boats nominate the speed they are going to travel at to get to the finish line in an allotted time. First in after the allotted time wins; anyone over the line before then is disqualified.

As well as spending plenty of time in the gulf, Alan and Nicky take Lucille cruising further afield. Here she can be seen moored off Cathedral Cove in the Coromandel.

The couple have taken part in displacement boat races, which Alan says are funny because they're so slow. When I met Alan he was about to head out to the annual 'Round Rangi Cake Day and Race', which is a tradition upheld by the club and harks back to the days when boating was a gentleman's domain and ladies stayed at home – except when invited to special events where they dressed up in their frocks and baked cakes to be judged and then promptly eaten at the finish line. These days it's a fun event – yachts and launches race around Motutapu and Rangitoto before finishing at Islington Bay. The crews come ashore for the fiercely contested cake competition and then relax, have a barbecue and hang out with friends for the afternoon. The boating community are a friendly bunch and it's as much about the people socialising and having a laugh and a bit of banter as it is about boating or racing. Sometimes, they dress up in smart suits, prepare food, and come ashore on a red carpet for the usual high jinks and post-race party. One particular day they did this, other visitors to the island thought they were witnessing a wedding.

The CYA have a group of members who travel to Melbourne each year where they're hosted by a local yacht club who organise a regatta over three days. The New Zealanders have a blast, and take turns to sail on the various Australian vessels, enjoying different boats, races, and meeting new people as they sail as part of their new crews. The New Zealand members compete against each other, with an aggregate points system, and the regatta culminates with one winner who returns victorious with the Trans-Tasman Trophy. The trophy is then fought for the following year when the Aussies visit New Zealand

Alan with the Ponui Island donkeys.

to be hosted for a similar few days of racing and socialising.

The Melbourne boaties love coming to New Zealand. They really enjoy sailing in the gulf as the geography and conditions are so different from those to which they are accustomed. Around Melbourne they don't have a sheltered gulf to protect them from the ocean swells or a network of islands to sail to and explore. There's a high volume of shipping that goes in and out of Melbourne so it's busy out there, which is why they really appreciate the Hauraki Gulf as a boatie's paradise.

I ask Alan if he had any favourite places in the gulf. He tells me that last summer he and his wife had a wonderful couple of weeks in the gulf around Waiheke, Ponui and Rotoroa islands. They particularly enjoyed anchoring off Waiheke and going for walks although, whilst cruising, they encountered a lot of rubbish along the shoreline at Ponui, as well as at Man o'War Bay on Waiheke. Perturbed by the scene, they came ashore and collected it. A reminder that the gulf is a precious natural environment and its sustainability requires constant consideration and protection.

They often take friends out on trips to Waiheke, where one of their favourite places is Owhanake Bay, which boasts great walks up past the Auckland University Vineyard and to Oneroa. Other Hauraki Gulf highlights have been swimming and snorkelling in the clear water around Motuketekete and visiting the wreck of the *Rewa* at Moturekareka. They also recommend snorkelling around Leigh as a good way to see marine life – especially the ever-fascinating seahorses.

Trips out in the gulf are not always predictable. Sometimes unexpected changes mean altering plans. The weather can change quickly and so routes and destination plans have to adapt. Alan recalls a day trip out to Waiheke where en route he caught a 60-pound kingfish! His wife had been asleep on board and was quickly awakened to take over control of the boat whilst Alan wrestled with the kingie and reeled it in. With it being such a splendid catch they decided to return home to deal with it. They had nine people round for dinner and still had plenty left over.

After many years of being around boats, Alan felt he knew a fair bit about boating and was surprised at just how much more there was to learn after attending a boat master's course. He studied navigational details and charts, while gaining an appreciation for the depth of knowledge required relating to safety and being responsible for your entire crew.

Another experience which Alan highly recommends taking on, if you're interested, is building a boat. Unbeknown to Alan his wife, whilst in the UK, bought him the plans for a small dinghy as a Christmas present. She brought back the plans and enrolled him into the Traditional Boat Building School to begin construction. As part of a small group of people who were restoring and building new boats, Alan began building his beloved *Maggie*. Having a tutor to assist and a mentor available when needed, along with all the tools and gear on hand, meant it was a great experience. 'I reckon every guy should have a go at doing something like that because you learn so much.'

With good DIY skills to start with, Alan built the hull at the boat-building school and then was able to do the rest from home. With a couple of versions of the dinghy building plan, Alan chose to build the clinker version (a boat-building method where hull planks overlap). A few of the all-important board measurements were incorrectly listed, which meant he had to customise the design (improving his craftsmanship even more in the process!) to make it work. Apparently a blessing in disguise, the dinghy now has 14 boards instead of 12 and is slightly larger and stronger for it. Alan made the mast, oars, sails, and the patterns for the brass work. He used 13 different types of timber – some pieces of family heirlooms were incorporated. It was a labour of love and *Maggie* is now a precious member of the family as well as acting as tender for *Lucille*. She looks great being towed behind *Lucille* as she's got the same character, style, and old-world charm. Alan often takes *Maggie* out for a sail when they're away on *Lucille* for extended trips.

In addition to building boats, Alan has also successfully built up a business which is environmentally friendly and relevant to the marine industry and environment. His paper products, Rockstock, are made from waste stone offcuts from the building industry, with very low carbon emissions. This rich mineral paper is coated and waterproof, recyclable, photodegradable, and requires significantly less energy to produce than paper made from wood fibre. It can even be written on underwater. It is ideal for maps, charts, and leaflets – anything that benefits from being hardwearing or environmentally friendly. Alan's company makes a range of products including carry bags and singlet bags – made from rich minerals (calcium carbonate) and a small amount of non-toxic resin. These products are a no-brainer for reducing our carbon footprint and taking care of our environment. With plastic pollution in the ocean at a frighteningly high level, and trees still being felled to make wood fibre paper, I was surprised and excited to hear that there are alternative products made from waste materials which are better for our air, land and water quality – all thanks to innovative ideas and good people who put them into practice.

Alan sailing Maggie, *the dinghy he built from scratch.*

Lucille.

Grapes growing in the Ponui sun.

Ponui Island

HOME TO DONKEYS AND KIWI

Ponui means 'the great extended night' in Maori. The context of Ponui is believed to relate to the Maori story of creation where Ranginui (the sky father) and Papatuanuku (the earth mother) lay in an embrace for a long period of darkness – the great extended night – before the heavens were made light as they were separated by their children.

Ponui Island is mostly farmland and vineyards. Privately owned and with access by permission of the landowners, the island lies 1.3 kilometres off the east coast of Waiheke Island and 18 kilometres from downtown Auckland. Ponui is one of the larger Hauraki Gulf islands and covers 18km². The island, also known as Chamberlins Island, has been owned and farmed by the Chamberlin family since 1853.

There are other landowners on Ponui but not many – the late John Spencer was one of them. Spencer, a multi-millionaire businessman whose family business interests own the Man O' War winery on Waiheke Island, owned a third of Ponui Island. Vineyards were established, producing a substantial amount of pinot gris grapes which are harvested and then delivered by barge to the winery on Waiheke. The wines produced from the Ponui vineyards include a Bordeaux-style blend called 'Warspite' (60 per cent cabernet franc, 30 per cent merlot and 10 per cent malbec); another named 'Exiled' is made from 100 per cent pinot gris grapes also grown on the hillside vineyards at Ponui. The island may not be accessible to explore, but we are able experience a taste of Ponui's produce.

Aside from farmland and vineyards the island boasts the Ponui donkey. These donkeys are classified as a rare breed and are New Zealand's only donkey breed. They are descended from three donkeys which were imported from Australia in the 1880s by the Chamberlin family. Ponui donkeys are mostly a light grey colour with a darker stripe down their backs; they have a very pure bloodline and docile temperament. They live as part of an established herd on the island and are considerably better off than their Australian counterparts who are mostly considered to be pests and are culled by landowners who shoot them from helicopters.

valued and kept by pioneers and farmers were set free to fend for themselves. This is how they became to be known as 'feral'. So if you're lucky enough to be on Ponui and see the donkeys, you'll be glad to know they're way better off in the Hauraki Gulf than their ancestors in Australia.

Not only are they better off, they're also doing their bit for the global donkey gene pool. The Rare Breeds Conservation Society of New Zealand recognise Ponui donkeys as valuable in playing an important role in preserving genetic diversity within the world's livestock species.

Another species to call Ponui home are the North Island brown kiwi and Coromandel kiwi. Thirteen kiwi were released on the island in the 1960s in the hope that they would survive and breed. Not only did they survive, the small population increased rapidly. In 2006, when scientists checked on the kiwi population, the island was thought to be almost full to kiwi-capacity with around 1500 birds – an incredible 6 per cent of the brown kiwi population in New Zealand at the time. Since then kiwi from Ponui have been relocated to other safe havens in the gulf in the hope that they will continue to thrive in other locations.

Ponui Island bays can be popular with boaties, particularly in the summer months and on weekends. The northern shore of the island is particularly popular in summertime with boats converging on Chamberlains Bay, also known as North Harbour. As well as a busy summer hangout spot, North Harbour is also a good overnight cove to shelter from sou'westerlies. Alternative anchorages include Bryants Bay, Te Kawau Bay and Apuapu Bay on the southern side of Kauri Point.

The term 'feral' has negative connotations and seems unfair in the case of this particular donkey breed. Donkeys were shipped in to Australia in the late nineteenth century by the British. Pioneers used them to haul goods and equipment through the outback whilst searching for minerals and land to farm. Back then, donkeys were regarded as useful imports but once motorised transport came about in the 1930s they began to be considered redundant pests and were even classed as vermin on the grounds that they were not indigenous. A bit of a cheek considering they'd been imported only a few decades earlier. The donkeys that were once

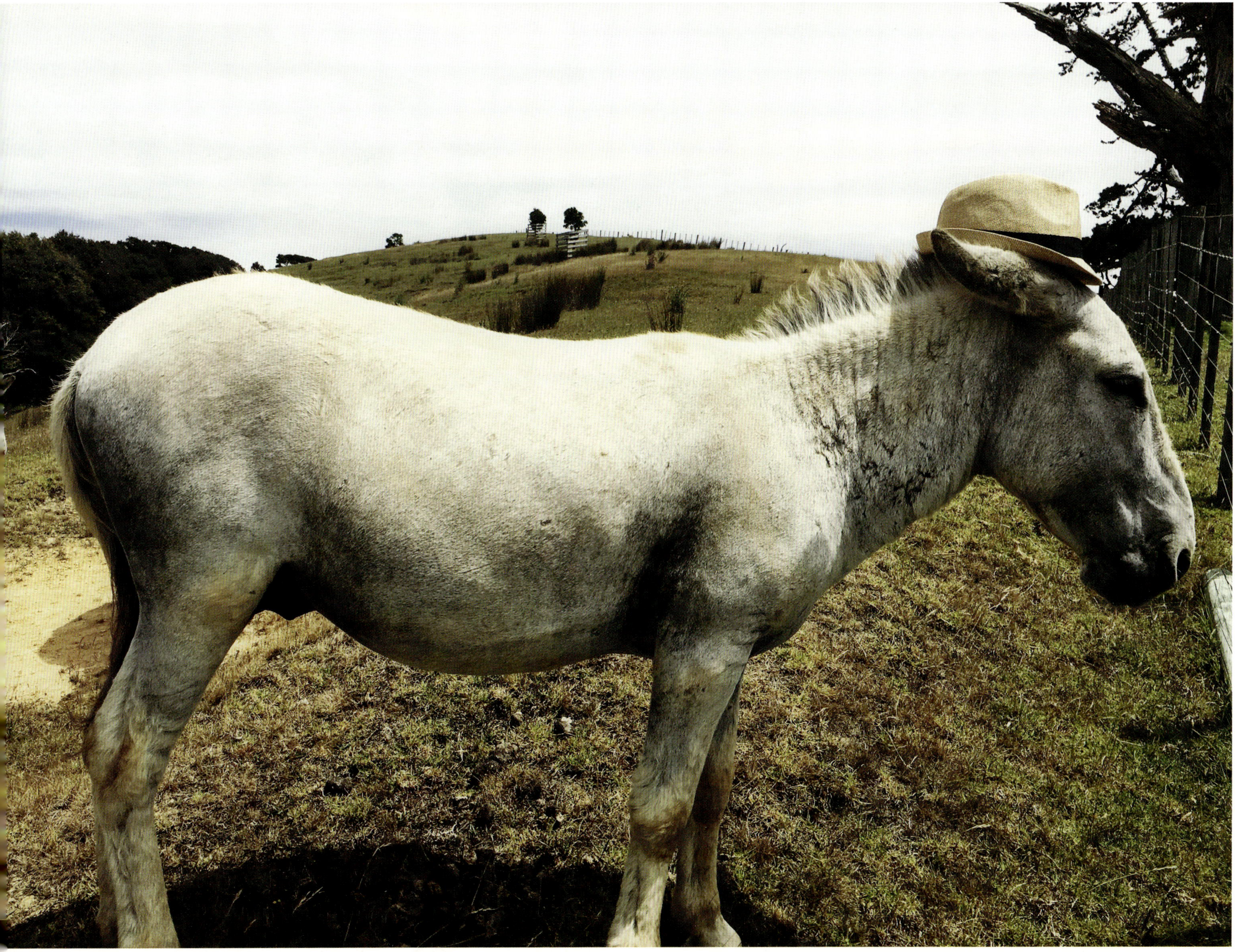

The Mansion House on Kawau Island.

Kawau Island

A COLONIAL CHARMER AND SAILING WONDERLAND

Kawau Island is one of the Hauraki Gulf's larger islands and has a unique charm and relaxed atmosphere. Visitors arriving for the first time at Mansion House Bay are often struck by the curious botanical display that greets them. An eclectic mix of exotic trees and plants from all around the world surround the grand Victorian mansion house. The scene is untypical of New Zealand and the ambience of the place feels different, yet alluring.

A world away by boat

The island is situated conveniently close to the mainland and is a favourite destination for boaties. For visitors without a boat, Kawau is a 30-minute ferry or water-taxi ride from Sandspit Wharf, near Leigh. Its mostly uninhabited 2000 hectares are approximately 8 kilometres long by 5 kilometres wide and with no public roads and very few vehicles.

Kawau is best seen from the water, which is fortunate because boating is the only way to get around (almost all of the residents are also boat owners) and a cruise along the western side of the island is a great way to discover serene bays that you'll likely want to revisit.

There are plenty of sheltered anchorages within the clear blue water of the five fingers of land that extend out from the island's western side. There are safe harbours and inlets at Vivian Bay, North Cove, Bon Accord Harbour, South Cove and Bostaquet Bay. Most of the residents on Kawau have homes close to the shoreline on the western side. The eastern coast is uninhabited and flanked by many high cliffs and steep-sided hills, making the coast inaccessible by boat for the most part.

The Kawau Island Historic Reserve, accessible via Mansion House Bay, is managed by the Department of Conservation and comprises roughly 10 per cent of the island including most of the historic buildings, attractions, sheltered coves, forest and bush walks. The remainder of the island is privately owned.

Kawau, a paradise for boat and fishing enthusiasts, is also one of the most popular gulf islands for visitors and day trips. The famous Kawau Island Boating Club, which used to be called the Kawau Island Yacht Club (and at one time had the most members of any yacht club in New Zealand) is popular with boaties who can refuel, have a bite to eat in the restaurant or relax in the Bon Accord Bar. Members and non-members also enjoy improved facilities with showers, laundry, wi-fi and even a library where books can be swapped.

The Royal New Zealand Yacht Squadron has recently installed a new playground on the lawn at Lidgard House nearby which is enjoyed by the families of many Kawau Boating Club members.

Many yachts and boats make trips to Mansion House Bay in the summer months. It is a popular spot for late afternoon and early evening sundowners whilst enjoying a view of Mansion House and its exotic gardens.

A variety of water-based activities such as fishing, paddle-boarding, kayaking, swimming and snorkelling are popular on Kawau. Kayaking around the coves is particularly nice at high tide as the water is beautiful and still. There are often rays in the shallow water so it is sometimes possible to see these whilst kayaking.

There are a variety of accommodation options available on Kawau for those with time to linger. Kawau Lodge at North Cove and The Beach House at Vivian Bay are popular luxury options with beautiful views and peaceful surroundings.

A rich history

Kawau Island is believed to have been discovered by explorer and Maori ancestor Toi Te Huatahi. He named the island after the many shags that inhabit the shorelines – Te Kawau Tu Maro, 'Kawau the island of the motionless shag'.

The island has a rich and action-packed history. There isn't much that happened in New Zealand that didn't also happen on Kawau: Maori tribal wars, land disputes and destruction, piracy, cannibalism, drunken debauchery, fishing, shooting, farming, mining, building, colonisation, royal visits, fancy picnics and eccentric Europeans getting up to all sorts.

The early seafaring Maori tribes settled on Kawau from around the time of the first migration to New Zealand. The Ngati Tai and Ngatiwai tribes built villages and enjoyed the island's warm climate, shark fishing, and strategically positioned views of the gulf. The outlook across the gulf was particularly important to the Maori tribes; being able to see approaching seafaring vessels was a huge advantage and enabled them to identify any incoming enemy canoes or craft.

The island offered little in the way of land that was good for farming, but the surrounding waters were abundant with fish (particularly muru and little spotted sharks), so much so that the first Maori settlers soon had competition for the island.

Ngati Tai and Ngatiwai were continually invaded by Kawerau iwi; many battles took place throughout the seventeenth century and as a result the island was resettled many times. The land was so sought after that mainland tribes joined forces to launch large-scale, savage attacks. Vicious fighting ensued and the attackers were successful in taking over the island and slaughtering those who fought or could not escape. The Kawau tribes had a particular reputation for cannibalism and there are many tales and much evidence of human bones on the island which substantiate this.

Following a particularly gory battle at Bostaquet Bay on the south-eastern side of the island, it was said that the invading tribes celebrated their success by feasting on some of the inhabitants they had killed. The last known battle on Kawau was in 1832. It marked a long overdue end to many years of bloodshed and destruction.

In the early 1830s Europeans sailing from Australia to New Zealand stopped by Kawau hoping to be able to trade with the locals. They found the island uninhabited but later discovered a group of Maori who claimed to have ownership of the island. A deal was agreed between Maori and Mr Wheelan, of the vessel *Sucidan*, and the island was unofficially purchased in exchange for muskets and gunpowder.

A few hours' catch off Kawau Island in 1901.

Even the mail comes by boat on Kawau Island.

Mansion House gardens and pagoda

In the 1840s, Kawau was bought by the British Loan and Investment Company whose intention was to invest in the land for farming. Livestock including cattle, sheep and donkeys (the first donkeys ever to set hoof in New Zealand) were shipped in and the agricultural development of the land began with Mansion House Bay as the main farming settlement.

A few years later the accidental discovery of manganese meant that farm workers were enticed to work in the mines. Copper was discovered a year later and the mining of manganese was abandoned for the more lucrative copper. The Kawau Mining Company brought miners and their families all the way from England and Wales, expanding the local community to around 300.

The copper mine shafts at Dispute Cove were dug well below the seabed to a depth of 60 metres and large steam-driven engines were required to pump water out. The mining companies took great risks driving mine shafts out under the seabed beyond the tidelines, and some miners were said to have drowned.

Kawau Island operated the most productive copper mine in New Zealand at the time producing over 3000 tonnes before closing in 1855 when the discovery of gold and the lure of more lucrative mining at Coromandel brought the island's copper mining to an end.

The remains of the island's copper-mining industry still exist to explore. Turquoise streaks, representing the presence of copper ore, can be seen within the rock at Copper Mine Point. The copper mine chimney and part of the engine house stand tall on the coastline as a historic landmark visible from the mainland. The chimney (20 metres high) was modelled on Cornish-style chimneys, constructed with bricks, whilst the engine house was built, surprisingly, of soft sandstone from Matakana. Driving rain and gales eroded the sandstone quite quickly and reinforcements were needed to keep the buildings from collapse.

On a hill above Schoolhouse Bay there is a small cemetery for the mining families whose village remains lie buried in the undergrowth at the foot of the hill. The remains of other mining settlement buildings are also visible at Miners Bay.

The gothic-style smelting house ruins, which would have housed big roaring furnaces, can be seen at Smelting House Bay on Bon Accord Harbour. These ruins are important historically – they represent the very first minerals to be mined in New Zealand. At the time of operation, gold and coal had not yet been discovered.

In 1862, George Grey bought Kawau Island. The hard-working industrial days were over and the era of Victorian pomp and circumstance was just beginning (see page 192).

On the water

Jetties and wharves are a 'must-have' for residents who need access to the mainland for supplies and to other bays to visit friends and neighbours. On the approach to Kawau Island you can see dinghies and kayaks lined up by the water's edge and various wooden jetties and wharves connecting quiet, tree-lined gardens with the outside world via the clear waters of the bays.

The tranquillity of Kawau is immediately evident when approaching any of the sheltered bays. The water is often glassy and a deep emerald colour which is characteristic of Kawau. There are a number of luxurious-looking homes, all with plenty of

The ruins of the copper smelting house.

surrounding land, dotted around the water's edge, almost all with vistas of the water and surrounding bush. There are also older wooden houses and baches, with more character than swank, but these are fewer in number. The large, sleek yachts and launches sit majestically, and still, in the sheltered coves – some of them large enough to live on. Many residents have boats they can cruise and sail on for months at a time.

The Kawau Island Boating Club has always been a popular Hauraki Gulf destination. Boaties who were going on longer trips would often stop at Kawau for the night or to get fuel and supplies. The club's future became uncertain in 2011 when the Royal New Zealand Yacht Squadron announced they would be closing the club, as the maintenance costs for the yacht club building and facilities were too high. Not wanting to lose their precious club, a small group of locals formed a steering committee and organised to take over the club's lease. The club reopened in December 2014 and welcomes islanders and visitors alike, hosting local events, activities, meetings and local groups. The fuel pump,

Yachts and launches congregate in Mansion House Bay before the 1939 Kawau Island regatta.

bar, cafe and store are all doing good business, which is a great relief for boaties who sail and cruise around the Hauraki Gulf and beyond. They are grateful for the prospect of a great place to stop for the night, and the anticipation of a meal and cold beer or glass of wine are still a happy reality.

The Kawau Boating Club hosts fishing club competitions and boat and yacht races throughout the summer. Races to Kawau have always been popular dates in yachting and boating calendars. Many affiliate clubs organise races over a couple of days so that crews can enjoy a series of adventures and fun out on the water as well as have time on the island. Races out to Kawau often involve skippers texting their start and finish times, rather than trying to co-ordinate all boats at a race start line. The focus is almost always on ensuring everyone has fun, with families and friends coming along for the ride, and enjoying the social gatherings that take place in the evenings. The after-race gatherings are full of friendly banter and there are often amusingly named spot-prizes and awards for the best catch of the day, and best racing story.

Auckland Anniversary Regatta is another big day for the Kawau Boating Club – they host the start-line of one of the regatta's passage races. Sandspit Yacht Club also celebrates Auckland Anniversary Day with races to Kawau – it's an action-packed and exciting day.

Kawau is also host to two of the five races that make up the

Two yachts moored off Kawau Island.

Elan Yachts Commodores Cup Series – one of the Royal New Zealand Yacht Squadron's most prestigious racing series. Race 2: The Night Race to Kawau from Westhaven, followed by Race 3: Round Kawau, are both hotly contested by a 'members only' line-up. These races are held in February as part of the Squadron weekend where many of the club members converge on Kawau to coincide with the race celebrations and annual Squadron barbecue and party. The 2016 event saw Lidgard House become party central with over 500 members, friends and families attending the evening merriment.

For those visiting the island without their own boat, the Kawau Cruises Royal Mail Run Cruise is a relaxing way to see Kawau Island and learn about the island's people and history – it is the largest mail run by water in the southern hemisphere. The spacious ferry departs Sandspit, an hour north of Auckland, daily and tours the eastern-facing bays of the island, dropping off mail to residents along the way, before finishing up at Mansion House Bay.

The experience is fun and intriguing – exploring different coves and bays and approaching a range of wharves and jetties, waiting to see who will come and collect the mail. Sometimes nobody does and the ferry staff leave the mail in watertight mail boxes at the end of the jetties. More often than not, island residents stand waiting, keen for a quick chat about the weather or joke with those on the bow.

In addition to meeting the island's land-based residents, marine mammals such as common and bottlenose dolphins and blue penguins are regularly seen from the Royal Mail Run boat. Occasionally orca are spotted; they have recently been seen in a couple of bays at Kawau, hunting rays by driving them into the shallow water – which makes them easier to catch.

On the land

Kawau has beautiful bush walks in the historic reserve linking the island's attractions. The walking tracks are mostly family-friendly and shaded from the sun by the regenerating forests. For those who enjoy peaceful walks to the tune of birdsong, this place will not disappoint. You may even see a wallaby if you're quiet enough to sneak up on one.

The network of walks within the historic reserve allow visitors to explore the remains of the copper-mining industry, as well as Mansion House and its gardens, within a day. Ladys Bay, a secluded sandy beach, is also worth a visit. The bay used to be a ladies-only swimming spot and is a superb location for a picnic and a swim.

Mansion House is a 'must-see' for those interested in a slice of New Zealand's history. The house, originally built for the manager of the copper mine, was extended by George Grey in 1862 when he bought the island. The large, sweeping balcony, which wasn't there in Grey's era, provides renewed grandeur as well as an indoor-outdoor flow that Grey's cocktail parties could have benefited from! The elevated position is an ideal spot to contemplate the views out onto the glistening turquoise water of the bay.

Mansion House, having been through multiple owners and transformations since Grey's ownership (as a hotel, guesthouse, resort and pub), has been restored and replenished with Victorian furnishings that represent Grey's residence as it would have looked during the time he lived there. Visitors can walk through the house and gardens and get a sense of what a wealthy Victorian gentleman's estate was like.

The grand rooms of Mansion House have a colonial style and contain some of Grey's paintings, statues, sculptures and books which are part of the Grey Collection owned by Auckland Museum. The objects in the house tell the story of a well-travelled man – Australian, African and Maori artefacts adorn walls and floors. Each room is crammed with character and there are portraits of Grey throughout his life as well as a large bust of him, in marble, in the drawing room.

The solid marble bust of Grey was a carved by American sculptor Pierce Connelly. The bust had been a gift from John Logan Campbell who had commissioned the work to show his admiration for Grey's work as an MP for Auckland. The bust is believed to have stood in Mansion House since Grey lived there. In subsequent years when Mansion House became a hotel, the bust was stolen on numerous occasions. Boaties had pinched it and used it as an anchor. On one occasion the bust went missing, it was found on rocks at Mission Bay and had to be brought back to Kawau by the flying boat service.

Walking through the gardens at Mansion House is similar to experiencing a mini botanical garden. An eclectic mix of hundreds of different exotic plants, shrubs and trees from all over the world

A chimney among the ruins of the old copper mine.

The historic cemetery at Schoolhouse Bay.

still thrive. Visitors can stroll around the orchards, olive groves and lily ponds that George Grey developed and wonder at nature's design of the regal-looking, vibrantly coloured peacocks that roam the gardens.

Kawau is covered with forests and bush predominantly populated with manuka and kanuka trees. The 'tea trees' were so called by Captain Cook – the leaves were used to make a kind of substitute tea. For those preferring a stronger brew, they also used twigs brewed with rimu to make beer. You have to admire the credentials of a tree that can provide both tea and beer.

The manuka and kanuka trees were considered a nuisance by early settlers who tried to clear the land for cultivation. Maori used the robust red manuka wood to make weapons, tools and waka paddles, and for building. The trees are more highly regarded these days as an important catalyst for forest regeneration. Manuka, especially, are capable of growing in both wetlands and dry soil, acting as canopy and shelter from the elements which protects smaller emerging forest trees and plants, allowing them to grow. Once new plants and trees exceed the height of the manuka, the trees sometimes die off – their work has been done.

As well as tea trees, there are also puriri groves and smaller pockets of kauri trees remaining on Kawau. As with many of the gulf islands, pohutukawa trees cling to the island's shorelines and bloom with vibrant red flowers in December. The pohutukawa tree, New Zealand's endemic Christmas tree, blushes red above the turquoise waters of the gulf island bays and signals the start of long, sunny summer days. Whether choosing to walk in the bush, relax on the beaches or head out onto the water, Kiwis are some of the luckiest people on the planet, living within reach of such a beautiful, natural playground.

Many of the island's native plant species were damaged as a result of George Grey's exotic plant and wildlife imports; judged 'sensational' at the time, no one could guess the damage they would cause in years to come. Grey believed that by adding to what was already there he was 'enhancing' the environment and 'helping nature'. Sadly, quite the opposite was true. A quick look at the numbers tells the story of botanical destruction that occurred as a result of Grey's imports. In 1877, a visiting botanist recorded 348 native plant species in close proximity to Grey's Mansion House. In 1971, there were six native species clinging on to life.

The present native bird species on Kawau are a small subset of the original inhabitants whose environment was compromised by the introduction of wallabies and possums. Some of the usual suspects can be found on Kawau: fantails, tui and kereru, as well as grey warblers, kingfishers and silver-eyes. The largest population of weka in the North Island exist on Kawau and some of them are quite bold. They are often seen at the café in Mansion House Bay hoping to save themselves a little foraging. The not-so-usual suspects originating from Australia are the brightly coloured and vocal rosellas and kookaburras. There are kiwi on the island whose call can sometimes be heard at night along with the distinctive call of the morepork. Kawau is so peaceful that birdsong can be heard everywhere throughout the day. It is one of the most endearing characteristics of the island. At any point in time you can stand still and hear nothing else but birdsong.

Today, the island's damaged ecosystems are improving, with conservation efforts successful in eradicating many, but not all, of the introduced pests. Native plant and wildlife species have been recovering and regenerating but the remaining wallabies and possums on Kawau are still slowing the revival process down considerably. Possums destroy the trees and wallabies consume the seedlings, grass, new shrubs and plants that grow beneath the forest canopies. As a result, the forest regrowth is stunted, which means there are fewer insects and less food for foraging kiwi and weka. Many locals have constructed wallaby-proof fences to preserve their gardens.

Paddling in Bon Accord Harbour.

The potential to reintroduce native birds that were lost many years ago could become a reality if the wallaby population numbers could be kept low or eradicated completely. The Department of Conservation and the Pohutukawa Trust (a charitable trust set up by Kawau Island's private landowners) would like to eradicate wallabies and possums entirely from the island but it is easier said than done. In the 1990s, great efforts were made by local residents to save the pohutukawa trees that were almost all destroyed by possums. There is much work still to do but progress is gradually being made.

The jetty in front of the Mansion House, taken from the upstairs balcony.

Of all of the exotic birds and animals introduced by Sir George Grey, peacocks and wallabies were among the few that survived.

CAMP BENTZON

Camp Bentzon is situated on 11 hectares of land in Kawau's North Cove, and was gifted to the young people of New Zealand by a sea captain from Denmark. Nicolas Bentzon emigrated to New Zealand and enjoyed fishing in the gulf and living on his small boat, which he frequently anchored in the cove.

Bentzon purchased land at North Cove but did nothing with it until he became too old and arthritic to live on his boat. At 80 years of age he had a small cottage built there. When conditions on the boat were too cold and damp he sometimes slept on the floor of his cottage, as he had no bed.

Bentzon died in 1935 and he left the land to the Education Board. He had wished to enhance the lives of young people by offering them education and recreational experiences that would benefit their growth and development.

In 1936, a small schoolroom was brought over on a barge and classes were attended by a small number of Kawau schoolchildren. Sadly, the pupil numbers decreased and the school was closed. In 1969, the Education Board worked together to organise funding, sponsorship and volunteers to help establish a youth camp. Nicolas Bentzon's gift is still alive and well today – school trips and youth groups can hire the camp or attend organised programmes run by the camp staff.

The camp facilities can accommodate around 120 people providing opportunities for groups to take part in a variety of different activities including kayaking, rowing, sailing, paddle-boarding, snorkelling, rope climbing, bush walks, bivouac building, climbing and swimming. There is also an adventure playground for children of all ages. The camp is a wonderful facility and legacy – situated in a sheltered and beautiful spot, the land has been designated for education and recreational purposes, and cannot be sold to private owners.

BEEHIVE ISLAND (TAUNGAMARO)

This tiny island south-west of Kawau could easily be mistaken for an island in the tropics. The only aspect that gives it away is the strange-looking pine trees that grow there. The white sand, consisting of crushed shells, surrounding the island reflects an attractive bright white aura which contrasts with the blue ocean and entices you towards it.

Beehive Island is a pest-free recreation reserve with the safest access by boat via the northern side. The island has a reef system and boats should take care on approach. The surrounding rocks are a great environment for snorkelling and exploring the kelp and marine life. The island can be walked around in minutes it is so small. It is home to many birds including the New Zealand dotterel, Caspian terns, variable oystercatchers and shags.

Beehive Island.

SIR GEORGE GREY — CONTROVERSIAL LEADER

If one person were to be singled out as the most influential character ever to have lived and worked in the Hauraki Gulf (and possibly New Zealand), it would likely be Sir George Grey. Grey was a momentous game-changer for New Zealand politics, people and nature. He was a soldier, explorer, governor, politician, philanthropist and one of the most colourful and controversial characters New Zealand has ever seen.

Born in Portugal in 1812, George Grey grew up and was schooled in England. As a young boy he was sent to boarding school in Surrey, which he hated. He ran away from school and was then tutored at home by theologian Richard Whately, who was known as a 'liberal idealist' and social reformer. After completing his schooling George attended the Military Academy at Sandhurst — a royal institution where British Army officers are trained. On completing his training at Sandhurst he joined the army and served six years in Ireland in the 83rd Foot Regiment.

George's father, Lieutenant Colonel George Grey, died a week before George was born. He had been killed in Spain whilst fighting with the Duke of Wellington's army against Napoleon's soldiers. George's desire to follow in his father's footsteps and join the military did not work out well for him. Despite his early success and promotion to lieutenant, he detested army life and was appalled at the way fellow officers treated the Irish people.

Whilst serving in Ireland he was horrified by the poverty he witnessed and felt the Irish people's situation to be hopeless. His sympathies with the extremely poor compelled him to try to find a way to help provide better opportunities and living conditions for them – an admirable and challenging pursuit. Grey had been interested in systematic colonisation (an approach to colonisation which involved attracting capitalists and their associated workforces to new colonies) and considered this a solution for the Irish. He felt sure their only chance of a better life would be offshore.

After taking an interest in British explorer Charles Sturt's exploration in Australia, George Grey took it upon himself to investigate lands far away that would offer a better life for people like the Irish. An idealistic goal and simplistic approach may well have been reflective of his childhood tutor Richard Whately's influence, but he managed to convince the Secretary of State for the Colonies in 1836 to finance a couple of expeditions to north of Perth, Western Australia, to explore and identify land and natural resource potential for colonisation.

Between 1837 and 1839, Grey led two expeditions financed by the government and supported by the Royal Geographical Society. The expeditions can be described as nothing short of shambolic. The combination of Grey, an inexperienced and single-minded leader, and a rookie crew was a recipe for a series of disasters. The explorations were delayed by floods (it was the rainy season but that hadn't been taken into account), and the exploration progress was repeatedly delayed as the men were split up en route whilst fleeing ambushes from hostile Aborigines. Their inexperience led to supplies and stores being lost along the way and no useful geographical findings were made in the name of identifying colonisation potential.

To add insult to injury, or perhaps the other way around, Grey was critically injured by an Aborigine who speared him during an attack. Once he recovered from his wound, the expedition continued. The explorers went on to name rivers and mountains before being picked up by the Royal Navy ship HMS *Beagle* and taken to Mauritius to recover from the ordeal.

If you think Grey's first expedition in Western Australia was an epic fail, hold that thought. The second may require you to reassess the first as mildly successful in comparison.

Grey's second expedition involved a new team of explorers and three boats. (Hold on to your hats, this is going to be quite a ride.) In February 1839, Grey and 10 men started out at Bernier Island, Western Australia, with three boats. The intention was to sail north to explore the North West Cape.

Bad weather and gales hit almost immediately and delayed their voyage; to make matters worse they found that Bernier Island had no fresh water. Forced to return to the mainland in desperation, the boats were damaged in the storms and supplies were mostly lost or ruined. The journey north was abandoned and Grey decided they would venture south to Perth. In March, despite knowledge that the planned voyage was dangerous due to there being no safe places to land for 160 kilometres, Grey led the expedition southwards and chaos reigned.

During more storms the boats were wrecked and Grey and his men were stranded with the not-so-attractive prospect of a 480-kilometre walk back to Perth and few supplies to keep them fuelled. Grey describes his desperation in his diary: 'A disinclination to move pervaded the whole, and I had much the same desire to sink into the sleep of death ... My life was not worth the magnitude of the effort that it cost me to move; but other lives depended on mine, so I rose up weak and giddy, and by degrees induced the rest to start also.'

Already exhausted by their stormy-sea battering, the expedition began their 480-kilometre walk with what must have been immense trepidation and irritation. The expedition split up with the stronger men planning to go ahead and get help for the others. Almost a month later (21 April 1839) Grey arrived in Perth and sent out a rescue party to find the others.

They were eventually found and all but one man had miraculously survived. Frederick Smyth, a 19-year-old Englishman and cousin of Florence Nightingale, had travelled to Australia specifically to join Grey's expedition. Smyth managed to trudge 336 kilometres but his body was found 125 kilometres north of Perth. Grey was distraught at the loss of his comrade but it was clear for all to see that the responsibility for the fiasco lay squarely on his shoulders.

In an embarrassing turn of events a few years later, Grey was to be reminded of his blundering Australian expeditions when, to his surprise, in a package of papers he had received from London, he discovered a letter from none other than the highly reputable naturalist Charles Darwin.

The letter had not been written to Grey, but it had been mistakenly (or otherwise) included in the package from John Stokes, a British government surveyor, who had reviewed Grey's expedition reports and returned them by post.

Stokes had recently undertaken an expedition to the same

Top and bottom: Sir George Grey's international tastes are reflected in the interiors of the study and dining room at the Mansion House.

areas of Western Australia and had been highly critical of Grey's expedition reports. He had shared his critique with his friend Charles Darwin and somehow their correspondence had ended up in Grey's parcel.

The letter was not dated but was believed to have been written by Darwin in late 1845. (Letters between the hemispheres in the 1840s could take around seven months to arrive by sea.)

Down, Bromley, Kent.
Sunday.

My dear Stokes.
I do not think the most sensitive person has the smallest right to take offence at what you have said. You could hardly have corrected, as you were bound to do, what apparently has been a gross error, with more delicacy.

Poor Grey has made a very amusing book, but what a catalogue of mishaps & mismanagements. The whole expedition was that of a set of School Boys.

Ever Yours,
C. Darwin.

George Grey received the above letter, mistakenly included in a parcel addressed to him. He would, inevitably, have been mortified but responded politely and with diplomacy:

Govt House. Auckland. New Zealand.
May 10th 1846.

My dear Sir.
The enclosed note which I believe bears your signature, having been mysteriously sent to me (by whom & for what purpose remains unexplained) I have thought it proper to mention the circumstance to you and at the same time to return the note.

I ought perhaps to apologize for having read it, but it was so folded that my own name first caught my eye—and I concluded therefore that it had been sent to me with the intention that I should peruse it.

Believe me my dear Sir.
faithfully yours.
G. Grey.

Charles Darwin, on receiving this response from Grey, relayed the mishap to Robert FitzRoy, the Governor of New Zealand at the time. An excerpt from the letter from Darwin to FitzRoy read:

I have had a disagreeable incident with Governor Grey of New Zealand;—when Stokes was writing his book he sent me a proof, asking me my opinion whether he had contradicted some statement of Grey's civilly to which I answered in the affirmative, &

ended my note in these words— "Poor Grey, what an amusing book he has written—but what a catalogue of mishaps & mismanagement; it was an expedition of a set of School Boys."—Well, some malicious scoundrel, without Stokes' knowledge, sent this note to Grey—, who returned it to me with a short, though civil note! Is not this disagreeable and the more so, as if I had expressed my whole opinion it would not have been so contemptuous; thank Heaven, I hope I shall never see him again.

Charles Darwin, with his naturalist tail between his legs, replied to George Grey begging for his forgiveness and pandering to him with compliments:

Down, Farnborough, Kent
Nov. 10 1846

My Dear Sir
I beg to thank you for the courteous tone of your communication of the 10th of May 1846, considering the circumstances under which it was written. I enclose a letter which I immediately wrote to Capt. Stokes & his answer; this will, I trust, exonerate us of intentional impertinence. Some most malicious person must have sent my note to you. I have been much mortified by perusing it, & though I am not presumptuous enough to suppose that you can care much for my opinion of your work on Australia, it is a satisfaction to me to be enabled to name to myself many individuals to whom I have expressed my strong opinion of the many high qualities shown in your work, of which the amusement it afforded, was but a small part. Your account of the aborigines I have always though thought one of the most able ever written. As we are not likely to have any further communication, permit me to add that I have a most pleasant recollection of our former acquaintance. — With much respect, I beg to remain

Yours faithfully
Ch. Darwin

The series of letters did not end there. George Grey responded kindly again, Darwin was a hero in his eyes, and the two continued to correspond over natural history research topics. Darwin quickly seized the opportunity to ask Grey to help him gather research information about some limestone caverns he was unable to get into during his visit to the Bay of Islands. Darwin also engaged Grey with questions and requests to help him study erratic boulders and pigeons! (The full collection of letters can be viewed via the Darwin Correspondence Database.)

Alarmingly, after the blundering expeditions that led to loss of life, Grey was promoted by the army to captain in June 1839. By August he was busying himself with a different role entirely, having being appointed resident magistrate at King George Sound on the southern coast of Western Australia. Grey took over the incumbent's role (Sir Richard Spencer) and promptly married his daughter, Eliza Lucy, three months later.

Grey continued his controversial career as magistrate and was

Sir George Grey and his adopted daughter, Anne Thorne George, in the drawing room of the Mansion House, circa 1870.

then ordered back to England where he published books, journals and papers on his studies of Aboriginal language and dialects, and his philosophies expounding the virtues of assimilating native populations. Grey thought that the only way to 'save' native people was to introduce them to Christianity and bring them under the control of British law. Such narrow-mindedness was characteristic of Grey and he would not listen to anyone who said otherwise. Onward he forged with his attempts to force compulsory assimilation in whatever struggling colony he could find – and he found many.

In 1841 Grey resigned from the army and was appointed Governor of South Australia. He and his wife moved back to Australia and sadly, within months of the move, their infant son of five months passed away.

Grey spent four years as Governor of South Australia and in that time created and weaseled his way in and out of a lot of contentious political situations. His attempts to tackle the struggling economy at the time were partly successful but not without a heavy-handed plan that caused many angry protests and demonstrations. Government House was invaded twice by angry demonstrators, and Grey angered the *Southern Star* newspaper to the point where they publicly threatened to burn Grey's effigy. Despite his insensitive and autocratic approach, he did have some success in assisting with rerouting the struggling economy at the time. Grey's tactics as governor led to much criticism. Frederick Weld, New Zealand's Minister of Native Affairs, described him as 'the artful dodger of governors'.

In August 1845, George Grey was appointed Governor of New Zealand. His list of challenges was extensive from day one, as he took on the responsibility of managing the unrest that was developing between the Crown, European settlers and Maori as a result of land claims.

Grey assured Maori that he would respect the terms of the Treaty of Waitangi and promised to ensure that Maori rights to land would be respected. In the eight years of Grey's governorship there was a reduction in the fighting and conflict over land. Grey continued to build relationships with Maori whilst the government purchased land, supposedly via mutual agreement, which was then sold on to European settlers for a profit. The Maori people respected Grey more so than any previous governor. Grey strived to offer them equal opportunities for prosperity and justice as this was recognised and appreciated by many.

In his efforts to improve Maori's prospects he set up schools, hospitals, and encouraged agricultural development. Despite his good intentions the budgets for these projects were often limited and, consequently, so were the overall successes.

In a letter from Florence Nightingale, Grey was thanked for his efforts to improve the health services in New Zealand. Nightingale wrote, 'God bless you! I wish I could have helped you more. You will do noble work in New Zealand.' She then went on to say 'you are nearly the only governor, except the great Sir John Lawrence, who has condescended to qualify yourself by learning the languages, the physical habits, and the ethnological peculiarities of the races you govern.' It would seem George Grey had at least one fan.

Despite the huge wave of criticism that continued to envelop Grey for refusing to follow instruction from the mother country, he was knighted in 1848. The reaction to this news was not supportive. Many New Zealanders were perplexed by the honour,

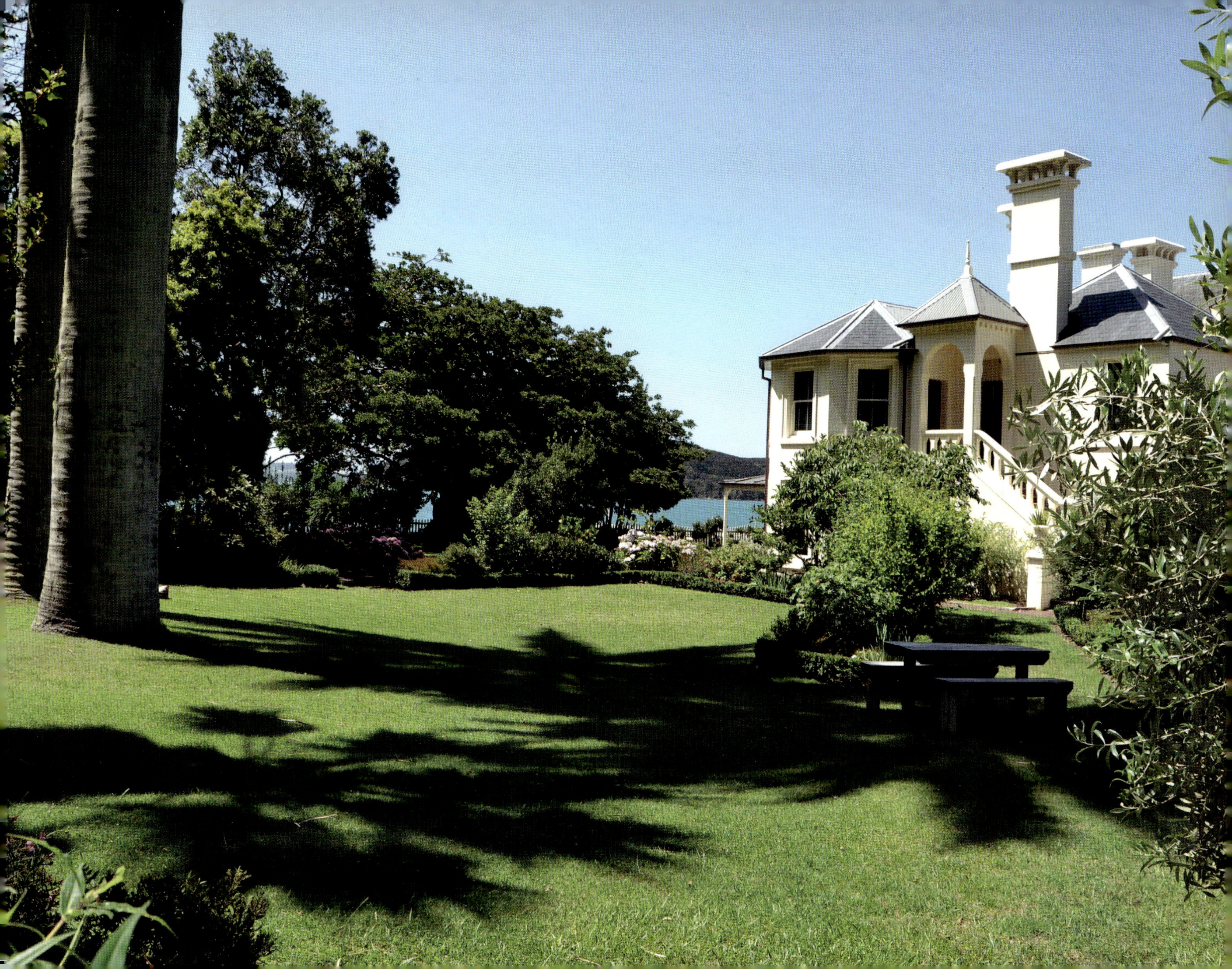

An early image of the Mansion House, taken during the 1860s.

which they vehemently believed he did not deserve. Grey continued his governorship, implementing policies that were in defiance of the British government's instructions and as a result he was recalled to London 1853.

Later in 1853, Grey was appointed to roles in South Africa as governor of the Cape Colony and high commissioner for South Africa. Grey continued to do his own thing and ignore the policies and instructions dictated to him by the British government. The story repeated itself and George Grey found himself being called back to London again to be reprimanded. By the time he arrived in London there had been a change in the British government and his supporter, the Duke of Newcastle, had been made Secretary of State for the Colonies. Grey, instead of being reprimanded, was reinstated. He returned to South Africa.

The return voyage to Cape Town was not a happy one from a personal perspective – Grey and his wife separated. Lady Grey had accused her husband of infidelity – supposedly right under her nose at their residence. Grey had seen his wife with an admiral on board the ship they were travelling on and had accused her of being unfaithful. Whatever the truth, Lady Grey was unceremoniously offloaded from the voyage at Rio de Janeiro and subsequently returned to England. George continued back to South Africa where he recommenced his work until offering to return to New Zealand in 1861 – an offer that was accepted.

Once again, appointed Governor of New Zealand, Grey returned to a very different country than he had left in 1853. War had broken out in Taranaki over land sale disputes, the European population had grown considerably, and the Maori population had decreased.

Grey had bad-mouthed the previous governor, Thomas Gore Browne, and oversold himself back into the role of governor by claiming to have 'mana' and to have built respect among some of the Maori people during his first governorship. He believed that his good relationships with the Maori people would assist him in diffusing the conflict between Maori and the colonists. This was not the case. Grey was unable to resolve the Taranaki wars that had begun in 1860, and in 1863 he approved a British army invasion of the Waikato region in revenge for the Europeans killed in the Taranaki wars. His actions led to more hard-fought land wars and loss of life, with no resolution to the land rulings and ownership issues in sight.

After a very unsuccessful period of turmoil and conflict, and after repeatedly disobeying the British government's orders to return the army regiments to Britain, George Grey was dismissed as Governor of New Zealand in 1868. He retreated to Kawau Island for a while before returning to England to seek new posts and stand for Parliament. He failed on both attempts in England and in 1870 returned to New Zealand.

Grey had bought Kawau Island in 1862 and, having been dismissed after 25 years of colonial service, he changed his focus and continued his passion for learning, specifically ethnography – the study of people and cultures. He focused on the development of his Kawau 'gentleman's estate', and his developments and experiments are yet another controversial legacy left by Grey.

Throughout the years that Grey remained in New Zealand, he took great interest in trying to acclimatise newly discovered plant and animal species – as did many Europeans around this time. A whole new world had opened up for them to discover and experiment with.

George Grey, having travelled and explored many continents, was intent on creating a global garden paradise; a private kingdom housing his extensive collection of exotic plants and trees sourced from botanists all over the world. Some of Grey's plantings included oak trees from Europe and America, silver firs from Table Mountain in South Africa, walnut and cork trees from the Mediterranean, elms from Siberia, China and Britain, and eucalyptus from Australia. Grey used his garden to study botany and as an elaborate venue for entertainment, hosting parties and gatherings for dignitaries to everyday folk – Maori and Pakeha. When not being used to impress visitors, the garden oasis served as a quiet sanctuary to retreat to, escaping the stress of work and politics.

European settlers had felt the need to 'improve' New Zealand by importing animals to farm, hunt and fish. Many species were brought to New Zealand with specific purposes: possum for fur; deer, wallabies, and rabbits for hunting; horses and bullocks for transport and farming; trout and salmon for fishing; dogs and cats for pets; and birds to hunt (mainly ducks and geese) and kill insects. Ironically, stoats and ferrets were brought for pest control purposes. They are now one of the biggest pests themselves. Hedgehogs were brought over as consumers of slugs and grubs that destroyed farmers' crops and pasture. Unfortunately, hedgehogs can also spread disease to cattle.

The Europeans did not consider the scientific and environmental consequences of introducing new species of plants and wildlife. It was not their intention to cause harm to the environment; they would likely be horrified to understand the extent of the damage their experimentations caused.

Unfortunately, by trying to create an other-worldly paradise, George Grey's 'enhancements' spoilt the native natural paradise that already existed. Between the possum and the wallaby, these critters gnawed and destroyed just about everything growing on Kawau Island at the time. The possums killed off vast areas of native forest, as they do throughout the country, and the wallabies polished off all the plants and grass at ground level.

The collection of animals George Grey imported went way beyond the range of animals brought over for farming or pets. He was quite the Noah-without-an-Ark of Kawau. His extraordinary menagerie of animals was notorious. Never before had New Zealand seen the likes of such two- and four-legged foreigners. The animals and birds he kept included monkeys, wallabies, deer, zebras, antelopes, gnu, peacocks and kookaburras.

In 1874, Grey returned to politics. He was elected Superintendent of Auckland province and Member of Parliament for Auckland City West. He was also Premier of New Zealand from 1877 to 1879. He then remained in government until 1890. As a backbencher, Grey continued to campaign for fairness and the welfare of all people.

Public disquiet concerning Grey's abilities as a politician and leader endured, but reports on the subject were often stifled. In a letter to the editor of the *Press*, in August 1879, the writer says, 'I observe in the reports of public meetings that when any speaker brings charges against his administration, someone generally requests that such matters may not be referred to.' The writer goes on to describe Grey as 'a person who ought to be got rid of. The recklessness of his words and acts, and the utter incompetency of which he has given evidence in administering the Government, prove that he is altogether unequal to the task set before him, of dealing with the Native difficulty and with the disordered state of the finances.'

Despite his propensity to fall short of achieving his goals, George Grey did manage a couple of undisputed political successes. He pushed for and delivered positive changes to the voting laws in New Zealand. In 1889, he abolished plural voting, which had allowed men who owned property in multiple electorates to vote in their respective electorates (only men were allowed to vote back then). He also helped put a stop to the multiple votes for rich men, which probably didn't go down too well with the affluent at the time, and in doing so brought New Zealand voting laws one step closer to being fair and equal.

Later in his career, Grey played a significant part in enabling equal voting rights for women. As a backbencher, he supported the women's suffrage movement in New Zealand. In 1893, New Zealand triumphed as the first self-governing democratic country in the world to allow women to vote in parliamentary elections. By comparison, the right for some women to vote in the UK was not allowed until 1918 and, even then, it wasn't until 1928 that all women were given the right to vote. The United States made an amendment to the Constitution to enable all women to vote in 1919.

George Grey returned to London in 1894 and reunited with his wife after 36 years of separation. Unsurprisingly, it was not a happy reunion and did not last. There was only one woman whom Grey had been devoted to throughout his life – he had worked tirelessly to serve the Queen of England throughout his career. The Queen recognised his efforts and honoured Grey by making him a privy councillor – an adviser to the sovereign.

In 1898, George Grey died within a few weeks of his wife, Lady Grey. Respect was bestowed upon him with a state burial at St Paul's Cathedral. At his burial a wreath and message from the Maori people was sent from four Maori members of Parliament at the time. Hone Heke (Northern Maori), Henare Kaihau (Western Maori), Tame Parata (Southern Maori) and Wi Pere (Eastern Maori) sent the following message of condolence: 'Horei Kerei, Aue! Ka nui matou aroha ki a koe – George Grey, alas! Great was our love for thee.' The Maori members of Parliament also requested that a wreath be adorned with a huia feather – a symbol of chieftainship. It was not possible to find such a rare feather from the huia bird, considered sacred by Maori, but the sentiment was not lost.

Miners Bay, Kawau Island.

HELEN AND DAVE JEFFERY — LODGE OWNERS

Originally from Christchurch, Helen and David moved to Auckland in 1985 and set up home in Half Moon Bay. They enjoyed life in the city's eastern bays and, as keen sailors, became part of the yachting scene enjoying sailing around the Auckland region and exploring the Hauraki Gulf. In later years, they set up a yachting charter business, hosting and catering for visitors on extended trips travelling around Waiheke Island, Coromandel, Great Barrier Island and the Bay of Islands.

They both had busy jobs – Dave had his own business in Avondale and Helen worked for a large city corporation for many years. They loved their home, friends and sailing opportunities, but after 17 years of Auckland traffic, getting worse by the day, they had grown weary of the commuting and the increased amount of time it was stealing from them each day.

Reading the newspaper one morning, a picture caught Helen's attention. It was an advertisement for a property on Kawau Island. Helen and Dave remember the ad vividly – the photo was a view looking across turquoise waters towards tree-lined beaches with a few properties tucked in amongst pohutukawa trees. The headline read: 'Wouldn't you like to wake up to this view every morning?' Dave responded instantly, 'That's what we should be doing, instead of sitting in traffic for two hours each night to come home – why don't we go and live somewhere like that?'

On a whim, they headed out to Kawau to view the property and liked the house very much. They fell in love with the island

and natural beauty of North Cove – but not with the price of the house. It wasn't long before they were informed of another property for sale in the same area. They eagerly went to see it. 'We were awestruck,' says Helen, 'we loved the situation and decided it would be perfect for us to run as a bed and breakfast lodge – something we'd done a bit of with our yachting charter business.'

It was love at first viewing with Kawau Lodge. The waterfront property, surrounded by trees and bush, overlooked the glassy waters of North Cove and, with its tranquillity interrupted only by birdsong, it was a dream come true. The character of the house and its unbelievable views bowled them over and they bought the place.

The couple lived on Kawau happily for 13 years, never tiring of the quieter lifestyle – still busy, but on their own terms. With only around 50 permanent residents on the island (rising to nearly 10 times this number during summer when the holiday homes are at full occupancy), the pace of life is definitely more relaxed. They've hosted visitors from all over the world and have met, and made friends with, many interesting people.

Helen laughs as she tells me the common scenario that would play out when guests first arrive. Dave often picked the guests up from Sandspit in his boat and brought them to the lodge's private jetty where they were greeted by Helen. After relaying to her their plans to head out and explore the island, they were often so taken with the tranquillity of the lodge they don't want to leave. Lulled into a state of relaxation by their pretty surroundings, they delay their plans for activity and choose to rest a while, kick back on the deck with a glass of wine and do nothing. 'It has that effect on you,' Helen smiled as she surveyed the 180-degree views of nothing but clear blue water dotted with gleaming white yachts, beaches and wooded hillsides.

Helen and Dave landscaped a beautiful garden at the lodge. When they first arrived they discovered that planting a garden was going to be more of a challenge than they had anticipated. To ensure that plants stayed in the ground for more than a day, they had to build a wallaby-proof fence. 'They would eat absolutely everything in sight,' Dave says. 'When we first arrived, at night-time you could shine a torch out into the back garden and there would be half a dozen of them chomping away on anything and everything ... and then you could shine a torch out the front and there would be half a dozen more.' There are fewer wallabies these days – residents would like to see them eliminated from the island and there are plans to get rid of them permanently but, as with any pest eradication project, it takes a lot of time and effort.

The residents on Kawau are a tight-knit community, and they mostly all know each other. Dave and Helen found themselves at its heart, understanding that island living relies on people working together and helping each other where possible, and as such they both contributed greatly to the island's community.

As well as being the lady of the house and reputable chef at the lodge, Helen became secretary for the Kawau Island Residents and Ratepayers Association and a member of the Matakana Coast Tourism Board, which incorporates the island. She also co-founded and organises Music in the Gardens – a popular annual concert at Mansion House, which attracts hundreds of visitors to the island.

Helen and her friend Lin conceived of Music in the Gardens in 2013; they felt it would be a great opportunity to celebrate the success of the Mansion House restoration project which had recently been completed. Having seen the success of a series of jazz concerts held at South Cove, organised by the Kawau Emergency Response Trust (KERT) to raise money for the volunteer firefighters, emergency response and civil defence teams on Kawau, Helen and Lin wanted to organise something similar to get the locals together, raise funds for KERT and to create an event which would attract visitors to the island.

Organising the staging, sound equipment and logistics, as well as finding a band, was no small undertaking. But they did a magnificent job, particularly on an island with only boat access. Music in the Gardens was a great success and the number of concert-goers has doubled over the three years it has been taking place. This year around 800 people enjoyed a perfect summer's day, sipping wine and picnicking in the shade of some of George Grey's exotic trees, with great music and a party atmosphere. 'We've had magnificent weather for all three years,' Helen says. Music in the Gardens takes place annually in February and is popular with locals and visitors who crowd the bays with their boats in great numbers.

The event has raised money not only for KERT but for the Kawau Coastguard, the Kawau Emergency Response Team, Camp Bentzon and the Kawau Boating Club, which badly needed a new generator – and got one thanks to Helen and Lin's venture.

The Kawau Boating Club, originally the Kawau Island Yacht Club, has always been a treasured boating, yachting and social hub for Kawau Islanders and was almost lost in 2013 when the Royal New Zealand Yacht Squadron shut it down. As a yacht owner and resident, Dave was determined to ensure the club did not close permanently and, together with a small group of like-minded people, they formed a committee to save the club. They took over the club's lease and arranged for essential maintenance work to be done – the building badly needed rewiring amongst other work – to ensure it was safe. There were issues around responsibility and ownership of the club, but the club members formed an alliance with the Yacht Squadron and worked together to keep it operational. They renamed it the Kawau Boating Club, to include boaties and fisherman and not just yachties, 'and it's become a destination again,' Dave says. 'It was a big deal – and it's been saved ... without the club there wouldn't have been any petrol from Gulf Harbour to Marsden Cove'.

The club has a history of having more members than the region's other clubs put together, because it is such a hub for stopping off overnight on the way to Great Barrier or the Bay of Islands. It is also a historic venue for the annual Auckland Anniversary Regatta races and the Yacht Squadron's own series of races – the Commodore's Cup. The club is happily very much back on the map.

Originally built by local volunteers with materials supplied by the Lidgard family, the club is now a thriving community hub, and the café and bar are open with new owners doing a wonderful job of catering to a variety of offerings, including coffee, freshly baked goodies, lunches and dinner. There is a small store selling basic supplies, a new playground for the kids, and club facilities that are improving all the time.

Dave played a number of roles on the island; he was a wearer of many hats – mostly voluntary. One of them is a firefighting hat. Dave was part of a small volunteer firefighting team with around seven others. The risk of fire on Kawau is an extremely serious one. The island is so dry that if a fire were to break out, it would be extremely difficult to extinguish. Covered with manuka and

Boats in North Cove.

kanuka – dry and oily trees which burn extremely well – the fire would burn extremely hot and spread very fast. Dave explained that the dry conditions cause similar threats and issues to those in the high-risk areas of Australia – trees containing natural oils burn with such intense heat that fire service helicopters dropping monsoon buckets of water from above are not effective, as the water turns to steam before it reaches the ground.

There is a fire ban on Kawau during the summer months, but residents would like to see it extended to all year round. There have been several fires on the island but luckily the team were able to put them out. The firefighters train for such emergencies, and Dave explains it's extremely physical work. The team have a pump which is capable of pumping sea water up through hoses, right to the top of the hills surrounding the bays and coves if necessary. 'The firefighting team run the hoses up the hillsides on foot. It is heavy work requiring a high level of fitness,' Dave explains. He said the last time he tried to run up a hill with the heavy gear, carrying a big backpack and hose, he almost collapsed. The team also have a canvas dam which they can assemble and pump water into halfway up the hill, then a second pump is used to push the water up to the top of the hill. Dave explains, 'If a serious fire broke we would probably have to evacuate the island rather than firefight.'

Dave was also a volunteer member of the Emergency Response Team who deal with medical emergencies. The team has been trained by paramedics and the Auckland Helicopter Trust. They get plenty of call-outs – fingers squashed in winches and badly gashed limbs all require treatment only available on the mainland. The Emergency Response Team do everything they can to ensure the injured or sick patient gets the best medical assistance possible before arranging for them to be taken to Sandspit by boat, and then on to the medical centre at Warkworth. Dave sometimes took patients to the mainland in his boat. He ran a water-taxi service (another hat) and has taken many trips of the medical emergency kind over the years.

Dave was also the harbourmaster – he's a busy chap! This involved liaising with the harbourmaster at Sandspit, keeping an eye on moorings, and checking any issues such as faulty lights on buoys. As if all that wasn't enough to keep him out of trouble, Dave was also a real estate agent on Kawau. The property market is relatively quiet on the island and, with many of the properties being holiday homes, there isn't the same urgency for buyers. The property prices peaked in 2005 when people were buying houses on Kawau without even having viewed them. The prices are gradually recovering, but like many other places (Coromandel being one) they are increasing again slowly.

'It forces you to relax – being here,' Helen says. The people who live on Kawau 'have an adventurous spirit ... they want something a little bit different,' she says. They certainly have something different – they have a peaceful, island paradise.

In late 2016, Dave and Helen sold Kawau Lodge and spent the summer months living aboard their 40-foot catamaran, *Fait Accompli*. The couple have since bought a house in Mapua, near Nelson, where they plan to spend the winter months. This summer they plan to go cruising to Great Barrier Island, the Mercury islands and wherever the wind takes them.

Dave walking back to Kawau Lodge.

Motuora Island and campground.

Motuora Island

A LITTLE CAMPING BEAUTY

Motuora may be a little island but it definitely punches above its weight when it comes to stunning campsite locations. Situated close to the mainland, 6 kilometres east of Mahurangi Harbour, the 80 hectares of Motuora are home to pretty beaches and short walks, suitable for families as they are not too long (up to two hours). One of the walking tracks meanders around Still Bay, which is a great spot for picnics and viewing marine life. The clear waters around Motuora are great for swimming, snorkelling, diving, and fishing, as well as exploring the island's coastline by kayak.

The island is a recreation reserve as well as a sanctuary for endangered birds and wildlife and is managed jointly by the Department of Conservation (DOC) and the Motuora Restoration Society. There is a delicate balance being maintained between keeping the island pest-free and welcoming visitors. The biosecurity guidelines are key to keeping sanctuaries safe and visitors should always check before they arrive on the island that they are complying with the pest-free regulations.

One of New Zealand's top five small islands for camping, according to the *New Zealand Herald*, Motuora's campsite is sweetly positioned right next to the beautiful white sandy beach at Home Bay. It is a great spot for families with children to camp during summer months. There is also a bach, which sits back from the beach and sleeps five people in bunks. Both the campsite and bach can be booked via the DOC website.

For most of the last century the land on Motuora Island, like many of the Hauraki Gulf islands, was cleared of native trees and bush and farmed intensively. As a result, the island had become bare and dry. The birds and wildlife thriving on Motuora today could never have lived on the island had it not been for the huge amount of work to restore native bush by the Motuora Restoration Society and their volunteers. Over the last 16 years, restoration work has replenished the island's natural ecosystem allowing native birds and wildlife to nest and breed safely. The restoration work is almost complete. When replanting began, the volunteers were managing to produce and plant 30,000 native seedlings each year from the island's own nursery. Up to 5000 trees were also planted yearly and the change in the island's ecosystem and appearance has been dramatic – in a really positive way.

Thanks to the success of the restoration of Motuora's ecosystem, the island is a sanctuary for flora and fauna as well as being home to a 'kiwi crèche' – part of a programme called Operation Nest Egg that raises endangered North Island brown kiwi chicks and provides sanctuary for them. The programme has been very successful in increasing a healthy and growing population of kiwi as well as other endangered bird species on Motuora. The island offers excellent bird-watching opportunities and those visiting during the evening or staying overnight may be lucky enough to hear or see kiwi.

Motuora has been a safe environment for the endangered birds since pest eradication programmes were successful in ridding the island of mammalian predators (feral cats, rats, ferrets, stoats and weasels). In recent years, other birds such as whiteheads, Pycroft's petrels and diving petrels were reintroduced. It is also possible to see the New Zealand dotterel and grey-faced petrel. Seabird numbers on the island are increasing.

In recent years a clever plan to attract gannets to the island was trialled – and it worked. A range of fibreglass gannet decoys were installed to make it look like a colony, and a solar-powered sound system was installed to emit a multitude of gannet calls. There were pretend nests made of seaweed and a few splats of white paint were dotted around to add the final touches of authenticity. The real gannets bought it. To give them credit it took them two-and-a-half years to be sure – but they have nested on the island since 2012, and in 2013 the first gannet chick was born on Motuora.

A similar tactic has recently been used to attract shearwaters to the island. Artificial burrows were created and the sound system put in play again with shearwater calls. Two pairs of fluttering shearwaters have taken up residence and the first fluttering shearwater chick was born at the end of 2015. A proud moment for the volunteers and all those who have contributed to this success story that provides much hope for the future.

A good way to see birds and wildlife on the island is to head out on the walking tracks. The Northern Loop Track (two hours return) starts at Home Bay and leads through paddocks up to the northern end of the island where there are great views of the Hauraki Gulf. The track then turns back and leads across cliff tops before returning to Home Bay.

There are no scheduled ferries to Motuora Island but it is a short journey by water-taxi or charter (from Sandspit Wharf near Warkworth), or private craft; or it is possible to kayak to Motuora. Kayaking takes approximately one-and-a-half hours from Mahurangi Harbour and is not recommended for complete beginners, as the open water can get choppy in the wind. There are kayaking operators who offer kayak rental and guided tours. The recommended place to land kayaks is at Home Bay beach. For those visiting by private craft, there are safe anchorages at Home Bay on the western side of the island and Still Bay on the eastern side, depending on the prevailing wind.

Looking towards Moturekareka and Motuketekete islands from the beach on Motuora Island.

Moturekareka Island. Remains of commercial fishermen's house and operations in the foreground.

Moturekareka Island

WHERE ONE OF BRITAIN'S LARGEST LADIES OF THE SEA TOPPLED OVER, NEVER TO GET UP AGAIN

Boaties and yachties who know the gulf will have visited Moturekareka, a small island off the south-east coast of Kawau. A pretty tree-lined bay on the north-western side of the island is sheltered and one of the most popular anchorages in the area. Pine trees line the hills and pohutukawa surround the rocky bay which has deep water close to the shore making this a unique spot. Close to the shore lies the wreck of the grand old lady *Rewa*, creating a lagoon behind her that makes it possible for small craft to anchor here.

The *Rewa* was a very tall ship; the largest British-owned sailing ship in New Zealand waters at the time. Originally named *Alice A Leigh* after the mayoress who christened her, she was later sold to a New Zealand businessman and renamed *Rewa*. She was a magnificent sailing ship – 25 metres long, 3000 tonnes of steel barque with four masts (54 metres high) that carried 31 sails. Built in Cumbria in the United Kingdom, she was launched in 1889 and sailed all around the world transporting cargo before completing her final voyage to Auckland in 1922. Sadly, her trading days were over – she was not able to compete with the new and faster steamships. She sat idle, moored at Chelsea Wharf near Northcote, for eight years until a man named Charlie Hansen bought her in 1931. She was towed out to the Hauraki Gulf, to the north-western bay of Moturekareka Island, where attempts to rest her across the bay further out to sea proved to be unsuccessful. She became stuck in the sand close to shore and would not budge. Whilst trying to reposition the *Rewa*, Mr Bennett, a caretaker who had been asleep on board, was rudely awakened and got quite a fright when the ship suddenly listed sharply from an upright position to 45 degrees. The *New Zealand Herald* reported the story on 11 July 1930, including an entertaining photo of the caretaker and two others standing precariously on the slanting deck after the ship keeled over.

After the *Rewa* toppled over there was no chance of moving her. She remained on her side, semi-submerged, soon to be partially dismantled and left to rust – a very sad end to an illustrious career.

The rusting remains of the Rewa *show no sign of the ship's shady past.*

There are differing stories about what Charlie Hansen intended to do with the *Rewa*. One story claims that he intended to use her as an offshore casino; a means to sidestepping the licensing and gambling laws that were strictly enforced on the mainland. It would have been a bit of a mission for potential gamblers to get out to the *Rewa*, only to place bets, lose a few chips and have to come back again. The official line, as reported by the *New Zealand Herald* in May 1932, was that the *Rewa* had been deliberately sunk and 'stranded two years ago to serve as a breakwater at Moturekareka'. Whether Charlie Hansen had intended the *Rewa* to act as a breakwater or a place to gamble, she remains half submerged and a very much reduced version of herself, but still a remarkable wreck to explore.

Moturekareka, meaning pleasant island, is open to the public and run by the Department of Conservation. Sightseers, private boats and yachts, snorkellers, divers, sea-kayakers and jet-skiers can explore the huge wreck and marvel at the impressive remains of a once regal ship.

A relatively shallow wreck to dive, the *Rewa* is suitable as a training site for scuba divers or freedivers. It is possible to get into her hull and on clear days the visibility is excellent and also good for photographers.

Moturekareka and neighbouring Motutara and Kohatutara islands are all joined and at low tide it is possible to see the rocky isthmus than connects them. There are endangered birds taking advantage of the safe seclusion this small island group provides – grey-faced petrels nest on Moturekareka, while red-billed gulls and white-fronted terns nest on Kohatutara.

Motuketekete is a privately owned island and access to the public is not allowed. Like its close neighbours, it is a pretty island – and could easily be mistaken for an island in the South Pacific. With clear, deep water close to shore there are good anchorages in coves on the western side. The island was once home to a copper smelting house before Kawau established its own.

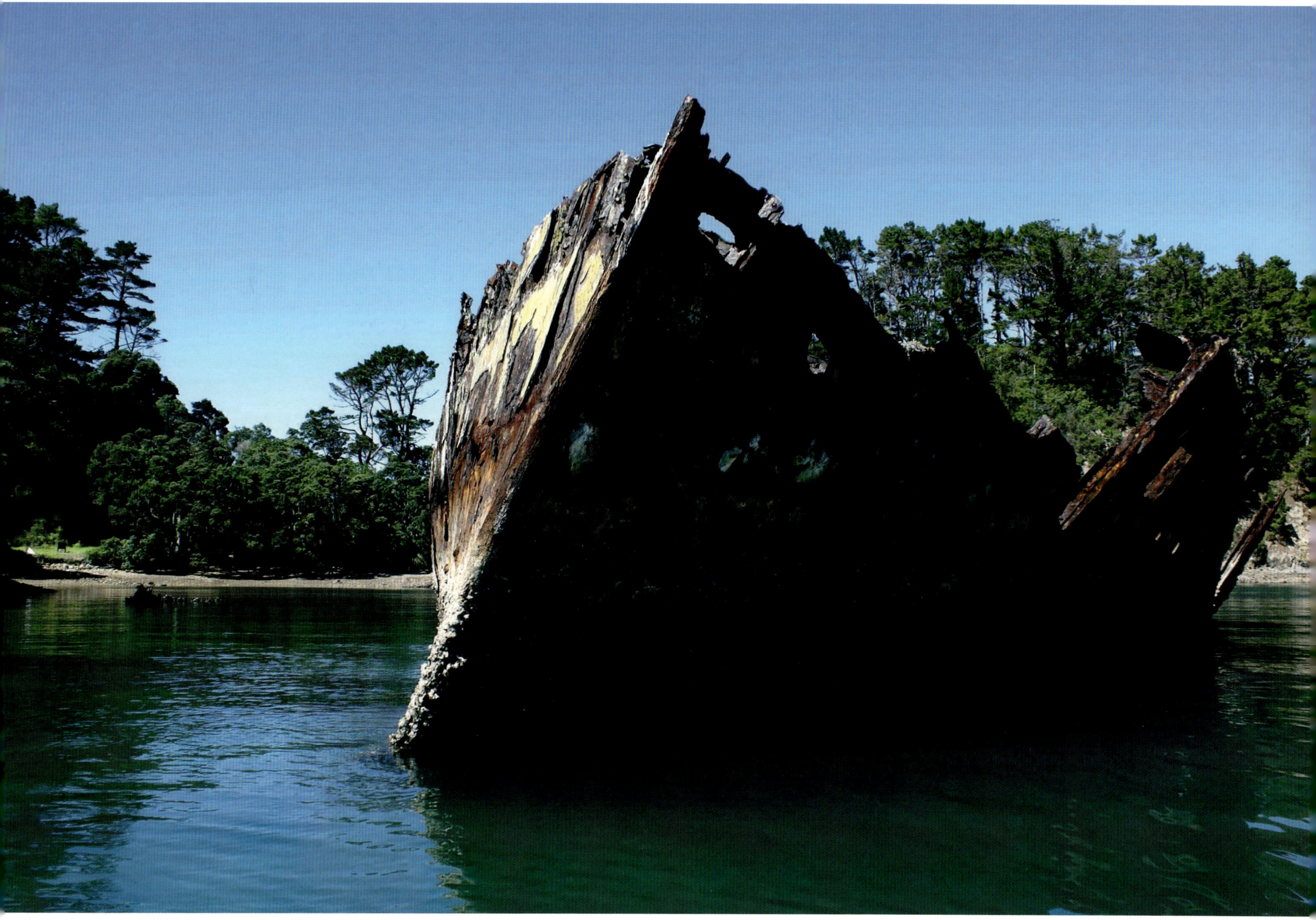

KAREN ELLIOTT AND DAN McGOWAN — COASTGUARDS

Dan and Karen welcoming visitors onto a Coastguard boat.

It is well known that New Zealand's Coastguard endeavours to save lives at sea, taking on search and rescue operations, and assisting people and vessels experiencing difficulties – but people are less aware that the Coastguard units are staffed entirely by volunteers. There are over 2000 Coastguard volunteers in New Zealand – all of them willing to take part in training, commit to being available and 'on call' day and night, to work as part of a larger team, and to serve their local boating community out on the water.

Coastguard Hibiscus President Dan McGowan and Crew Chief Karen Elliott shared some of their knowledge and experience relating to their respective roles and talked about the challenges and rewards that come with their work.

The New Zealand Coastguard is divided into a number of geographical regions – Coastguard Hibiscus is part of the northern region. Within the northern region there are 24 Coastguard units, nine of which serve the Hauraki Gulf area. These units are based at Great Barrier, Kawau, North Shore, Auckland, Howick, Maraetai, Waiheke, Thames and Whangaparaoa. There is also an air patrol team based at Ardmore and a communications team at the marine rescue centre in Auckland.

The Coastguard Hibiscus unit operates mostly in their local area – on the southern side of the Whangaparaoa peninsula, but they can be asked to travel more widely within the gulf if required. The unit has two vessels: *Hibiscus Rescue 1* – 9.5-metre Naiad stationed in the water at Gulf Harbour and *Hibiscus Rescue 2* –

a 7.7-metre Sealegs vessel (an amphibious craft which has wheels enabling transition straight from land into the water) based at Stanmore Bay.

Within the unit there are 50 volunteer crew who operate on the vessels at sea (known as wet crew). The crew train regularly and operate out at sea as and when required. There are also volunteers known as shore crew – these are often partners, husbands and wives of the wet crew, who manage the planning and organising of many social gatherings and fundraising events. A strong community spirit is central to the Coastguard Hibiscus team and their success.

The unit is run by a committee with officers responsible for the core pillars of work: training, safety, maintenance and volunteer recruitment. Dan, as president, is the public face of the unit. As part of his role he facilitates and ensures the unit officers are achieving their objectives. He also manages all relationships with the Coastguard's many different stakeholders, authorities, and volunteers. He is one of the operational crew, a trained rescue diver, father, self-employed businessman, and an experienced manager of people, which enables him to maintain the high levels of professionalism within the unit. Dan has been part of the unit for three years and president for one-and-a-half years. He enjoys helping people and giving back to the community. His role requires a continual balancing act between family, work, and other commitments. Some weeks he'll work up to 30 hours for the Coastguard, which means some late nights catching up on his own business work.

Many of the volunteers who make up the unit have busy lives. There are mothers and fathers who work and have small children, self-employed people, retirees, and others in part-time work. They all have many other roles that are important in their lives – but giving back to the community, saving lives, and helping people, is important to them. They don't necessarily have 'spare time', but they make time to volunteer and that often involves making sacrifices and compromises in other aspects of their lives. The volunteers put a lot in and get a great deal of satisfaction and a huge sense of achievement from their work – being able to help people in difficulty, and ultimately save lives, is enormously rewarding.

Karen gets a real sense of achievement from her role. 'I get such a buzz from seeing people achieve things they didn't think they could do.' She enjoys being part of an effective team. When crews return from training exercises or rescue operations they always have a team debrief, and this is often when Karen sees people realise and take stock of their growth, courage, skills, teamwork and achievements.

Dan and Karen agree that 'the rewards and challenges are, very much, a two-way street'. Managing volunteers adds a challenging dimension to their work – they understand and respect that they can only ask people to do so much. Each volunteer brings different strengths and abilities to the mix and has different limits of what he or she is capable of. Dan and Karen have to be good at being able to read people, understand their capabilities, be empathetic, and motivate them as individuals and as a team without pushing people too hard or putting them off. 'They're volunteers, after all, so it's a delicate balancing act and takes a lot of time and co-ordination,' Dan explains.

Karen has volunteered for the Coastguard for 11 years – including five years as skipper. As Crew Chief she works closely with Dan and the training officer to oversee and manage operations. She also looks after the crew, the vessels, and manages a lot of paperwork. Karen is responsible for ensuring all records and logs are complete and up to date for all of their core functions: health and safety, training, maintenance, and operations. There are constantly changing health and safety regulations with which they must comply and the unit is surveyed on a regular basis. Karen admits 'there is a lot to keep on top of'.

Karen is also a skipper, a role which involves total responsibility for the safety and operations of her crew. It is a lot to take on – being responsible for the safety of a crew of volunteers who are working together, often in difficult conditions, to ensure the safety of others. Karen is also involved with training days and training exercises with crews. She has logged 170 jobs and over 2000 hours on the water, and goodness knows how many hours in meetings, training modules, and completing documentation on land!

The kinds of incidents the wet crews attend are varied. They're often called out to assist boaties with mechanical issues, run-down batteries, anchors that have got stuck, and boats that are taking on water. Less frequently the crews attend more serious incidents such as fires on board vessels, injured or sick people, sinking vessels, and lost or missing people and vessels as part of larger search and rescue operations.

Incidents are controlled and co-ordinated from a central Coastguard base in Auckland. Each incident is managed by a central incident management team which, depending on the emergency, may involve multiple services and agencies such as Police, the Fire Service, St John Ambulance, Coastguard Air Patrol, and the Westpac rescue helicopter.

Coastguard Hibiscus crews can be called up to attend incidents in their area at any time of day or night and they are required to come together as a highly trained team to respond to any emergency.

Recently, one of the Hibiscus crews was called out to search for a boatie who was around 30 hours overdue returning from a fishing trip. The elderly man's family had reported that he had not returned home that evening but had no other information regarding his intended route, destination or when he planned to return. Air Patrol and two Coastguard units (Kawau and Auckland) had been searching for him that evening and throughout the night in rough weather conditions. The Hibiscus crew had been called out at first light the following morning to conduct a shoreline search north from Stanmore Bay. After an extensive search Air Patrol spotted a boat that they thought might belong to the missing man. They passed on the co-ordinates to the Coastguard Hibiscus crew who made their way to the boat at about 11am. They found the man flustered, but in remarkably good shape considering the conditions he'd been out in all night. The man had gone fishing, not told anyone where he was going or when he'd be back, had forgotten to take his mobile phone, and had no VHF radio on board. When he experienced difficulties with his boat, he was completely helpless with no means of communication. The problem had been his anchor – it had become stuck, and he had not been able to start the boat's motor.

The Coastguard crew helped the man, who was suffering from mild hypothermia, and towed his boat back to shore. The skipper then drove him home to ensure that he got back safely – a kind gesture that was above and beyond the call of duty. The rescued man was extremely grateful and embarrassed by the position he had found himself in. He had learned, the hard way, the importance of having adequate means of communication, ensuring that he let someone know where he was going, and when he expected to be back.

The Coastguard safety guidelines recommend boaties have at least two means of communication – a VHF radio and a mobile phone – ideally kept in a waterproof or ziplock bag. It is also recommended that boaties tell someone where they are going and when they intend to return. Additionally, boaties should have lifejackets for everyone on board and should wear them at all times.

Since the incident, the skipper has kept in touch with the man who has subsequently become a member of the Coastguard, bought a VHF radio, and attended a VHF radio course to ensure he knows how to use it correctly to log trip reports for future outings. He has also bought flares for the boat as a backup safety measure should his other means of communication fail. He also made a donation to Coastguard Hibiscus.

By becoming a member of the Coastguard (currently $115 per year for individual membership) the man also ensured that in any future emergencies he would be able to get unlimited Coastguard assistance for a year. With his VHF radio he could now log trip reports with the Coastguard every time he went out in

Coastguard Hibiscus out on the water.

his boat. Trip reports have multiple benefits – they allow boaties to log where they are going and when they intend to return with the Coastguard. Boaties then report back in when they return from their trip, closing the trip report. The Coastguard retains all member trip reports on file so if someone is reported as overdue, they can look at their previous history and know where to start searching.

Dan was keen to clear up any misunderstanding regarding the Coastguard's objectives. The Coastguard is there to help people who need it. They are not there to place blame, issue tickets or penalties. They are not part of Police, Customs, or Fisheries but they are a charitable organisation whose mission is to save lives at sea. Thanks to their more than 2000 volunteers, Coastguard New Zealand does exactly that. In 2015, the Coastguard brought over 7000 people home safely after an emergency on the water. 'People learn from their mistakes; it's not for us to judge them, we just want to help them and make sure they are safe,' says Dan.

Another important role the Coastguard fulfils when they're out on the water helping people, or when they speak to schools or community groups about what they do, is education. There are plenty of boaties who don't know enough about safety or the rules out on the water. 'It's a shame that anyone can go to a boat shop, buy a boat and launch it,' Karen says. It seems quite an anomaly that anyone can buy a boat without any understanding of how to operate, navigate, or maintain it safely, especially when you consider that the weather conditions in the region are so changeable. Dan and Karen say the best thing people can do is educate themselves – take a day skipper course run by Coastguard Boating Education.

When they're not skippering or crewing rescue boats, Dan and Karen both enjoy spending time in the gulf with their families. 'I grew up on the Hauraki Gulf,' Dan says. He lived on the North Shore as a child and learned to sail at Torbay Boating Club. He enjoyed getting out on the water at every opportunity. He remembers sailing to Waiheke with a friend who had family on the island and enjoying jumping off rocks and having a great time there. He also has great memories of a formative experience as part of a 10-day voyage on the *Spirit of New Zealand* (a three-masted, tall sailing ship run by the Spirit of Adventure Trust – providing the opportunity for young New Zealanders to learn leadership, independence, and community skills). At 18 years of age he, and other young crew, sailed to Kawau, then on to Great Barrier Island for a few days before returning via Waiheke Island. Dan remembers the adventure fondly and values the skills and knowledge he gained on that voyage. 'I have carried them with me over the twenty-three years since then,' he says.

Dan and his wife take their two children out to enjoy the gulf whenever they can. They recently went snorkelling just off Little Barrier Island and were looking forward to an upcoming trip to go snorkelling at Goat Island. Dan also enjoys spearfishing and freediving.

Karen loves fishing and used to have her own boat, but sold it a year ago when she realised she wasn't using it enough as she was out on the rescue boat so often! She loves getting her 'water fix' and if she doesn't get out on the water regularly she really misses it. A number of years ago she recalled a wonderful visit to Motuora Island where she camped at the DOC campsite, which is right on the water and close to a historic Maori pa site. Recently, she visited Motuora during the evening and was lucky enough to see eight kiwi.

When she owned her own boat Karen especially enjoyed taking overseas visitors to gulf islands like Tiritiri Matangi and Motuketekete; the visitors were usually blown away by the natural beauty and character of each of the gulf islands.

I ask them both where they would go in the gulf if they had a few days off and could go anywhere. 'Barrier,' they agree, 'love it there ... or Kawau ... anywhere, actually – it's all beautiful, Motutapu, Rakino ... Auckland is blessed to have the Hauraki Gulf on its doorstep,' says Dan.

COASTGUARD MEMBERSHIP

There are different Coastguard membership options – the most popular option is individual membership which covers a person rather than a vessel. The membership allows cover for you, your partner and any dependants up to the age of 18 on any vessel so wherever you are out on the water you are covered. (Individual membership is currently $115 per year.)

BOATING SAFETY CODE – KNOW BEFORE YOU GO

Before you go boating on our seas, lakes and rivers, get familiar with New Zealand's Boating Safety Code. Five simple rules will help you to stay safe, no matter what kind of boat you use.

1. *Lifejackets*

   Take them – wear them. Boats, especially ones under 6 metres in length, can sink very quickly. Wearing a lifejacket increases your survival time in the water.

2. *Skipper Responsibility*

   The skipper is responsible for the safety of everyone on board and for the safe operation of the boat. Stay within the limits of your vessel and your experience.

3. *Communications*

   Take two separate waterproof ways of communicating so we can help you if you get into difficulties.

4. *Marine Weather*

   New Zealand's weather can be highly unpredictable. Check the local marine weather forecast before you go, and expect both weather and sea state changes.

5. *Avoid Alcohol*

   Safe boating and alcohol do not mix. Things can change quickly on the water. You need to stay alert and aware.

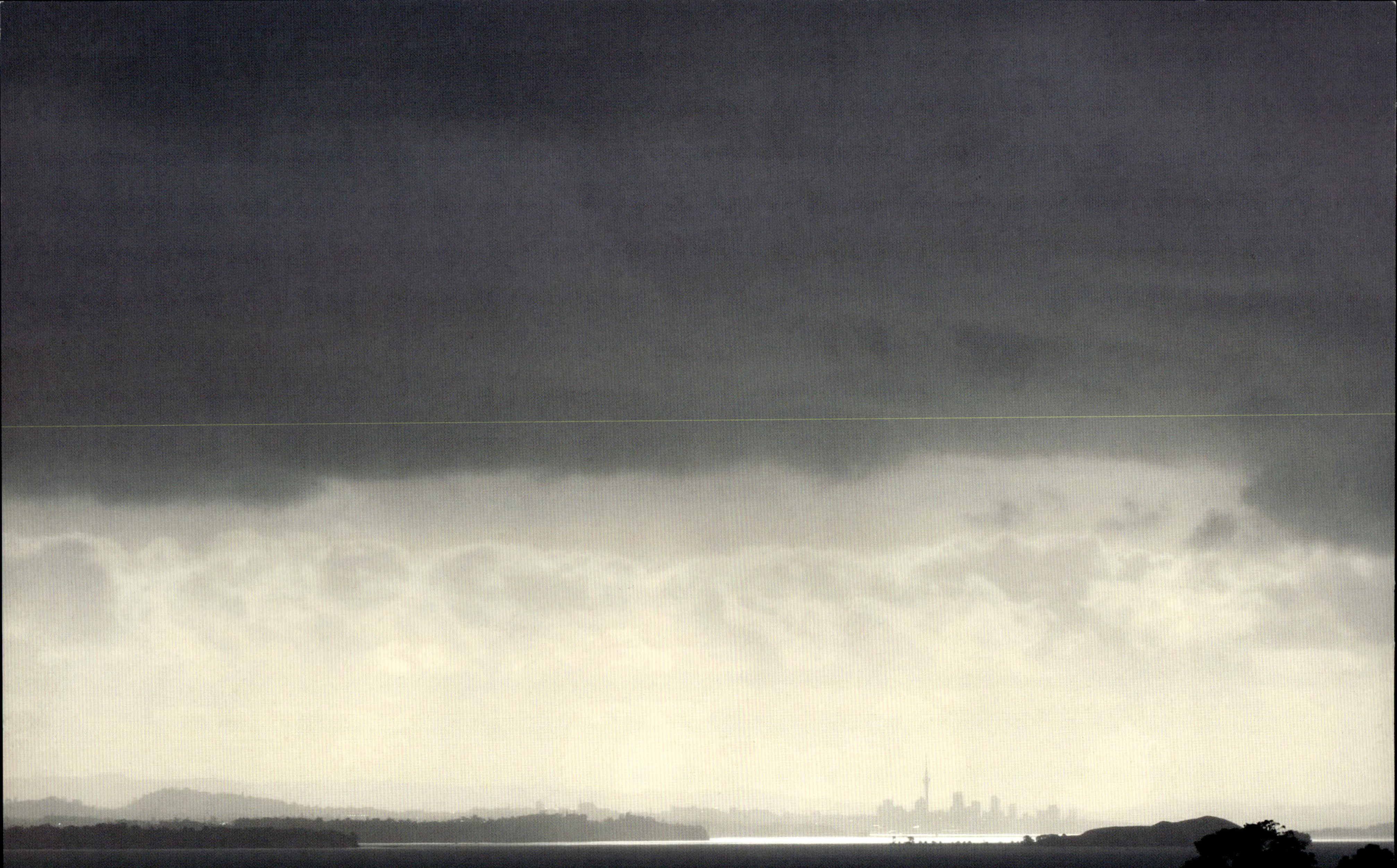

Lighthouse on Tiritiri Matangi Island.

A welcome resting spot for walkers on Waiheke Island.

Bibliography

Books

Armitage, D. (ed.), *Great Barrier Island*, Canterbury University Press, Christchurch, 2004

Baker, Ian, & Ryan, Michael, *The Gulf: New Zealand's Hauraki Gulf Explored*, New Holland, Auckland, 2002

Bercusson, Linda, & Walsby, John, *Exploring the Hauraki Gulf: from Bream Head to the Coromandel*, Craig Potton, Nelson, 2008

Burt, Biddy, *Native Trees and Shrubs of the Hauraki Gulf Islands*, J. Hunt, Inglewood, 2010

Butler, D., Hunt, J., & Lindsay, T., *Paradise Saved: the remarkable story of New Zealand's wildlife sanctuaries and how they are stemming the tide of extinction*, Random House, Auckland, 2014

Cook, James, *Captain Cook's Journal During the First Voyage Round the World*, Elliot Stock, London, 1893, Project Gutenberg, 2005 (www.gutenberg.org/files/8106/8106-h/8106-h.htm)

Darkin, John, *On Cook's Trail: a holiday history of Captain Cook in New Zealand*, Reed, Auckland, 2007

Duder, Tessa, *Discover Kawau*, Bush Press, Auckland, 1984

Duder, Tessa, *Seduced by the Sea*, HarperCollins, Auckland, 2002

Duder, Tessa, *The Story of Sir Peter Blake*, Oraita Media, Auckland, 2012

Ell, Gordon, *Wild Islands*, Bush Press, Auckland, 1982

Hall, Sue, *Walking the Hauraki Gulf – 20 Coastal Walks in and around Auckland*, New Holland, Auckland, 2003

Hamilton, Mary, & Whiting, D'Arcy, *Coastal Cruising Handbook* (9th edn), Royal Akarana Yacht Club, Auckland, 2002

Hauraki Gulf Maritime Park Board, *The Story of Hauraki Gulf Maritime Park*, Hauraki Gulf Maritime Park Board, Auckland, 1983

Hawkesby, John, *Waiheke: an island and its people*, Penguin, Auckland, 2013

Hayter, Rebecca, *Endless Summer – The Penny Whiting Story*, HarperCollins, Auckland, 2000

Ingram, Chas, & Wheatley, Owen, *Shipwrecks: New Zealand disasters 1795–1950*, A.H. & A.W. Reed, Wellington, 1951

Maddock, Shirley, *The Islands of the Gulf*, Collins, Auckland, 1966

McCloy, Nicola, *New Zealand Disasters*, Whitcoulls, Auckland, 2004

Moon, Lynnette, *Know Your New Zealand Birds*, New Holland, Auckland, 2006

Moon, Lynette, *The Singing Island: the story of Tiritiri Matangi Island*, Godwit, Auckland, 2003

Owen, William, *Hauraki Gulf: a fishing and cruising guide* (4th edn), David Bateman, Auckland, 2010

Radley, Paul, *Anchorages in the Hauraki Gulf*, David Ling Publishing Limited, Auckland, 1998

Rainger, Tim, *The New Zealand Good Beach Guide: North Island*, Clean Media, Auckland, 2011

Reed, A.H., *Great Barrier, Isle of Enchantment*, Reed, Wellington, 1946

Richardson, Brian, *Longitude and Empire: how Captain Cook's voyages changed the world*, UBC Press, Vancouver, 2005

Rimmer, Anne, *150th Anniversary of the Tiritiri Lighthouse*, Supporters of Tiritiri Matangi Inc, Auckland, 2015 (www.maritimenz.govt.nz/Commercial/Shipping-safety/Aids-to-navigation/Lighthouses-of-NZ/Tiritiri_Matangi_150th_anniversary_of_Lighthouse.pdf)

Robinson, Ian, *Hauraki Gulf*, David Bateman, Auckland, 2008

Siers, James, *Hauraki Gulf and its Islands*, Millwood Press, Wellington, 1981

Suisted, Rob, *Hauraki Gulf Destinations*, New Holland, Auckland, 2004

Thatcher, David, *New Zealand's Hauraki Gulf*, Captain Teach Press, Auckland, 2011

Thomas, Geoff, *Outdoors with Geoff*, Penguin, Auckland, 2012

Visser, Ingrid, *Swimming with Orca*, Penguin, Auckland, 2006

Wilcox, Mike (ed.), *Natural History of Rangitoto Island*, Auckland Botanical Society, Auckland, 2007

Articles

Duncan, Bruce, 'Waiheke's Bountiful Bottom End', NZ Fishing World, October 2015 (www.nzfishingworld.co.nz/latest/2015/10/waihekes-bountiful-bottom-end)

'German "Sea Devil" imprisoned in NZ', Ministry for Culture and Heritage, updated 17-Sep-2015 (www.nzhistory.net.nz/sea-devil-captured-german-naval-captain-count-felix-von-luckner-arrives-at-auckland)

Kidd, H.D. and Elliott, R.W. 'Logan, Archibald', from the Dictionary of New Zealand Biography. Te Ara – the Encyclopedia of New Zealand, updated 30-Oct-2012 (www.TeAra.govt.nz/en/biographies/3l10/logan-archibald)

Levien, Aaron, 'Kingfish Jigging – Beginners' Hotspots', New Zealand Fishing World, October 2015 (www.nzfishingworld.co.nz/latest/2015/10/beginners-jigging-hot-spots)

Lindsay, J., Needham, A., Smith, I., 'Rangitoto revisited: new insights to an old friend', Geoscience Society and University of Auckland, Auckland, 2010 (http://www.gsnz.org.nz/pdf/MP129B_FT3.pdf)

McClure, Margaret, 'Auckland places – Gulf islands', Te Ara – the Encyclopedia of New Zealand, updated 1-Jul-15 (www.TeAra.govt.nz/en/auckland-places/page-4)

Shelton, L.R., 'Kerridge, Robert James', from the Dictionary of New Zealand Biography. Te Ara – the Encyclopedia of New Zealand, updated 29-Oct-2013 (www.TeAra.govt.nz/en/biographies/4k10/kerridge-robert-james)

Sinclair, Keith, 'Grey, George', from the Dictionary of New Zealand Biography. Te Ara – the Encyclopedia of New Zealand, updated 2-Oct-2013 (www.TeAra.govt.nz/en/biographies/1g21/grey-george)

Wassilieff, Maggy, 'Seafood – Early Maori and settler diets', Te Ara – the Encyclopedia of New Zealand, updated 9-Jul-13 (www.TeAra.govt.nz/en/photograph/5096/sanfords-fish-market)

Wilson, John, 'European discovery of New Zealand – French explorers', Te Ara – the Encyclopedia of New Zealand, updated 13-Jul-12 (www.TeAra.govt.nz/en/european-discovery-of-new-zealand/page-8)

Websites

Auckland Council – www.aucklandcity.govt.nz
Auckland Libraries – www.aucklandlibraries.govt.nz
Auckland Libraries George Grey Collection – www.georgegrey.org.nz
Auckland Marine Services Directory 2016 – www.aucklandmarinedirectory.co.nz/
Auckland Zoo – www.aucklandzoo.co.nz
BBC Travel – www.bbc.co.uk
Coastguard – www.coastguard.nz
Darwin Correspondence Project – www.darwinproject.ac.uk
Department of Conservation – www.doc.govt.nz
GNS – www.gns.cri.nz
Kawau Island – www.kawauisland.org.nz
Little Barrier Island Trust – www.littlebarrierisland.org.nz
Man O' War Vineyards – www.manowarvineyards.co.nz
Maori Television – www.maoritelevision.com
Maritime New Zealand – www.maritimenz.govt.nz
Ministry for the Environment – www.mfe.govt.nz
Motuihe Island Restoration Trust – www.motuihe.org.nz/
Motutapu Restoration Trust – www.motutapu.org.nz
National Library of New Zealand – http://natlib.govt.nz
Navy Museum – http://navymuseum.co.nz
New Zealand Customs Service – www.customs.govt.nz
New Zealand Geographic – www.nzgeo.com
New Zealand History – www.nzhistory.net.nz
New Zealand Rare Breeds – www.rarebreeds.co.nz
Orca Research Trust – www.orcaresearch.org/
Papers Past (National Library) – http://paperspast.natlib.govt.nz
Penny Whiting – www.pennywhiting.com/
Rakino Ratepayers Association – http://www.rra.nz
Rangitoto Island Historic Conservation Trust – www.rangitoto.org/
Rimutaka Forest Park Trust – www.rimutakatrust.org.nz
Rotoroa Island Trust – http://rotoroa.org.nz/
Salvation Army – www.salvationarmy.org.nz
SOAS University of London – www.soas.ac.uk
Stony Batter Protection and Restoration Society – http://fortstonybatter.org/
Stuff – www.stuff.co.nz
Te Ara – www.teara.govt.nz
The Grid – http://thegrid.co.nz
The *Guardian* – www.theguardian.com
The *New Zealand Herald* – www.nzherald.co.nz
Tiritiri Matangi Open Sanctuary – http://www.tiritirimatangi.org.nz
Visit Waiheke – http://visitwaiheke.org.nz
Waiheke Museum – www.waihekemuseum.org.nz/

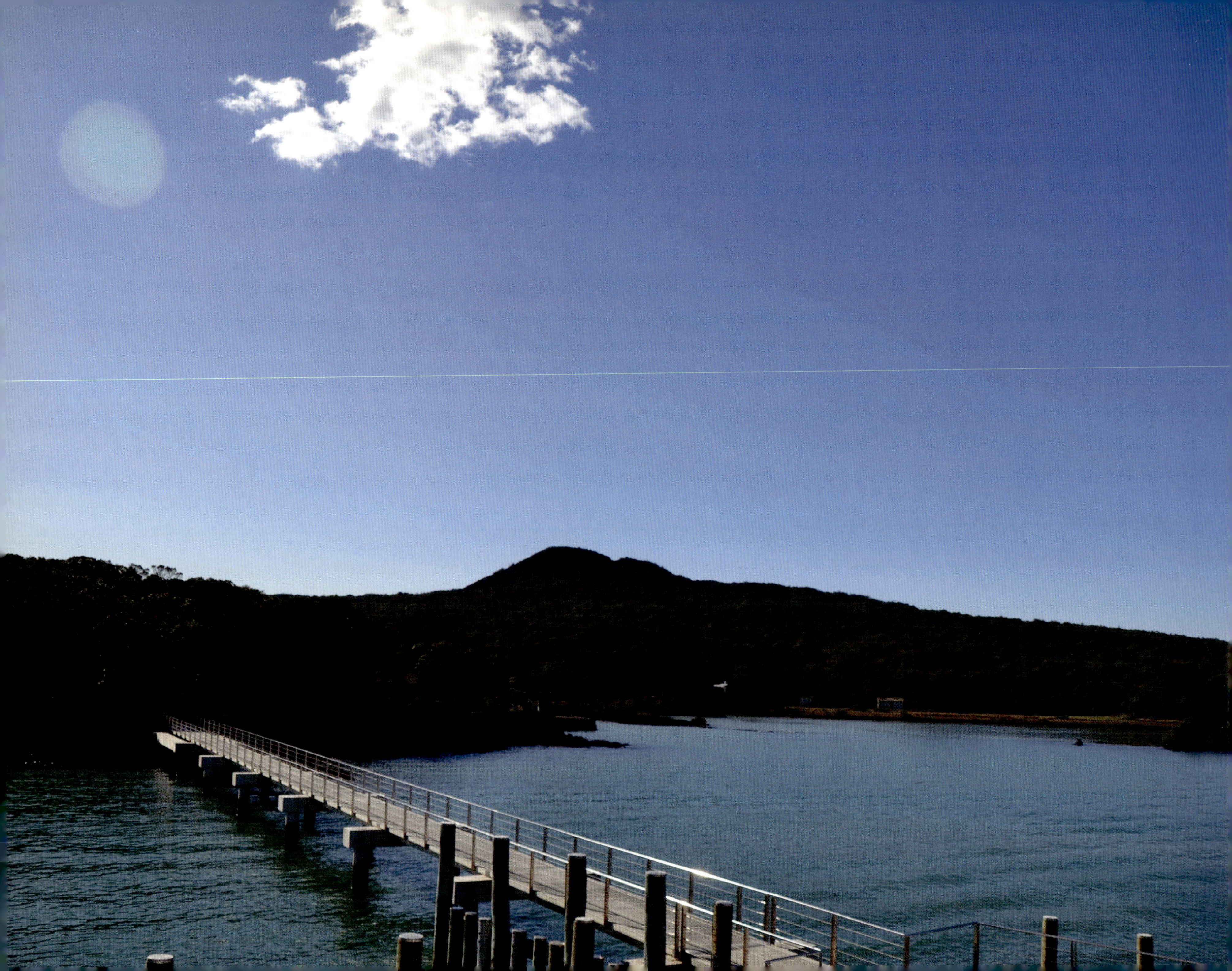

Image credits

All images are courtesy of the author, with the exception of the following:

Alan Good: pages 162, 164, 165, 166 (top and bottom), 168, 169, 172
Alexander Turnbull Library: page 29 (1/2-025589-F)
Auckland Whale and Dolphin Safari: back cover (dolphin), pages 107, 108, 111
Cliff Mail: pages 38, 61, 92, 210, 213, 214, 217, 225
Getty Images: pages 43 (Mark Minden/Minden Pictures), 45 (Michael Schwab), 102 (Mark Meredith), 105 (Mark Meredith)
Glenn Marvin: page 173
Helen Bucksey: page 62
Heletranz: pages 48, 50
Ingrid Visser: pages 118, 119 (top and bottom), 120, 122, 123, 125, 126

Karen Elliott and Dan McGowan: pages 218, 221, 222
Linden Images: pages 214, 216
Mary-Ann Rowland: back cover (saddleback), page 55
Penny Whiting: pages 146, 147 (top and bottom), 148, 150, 151
Ray and Barbara Walter: pages 67, 68
Rob Suisted/Nature's Pic: pages 81 (top) 95, 128, 134
Shutterstock: pages 132 (Karl Kolehmainen), 210
Sir George Grey Special Collections, Auckland Libraries: pages 28, 30, 31 (top and bottom), 41, 59, 97 (top and bottom), 99, 116, 117, 131, 138, 140, 177, 181, 182, 192, 197, 200

Acknowledgements

A huge thank you to everyone who has helped me with this book.

I am extremely grateful to Bill Honeybone and Nic McCloy for the opportunity to research and write this book. Thank you for your constant encouragement, support and good humour.

Thank you to the people who kindly gave their time to meet and share stories about their lives, careers, and adventures in the Hauraki Gulf: Ray and Barbara Walter, John Walsh, Penny Whiting, Andy Light, Sarah Harrison, Ingrid Visser, Helen and Dave Jeffery, Alan Good, David Watson, Steve Clarke, Karen Elliott and Dan McGowan.

Huge thanks to Cheryl Smith for the book layout and design.

Massive thanks to Mike Jones, my best friend and partner in crime, for helping and supporting me every step of the way.

Thanks to my mum and dad – Ray and Julie King – for proof-reading whilst visiting from the UK for a holiday!

A special thanks to Brad Kirner, General Manager of Auckland Whale and Dolphin Safari, for allowing me to experience the magic of the Hauraki Gulf on an Auckland Whale and Dolphin Safari, and for sharing some beautiful photos taken by his team.

I am very grateful to Mary-Ann Rowland, Helen Bucksey and Kay Milton, for their help with research and for sharing photographs from Tiritiri Matangi Island.

Thanks a million to Cliff Mail for help with my research and for sharing photographs from your boating adventures around the Hauraki Gulf.

And finally, thank you to Paula Charmley, Rachael Bright, Becky Kinross, Alex Bayes, John Eccleton, Mary Flaws, and Rendt Gorter for your help with research.